IMAGES
of America

JOHNSTON
VOLUME II

Johnston Historical Society

ARCADIA
PUBLISHING

ISBN 978-0-7385-8637-3

Published by Arcadia Publishing
Charleston, South Carolina

Printed in the United States of America

Library of Congress Catalog Card Number: 99-60292

For all general information contact Arcadia Publishing at:
Telephone 843-853-2070
Fax 843-853-0044
E-Mail sales@arcadiapublshing.com
For customer service and orders:
Toll-Free 1-888-313-2665

Visit us on the Internet at www.arcadiapublishing.com

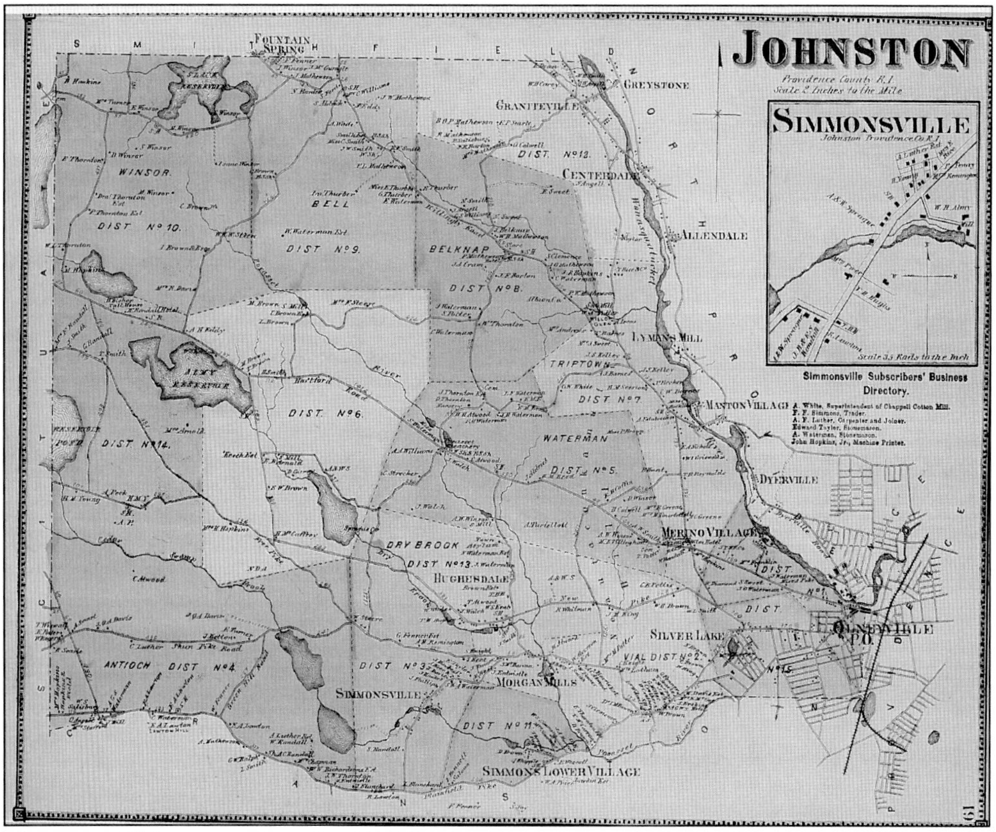

This map of Johnston is from the 1870 *Beers Atlas*.

IMAGES
of America

JOHNSTON
VOLUME II

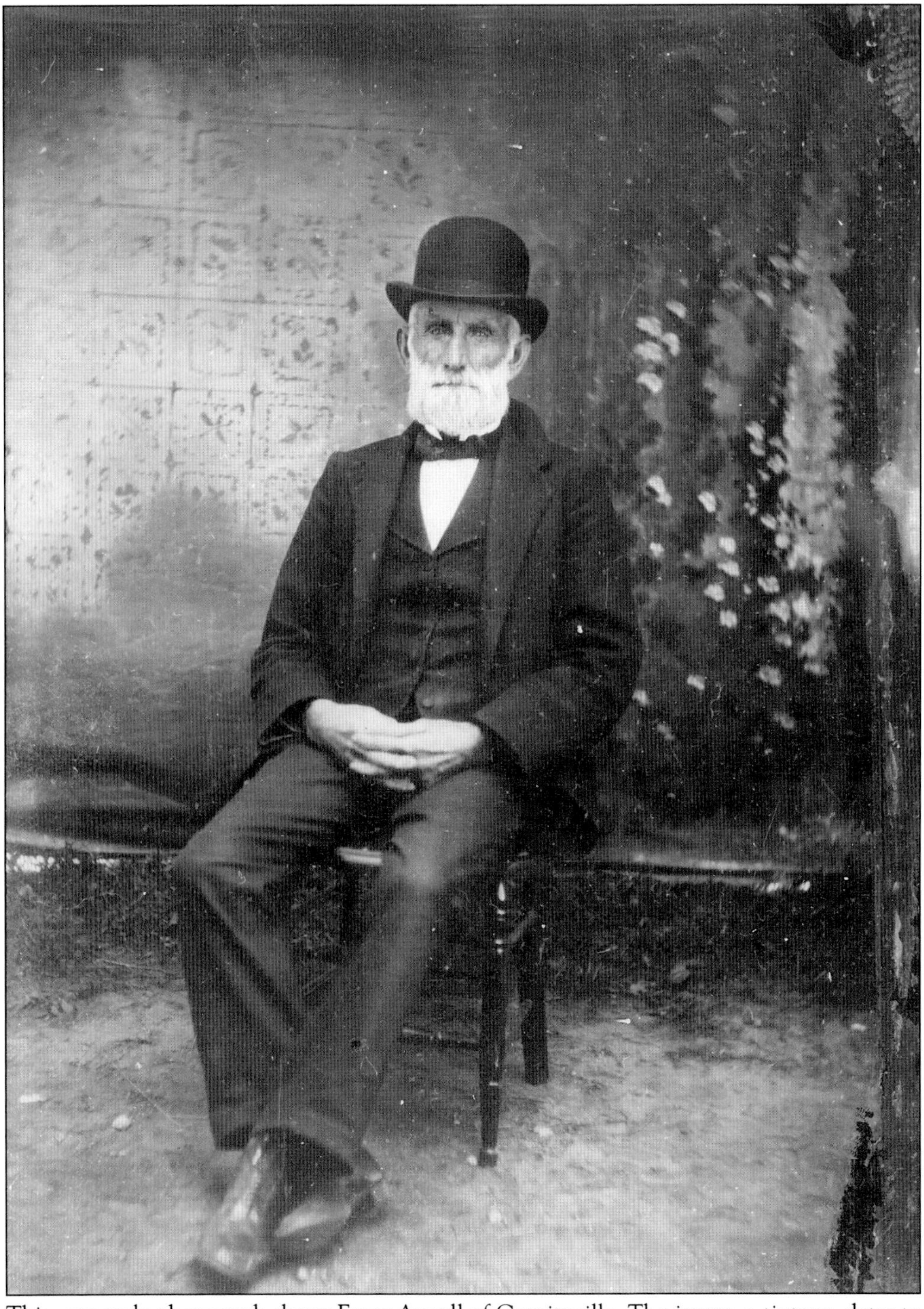

This very early photograph shows Emor Angell of Graniteville. The image, a tintype, dates to the 1850s or 1860s. His home, which he built along Putnam Pike at the corner of Pine Hill Avenue, still stands. He operated the granite quarry on Pine Hill in the village, and many of the foundations, walls, and granite steps in the village are cut from stone taken from his quarry. (Photograph courtesy of Steve Toro.)

Contents

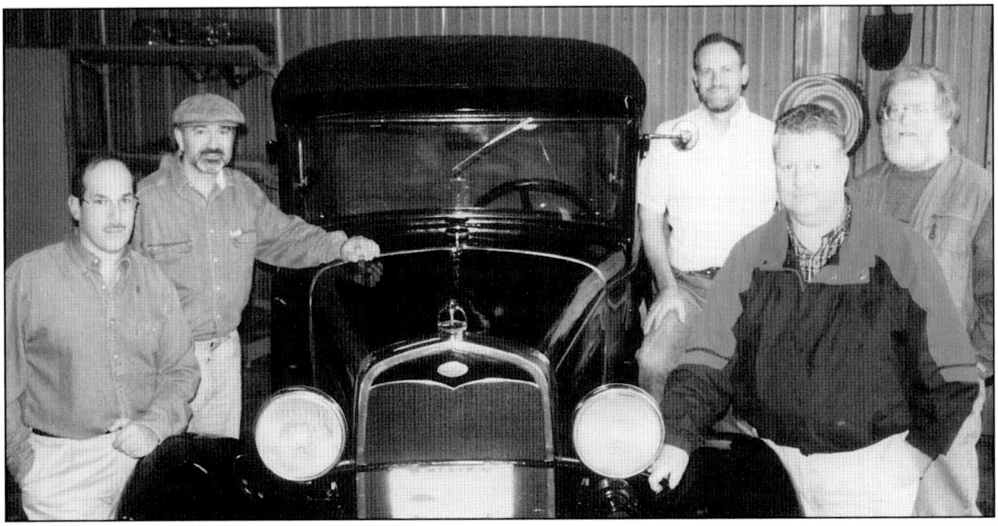

Five board members of the Johnston Historical Society put this book together. Shown here from left to right, they are Steve Merolla, Pasco Macari, Everett Cogswell, Dan Brown (in front), and Louis McGowan. The automobile is Everett's 1931 Model A Ford. (Photograph by Glen Fortin.)

ACKNOWLEDGMENTS

Continuing the search for old photographs of Johnston's past has culminated in *Images of America: Johnston, Volume II*. In combining oral history, written history, and photography we believe we have created an informative glimpse into the past of our town. Many enjoyable hours have been logged sitting and listening to residents reflect on the Johnston they remember. The stories associated with their family photographs are cherished.

Our appreciation is expressed to the following people, who have contributed time, information, and photographs: Sam & Lillian Coupe, Mabel Sprague, Harold & Judy Beaudoin, Keith and Raymond Crandall, Barbra McGuirl, Steve Toro, Bob & Arlene Russo, The Rhode Island Historical Society, Raymond Ricci, Vincent Acciardo, Susie Brown, Walter Nebiker, Anthony Ricci, The Rhode Island State Archives, Alan Iemma, James E. Mitchell, Cecile Morin, Kay D'Acchioli, Dot Baxter, Joe Coduri, Louis McGowan, Carl Rainone, the Rhode Island Department of Transportation, Jean Spina, the Holscher family, Nellie Dahlin, Lawrence Pezza, Nikki Gizzarelli, Louis Ullucci, Earl Newman, Millicent Newsham, Jim Shaw, Ralph & Tina Russo, Al Forte, Joseph Golini, Jean Arcand, Tony Petrucci, John Ricci, Bob Whittaker, Ernest Caloura, Laura Panicucci, Thomas E. Greene, Dorothy Wilner, Ray McGowan, Central Nurseries, Bob Stamp, Lora Clemence, Evelyn Beaumier, Gert Rice, the Newman family, Al Kimball, Francis Cox, Adam Macari, Charles Redinger, the Providence City Hall Archives, Arthur Harrington, Elaine Pereira, Charles Devaney, Joseph Russo, Millie Youde, Gary Lynn, Elizabeth Mowry, Bel Peters, Paul & Betty Russo, William Macera, James H. Waterman Jr., Herb Newman, Alfonso J. LaFazia, Mabel Hopkins, Dorothy Innocenti, Gladys DiMeglio, Linda Ruotolo, Christine Smith, John Rossi, the Criscuolo family, Fred & Martha Mikkelsen, Janice Rinaldi, Marie Florie, Joan Ventetuolo, Cecelia Cardillo, Margaret Pearson, Jim Geary, Sandra DeCesaris, Angelo Cappelli, Elizabeth Fleury, John Clark, Thomas & Eunice Hartshorn, Fred Iafrate, Dave Iannuccilli, Rich LaFazia, Robert Smith, Lee Swanson, Mario Ardente, and Carolyn Thornton.

INTRODUCTION

In *Images of America: Johnston, Volume I*, Louis McGowan and his three Johnston Historical Society associates explored the visual history of the town, as well as the development of its villages. Louis, Steve Merolla, Pasco Macari, Daniel Brown, and a new member of the team, Everett Cogswell, continue their probe into Johnston's history in *Johnston II*. This book looks back at the people, institutions, and architecture that gave Johnston its place in Rhode Island history.

Collecting photographs for this volume actually started with Volume I. We began slowly, as the process of acquiring them was new to us. Should we advertise, go to the local libraries or archives, or talk to elderly town residents? After trying it, we discovered advertising was not as productive as one-on-one contact. Through this latter means we were able to acquire the images we sought. Our growing collection of images of town residents, farm scenes, businesses, and houses no longer with us began to develop into *Johnston, Volume I*. After seeing the amount of photographs not used in our first book, we agreed that we needed to do a second volume. More views were needed, though. Following up on our original contacts and with many new leads, we were able to secure the unique collection contained herein, a collection that truly reflects Johnston's past.

After Johnston was founded in 1759, farming continued to be the most important component of everyday life, as it had been during the early days of the colony. Farms, ranging in size from a few to hundreds of acres, encompassed the area. Like its neighboring towns, Johnston trusted the bounty of the land to sustain its population. This was about to change. In the early to mid-19th century, as the effects of the Industrial Revolution took hold, farming began its decline. Its preeminence eroded because it was pitted against the new mills and the chance for farmhands to make a better living in the mills. Some families did, however, continue to operate their farms into the 20th century.

Manufacturing was beginning to replace farming as the basis of the Johnston economy. Johnston is blessed with abundant streams, which mills needed to power their machinery. English mill owners learned of this natural resource and built their factories here, resulting in the mill villages we continue to recognize today. As the town approached the end of the 19th century, there were a few large mills employing thousands of people. The mills, although started with English money and English workers, began drawing large numbers of their workforce from the tide of immigrants entering the town. While the big mills put money into workers' pockets, the many small businesses gave them places to spend it. The villages of Graniteville, Manton,

Upper Simmons Village, and Lower Simmons Village (later known as Thornton) held the greatest number of these establishments. Usually there was more than just one of each type of business, giving us many bars, barber shops, and markets in each village. Unfortunately, in this day of large chain stores and malls, the small businesses are disappearing, eating into the fabric of village identity.

When not working, residents took time to play and celebrate. Memorial Day parades and Fourth of July bonfires attracted large crowds. The celebrations or "feasts" associated with the Italian churches played an important role in the lives of the immigrant population. Sports were also very important to all town citizens. Cricket and soccer were popular in the early days, but baseball has been here all along, too.

The people of the town have been served by many institutions, two of the most important being the police and fire departments. Each of these departments is always represented in local parades, where townspeople can show their appreciation for a difficult job well done.

References to Johnston's earliest school date to the 1790s is Belknap. This school only admitted children of the institution's founders. Gradually, beginning in the early 1800s, education came to be viewed as a necessity. The town was divided into what became 16 school districts, and a school was built in each district. All children could now receive some type of education.

In the final chapter, we view the people of Johnston themselves, captured in images as they worked, played, and lived. The farmers, the mill workers, the store owners, and, of course, the women (many of whom raised large families) are all seen here through the eyes of the camera. It is to these people that we dedicate our efforts.

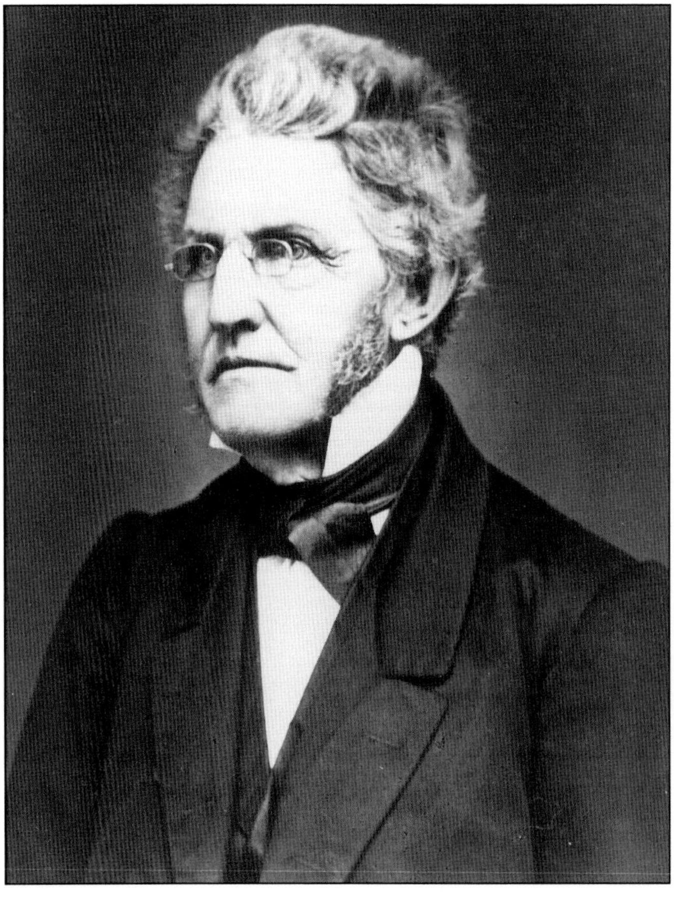

Probably Johnston's most famous figure, James Fowler Simmons moved to the town in the 1820s after marrying the daughter of a prominent Simmonsville resident, Samuel Randall. Simmons's primary means of livelihood was the textile trade, but he also went into politics and rose to become a senator from Rhode Island. His magnificent Greek Revival mansion still stands on Atwood Avenue in Thornton. At one time, two villages in the town were named for him, Simmonsville and Lower Simmonsville—now Thornton. (Photograph reprinted with permission of the Rhode Island Historical Society.)

One

Farms, Homes, and Other Buildings

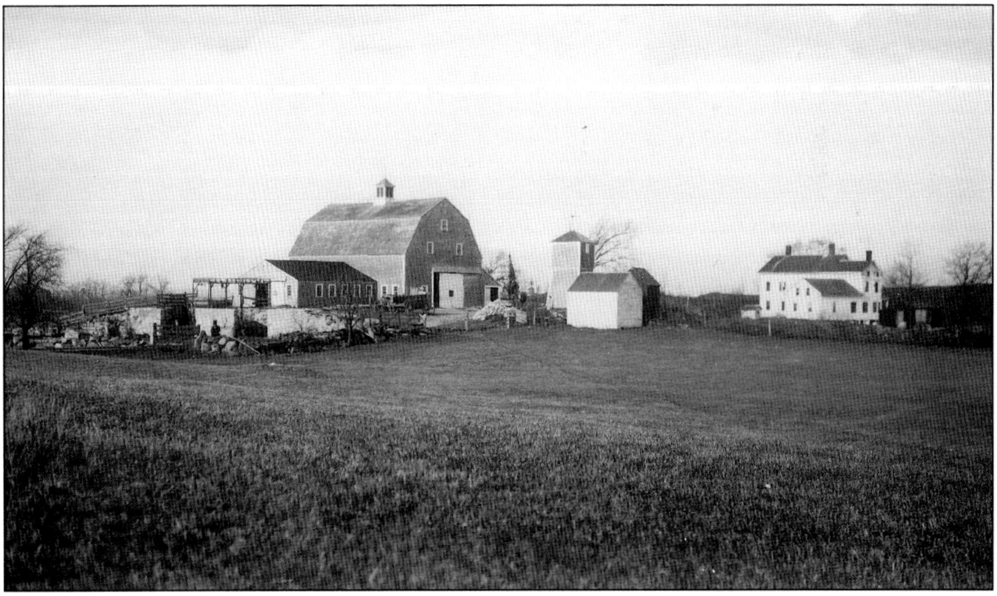

In 1868 Asa Tourtellot of Scituate purchased the 105-acre "Graves Farm," located southerly of Hartford Avenue and to the west of Borden Avenue. Present-day Route 195/Route 6 was the approximate southern boundary. The farm remained in the Tourtellot family into the 20th century. The house shown here was built by Asa, and the barn replaced an older structure that burned down. Only the house remains. It is located on the short stretch of Borden Avenue between Hartford Avenue and Route 195/Route 6. (Photograph courtesy of Harold Beaudoin.)

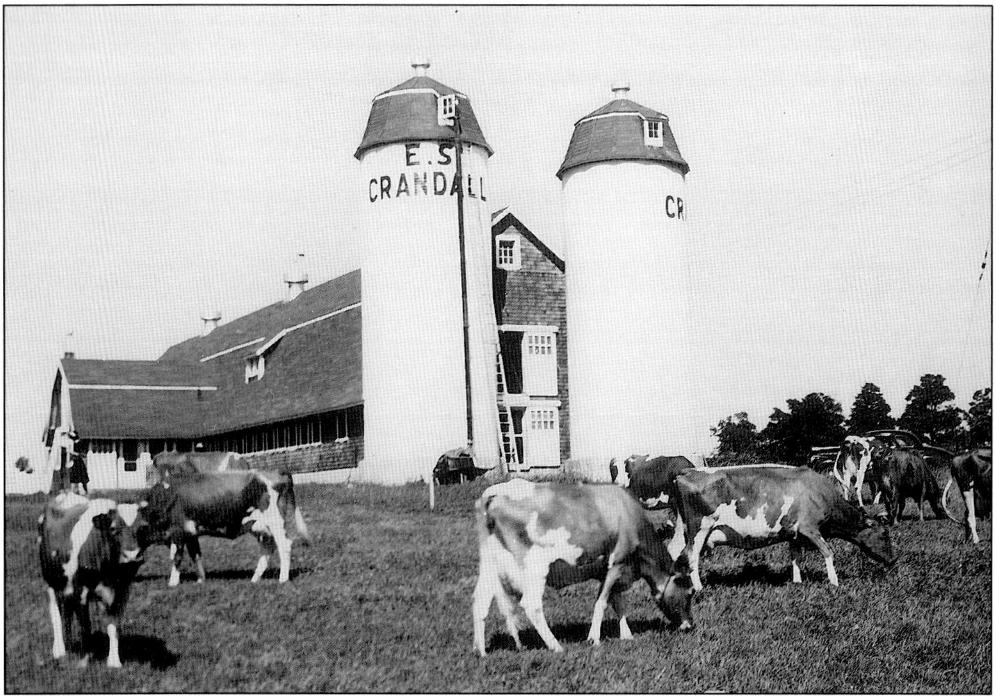

The picturesque Crandall farm is pictured here in the 1940s or 1950s on Morgan Avenue. Edward S. Crandall bought the former Frank W. Tillinghast farm in 1938, moving his dairy from Providence, where he had re-sold milk purchased from local farms. In Johnston he used his own herd of Guernsey cows for milk. (Photograph courtesy of Keith Crandall.)

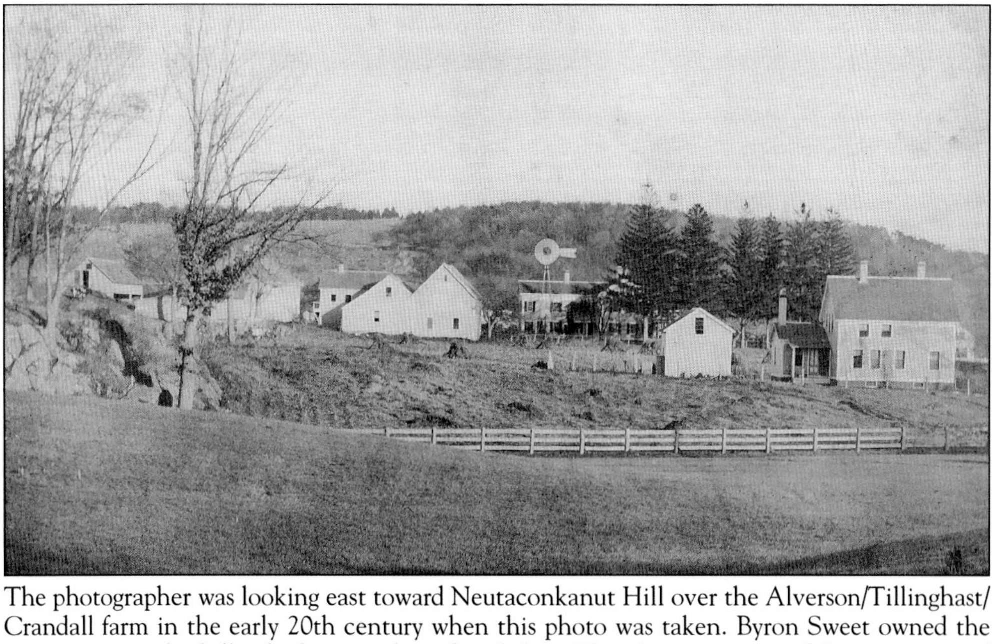

The photographer was looking east toward Neutaconkanut Hill over the Alverson/Tillinghast/Crandall farm in the early 20th century when this photo was taken. Byron Sweet owned the open areas on the hill, which were planted with hay. The above-mentioned farm was owned by Col. Frank W. Tillinghast at this time. He bought and sold cows and was a local textile manufacturer. (Photograph courtesy of Mabel Sprague.)

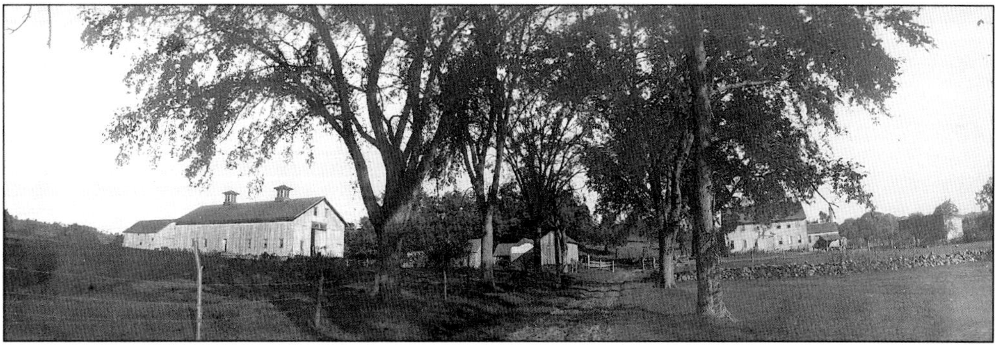

Encompassing an area of about 130 acres, the Tobey farm comprised the main part of the Allendale Insurance Co. property north of Central Avenue. The lane seen here is at the same location as their entrance on that road. The Thornton family owned the property in the late 1600s, at which time they built the house shown here. It was moved to Newport in the 1970s. The farm has been owned by many families including the Almys, Tobeys, Tourtellots, and Wilders. (Photograph courtesy of Harold & Judy Beaudoin.)

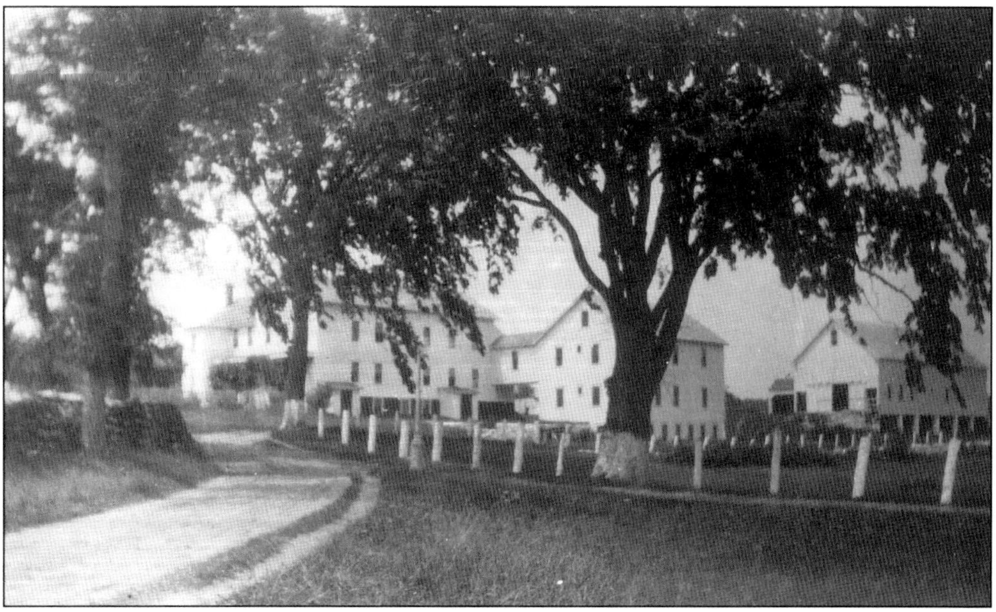

The Poor Farm or Town Asylum, pictured here about 1910, was located a little north of the present K-Mart plaza on Atwood Avenue. Town residents with no means of support could stay here and work for their keep. There were cows, pigs, and vegetable gardens on the site. The overseer of the poor and the keeper of the farm when it closed in the late teens was James Nichols. (Photograph courtesy of Bob and Arlene Russo.)

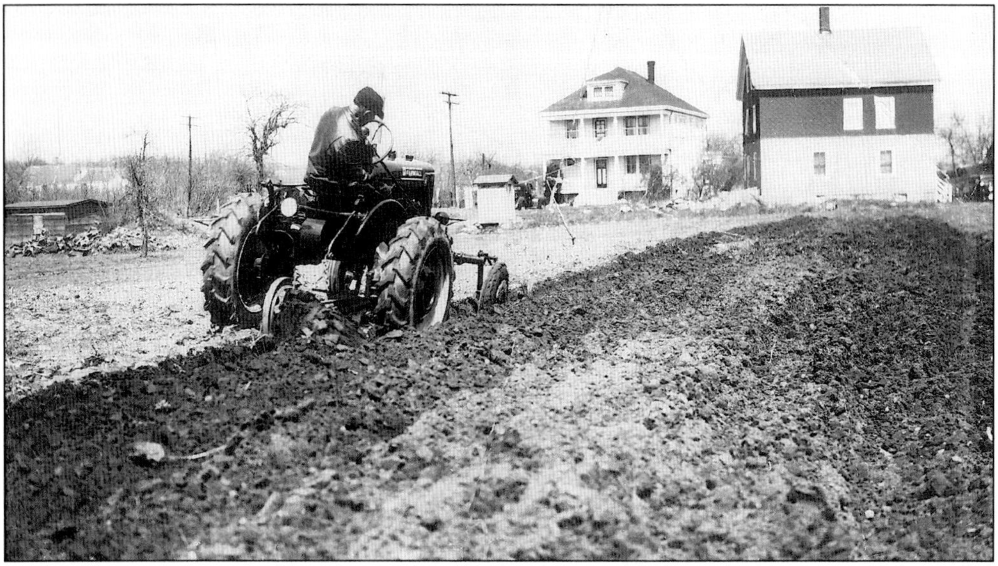

Albert Ricci worked a 6-acre farm located in the area of Old Simmonsville Road. Mr. Ricci trucked the produce he grew down to the Farmer's Market in Providence. The house on the right sits today on Old Simmonsville Road while the one on the left in the distance stands today on the new section of Simmonsville Avenue, which was laid out in the 1950s. (Photograph courtesy of Raymond Ricci.)

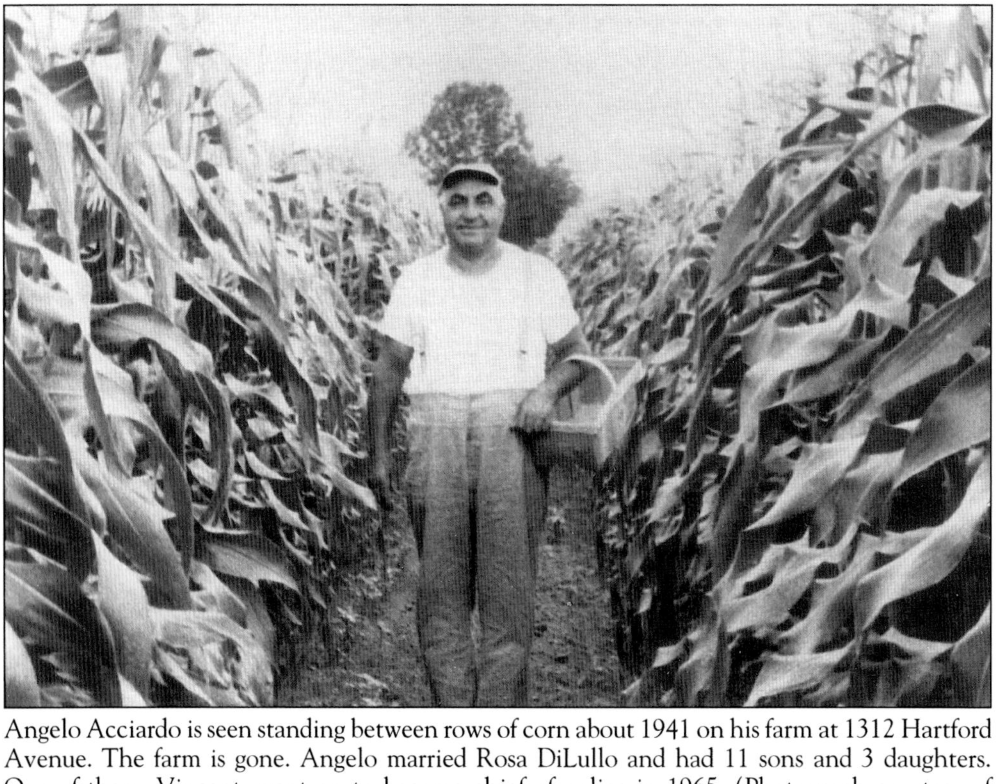

Angelo Acciardo is seen standing between rows of corn about 1941 on his farm at 1312 Hartford Avenue. The farm is gone. Angelo married Rosa DiLullo and had 11 sons and 3 daughters. One of them, Vincent, went on to become chief of police in 1965. (Photograph courtesy of Vincent Acciardo.)

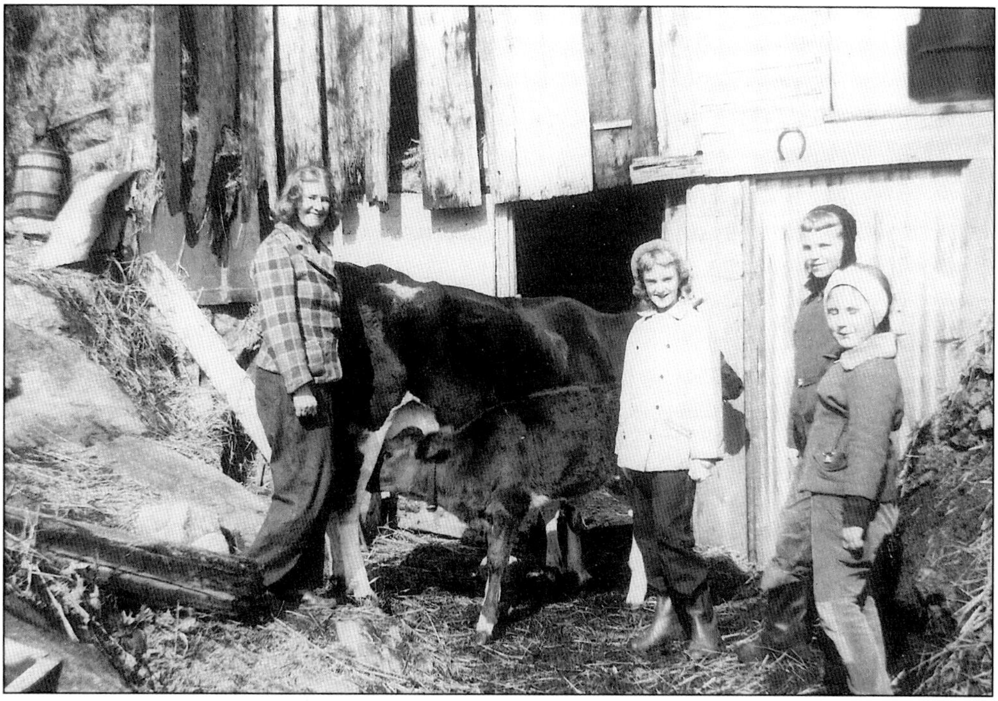

Susie Brown (left) and friends are gathered on her family farm on Belfield Drive about 1930. There was always something interesting for children to look at on a farm. Of course, there was always a lot of work to do, too. Susie, now in her 80s, has never lived anywhere else but on Belfield Drive, named after her mother for being the oldest resident on the old Snake Den Road. (Photograph courtesy of Susie Brown.)

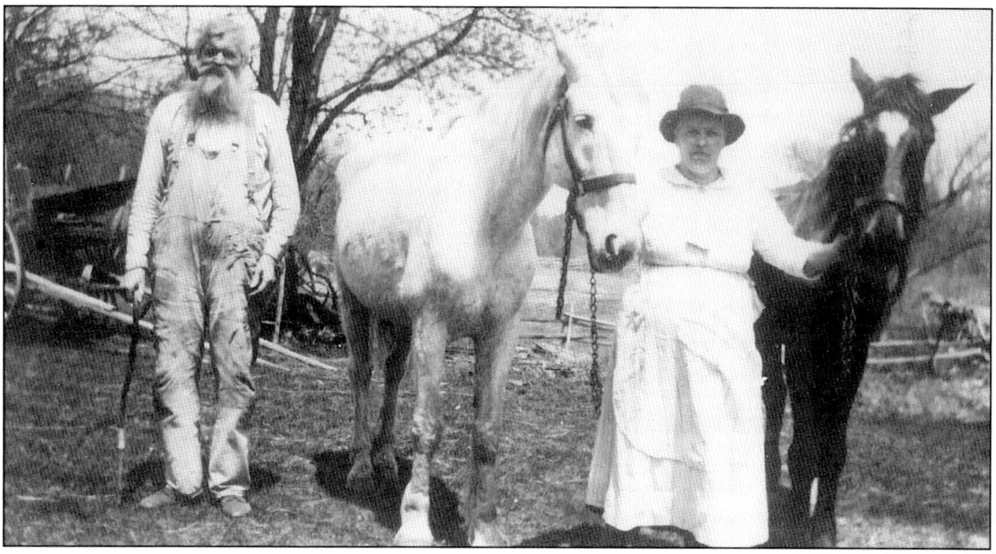

Zack Whipple and his daughter Esther pose with their horses in the early 20th century at their farm on the west side of Brown Avenue, about 1/8 mile past the site of the Brown Avenue Chapel. In 1895 Benjamin Whipple owned the house, which is no longer standing. (Photograph courtesy of Susie Brown.)

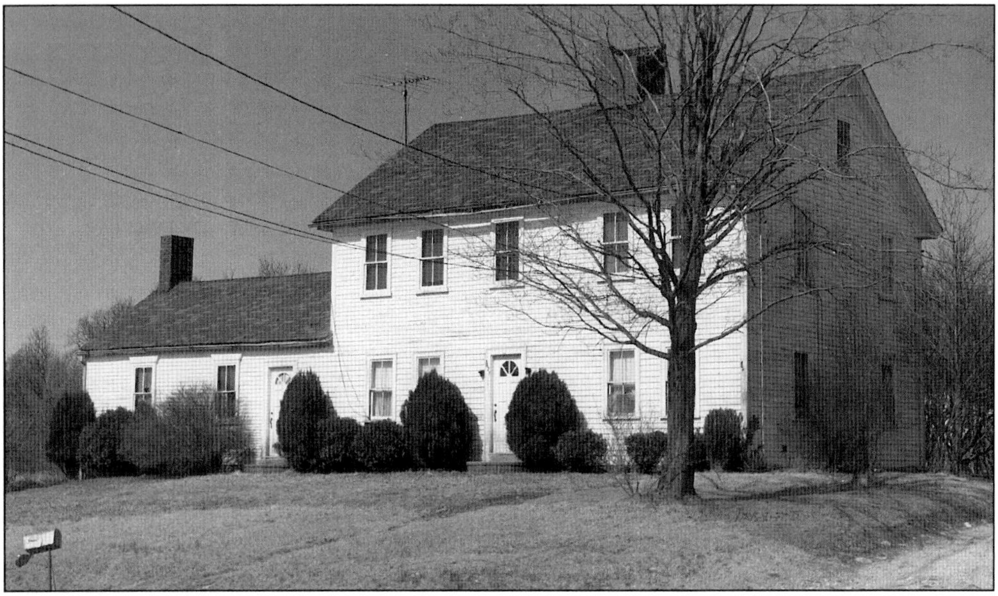

This house at 969 Hartford Avenue is now just a memory. Captured here in the late 1970s, it was torn down shortly after the photo was taken. It was owned by a variety of people over the years, including Miss S. Waterman in 1870; J. Fisk in 1895; F. & I. Gay in 1917; and the Parillo family in 1948. It is said to have been a tavern at some point during the Waterman's ownership. (Photograph courtesy of Walter Nebiker, RIH&HPC.)

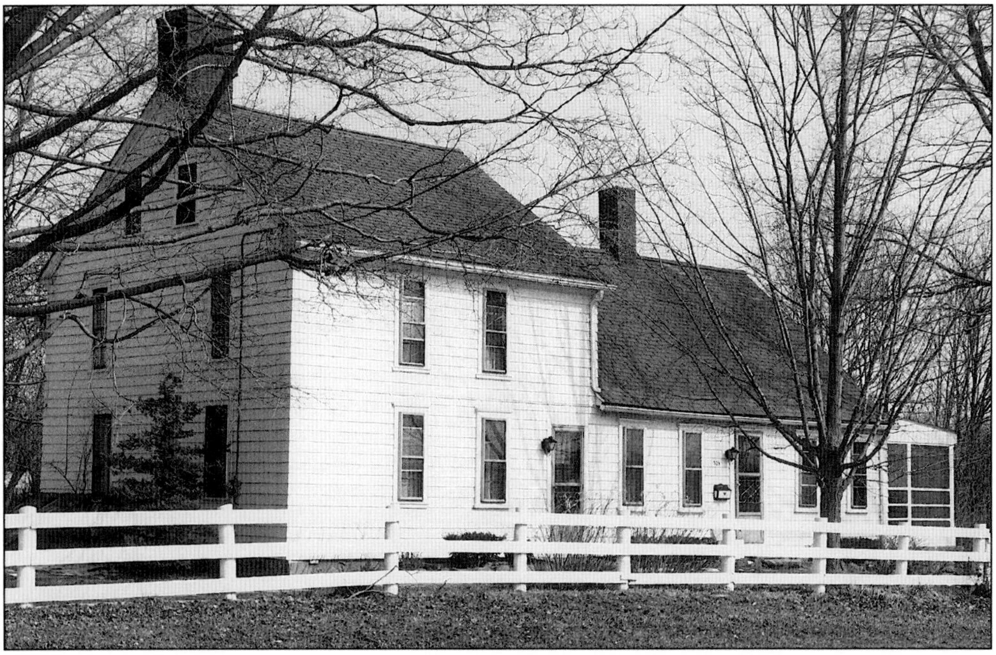

The Peter Randall House, 325 Cherry Hill Road, dates to the early 18th century and is still standing, although severely altered. Randall moved into this house in 1771 and remained here for the rest of his life. A descendent, Phebe, married Edward M. Evans, and his name can be seen on late-19th-century maps. Until recent times, the remains of a stone-ender chimney were still evident on the property. (Photograph courtesy of Walter Nebiker, RIH&HPC.)

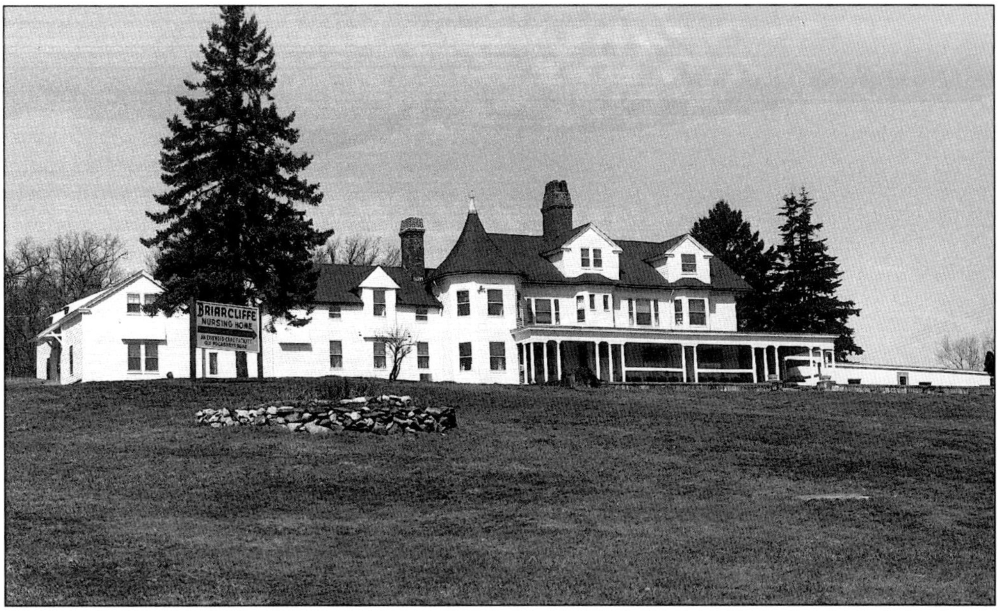

Joseph Redinger purchased this house and the surrounding farm, called the Woodlake Farm, from the Perkins family. The Redingers had an oval track on the property that they used for training harness horses until the 1950s. The main house possessed beautiful interior detailing, but was torn down in 1978 by the Briarcliffe Nursing Home. (Photograph courtesy of Walter Nebiker, RIH&HPC.)

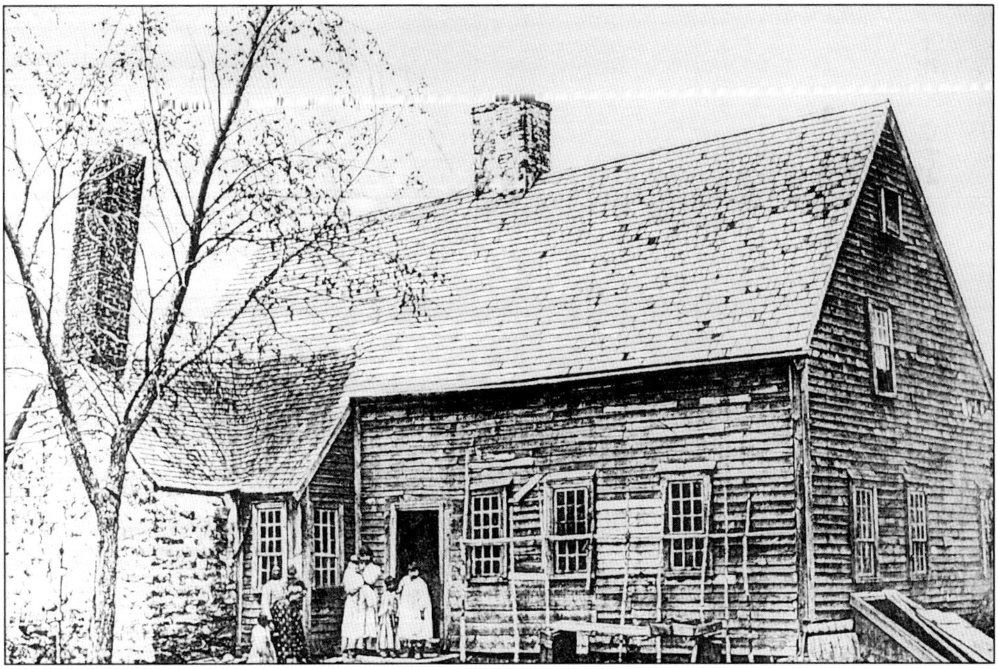

This ancient house, constructed c. 1700, once stood on Atwood Avenue in front of the K-Mart plaza. It was destroyed in the early 20th century. Though owned by the Waterman family for over 100 years (from 1770 to 1893), it was probably built by the Sheldon family, early residents of this area. It is often called the Nick Waterman or the Ben Waterman House.

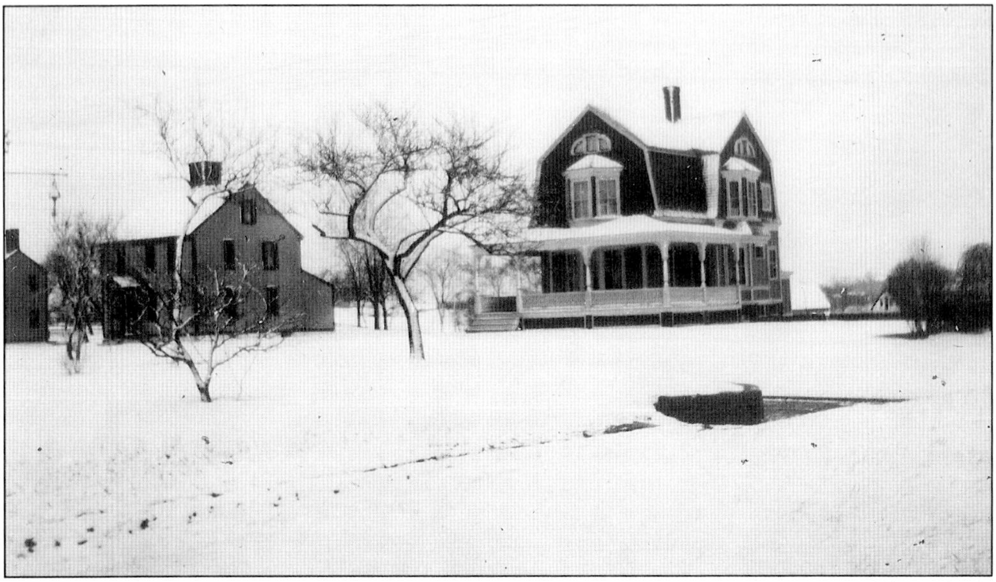

The house on the right is the Leander Peckham House, 278 Morgan Avenue. Peckham built the house in 1896 after he moved his shoddy business to the Morgan Mills. He and his wife, Josephine Bennett, enjoyed many happy years here. The house is still standing but has been much altered. (Photograph courtesy of Harold & Judy Beaudoin.)

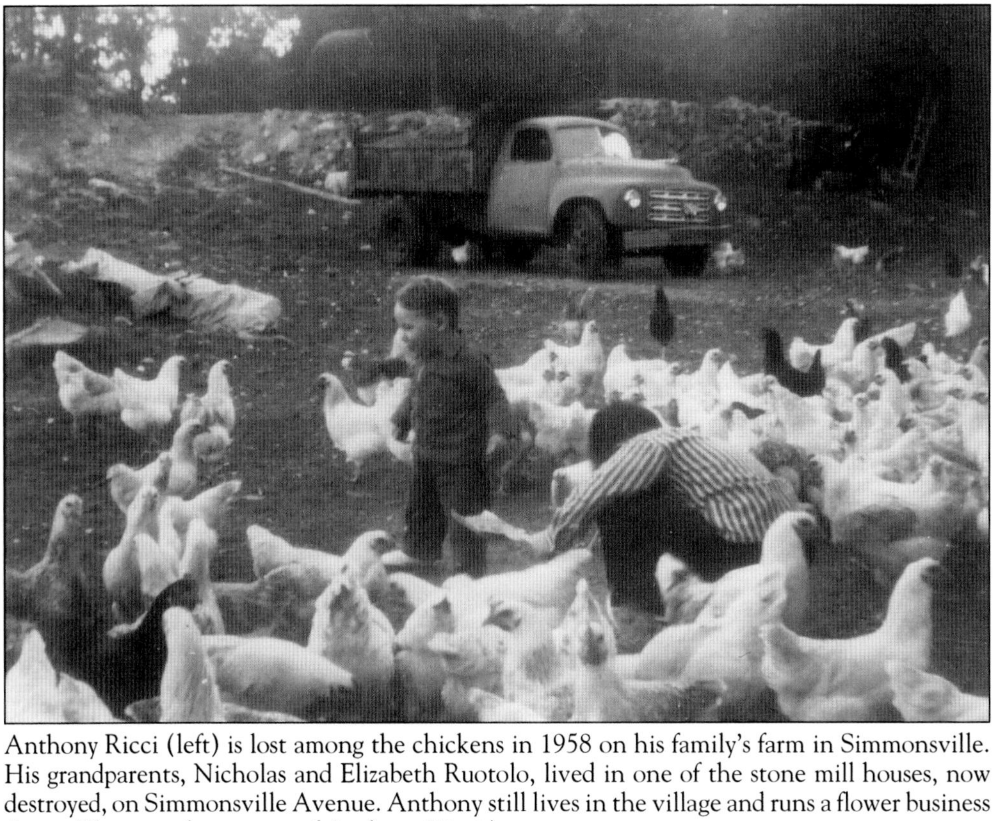

Anthony Ricci (left) is lost among the chickens in 1958 on his family's farm in Simmonsville. His grandparents, Nicholas and Elizabeth Ruotolo, lived in one of the stone mill houses, now destroyed, on Simmonsville Avenue. Anthony still lives in the village and runs a flower business there. (Photograph courtesy of Anthony Ricci.)

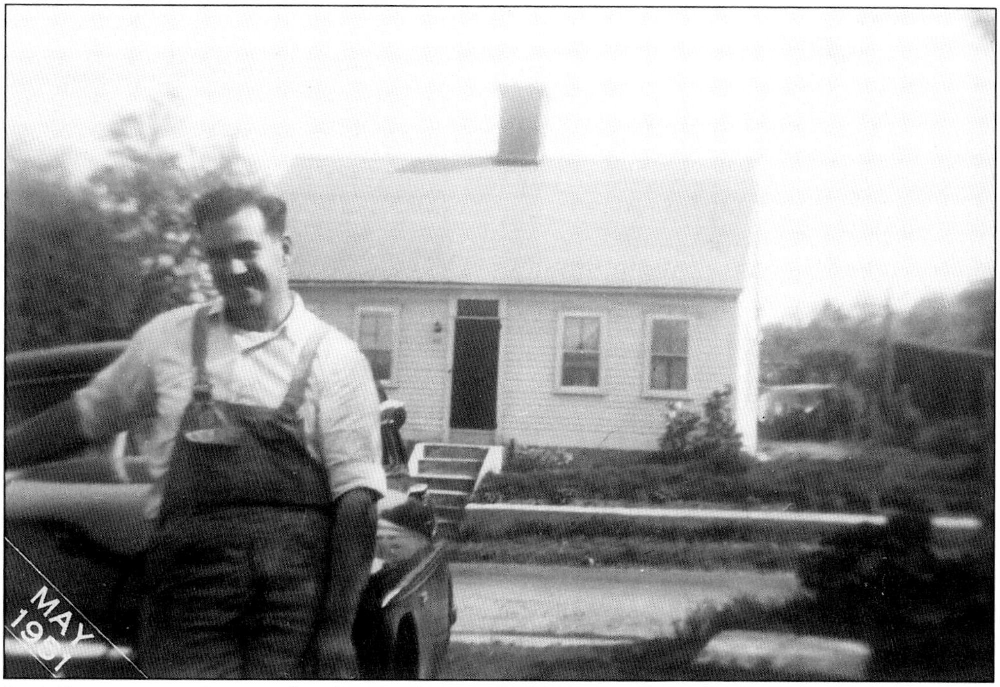

Paul Russo is standing on his family farm at 315 Morgan Avenue in 1951. The small cape across the street is still there but is slated to be torn down. In 1870 it was owned by Mr. A.E. Rathbone. In the 1950s Vito Bagalio lived there; after that the John Bizzacco family lived there. It is now owned by the Central Nurseries. (Photograph courtesy of the Russo family.)

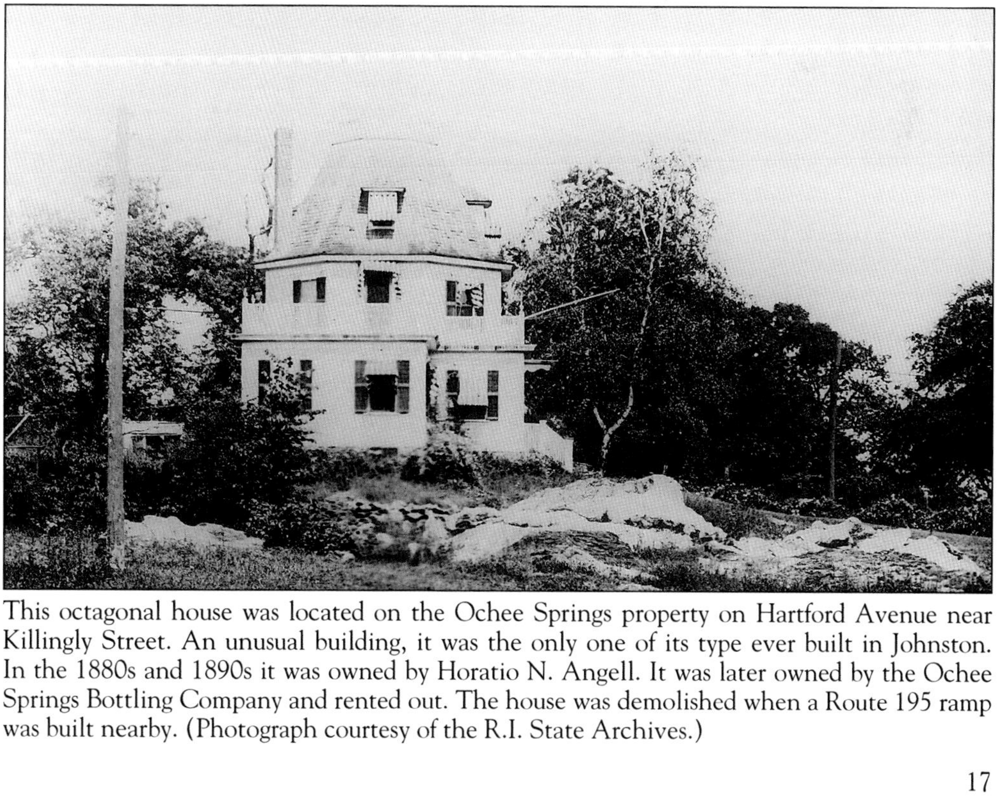

This octagonal house was located on the Ochee Springs property on Hartford Avenue near Killingly Street. An unusual building, it was the only one of its type ever built in Johnston. In the 1880s and 1890s it was owned by Horatio N. Angell. It was later owned by the Ochee Springs Bottling Company and rented out. The house was demolished when a Route 195 ramp was built nearby. (Photograph courtesy of the R.I. State Archives.)

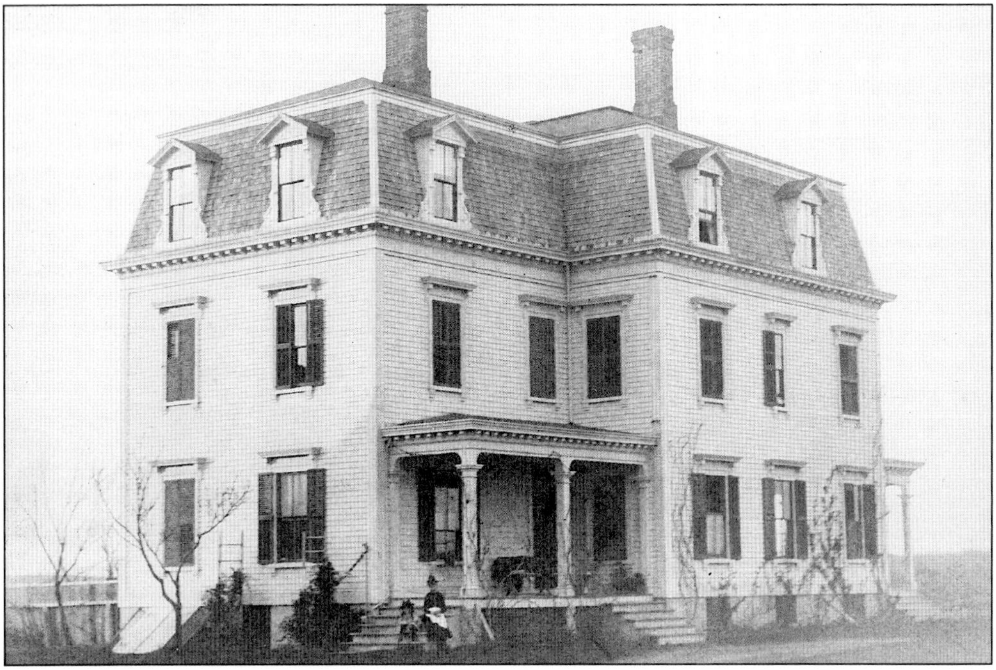

The George C. Calef Homestead stood majestically on Greenville Avenue across from Shaw's Garage until about 30 years ago. Reflecting Calef's status as a wealthy businessman, the house was built in the fashionable Second Empire style. Calef was a strong advocate of education, and the local grammar school was named after him in 1923. As a member of the school board he sought out good teachers from Providence, letting them board with his family if necessary. (Photograph courtesy of Alan Iemma.)

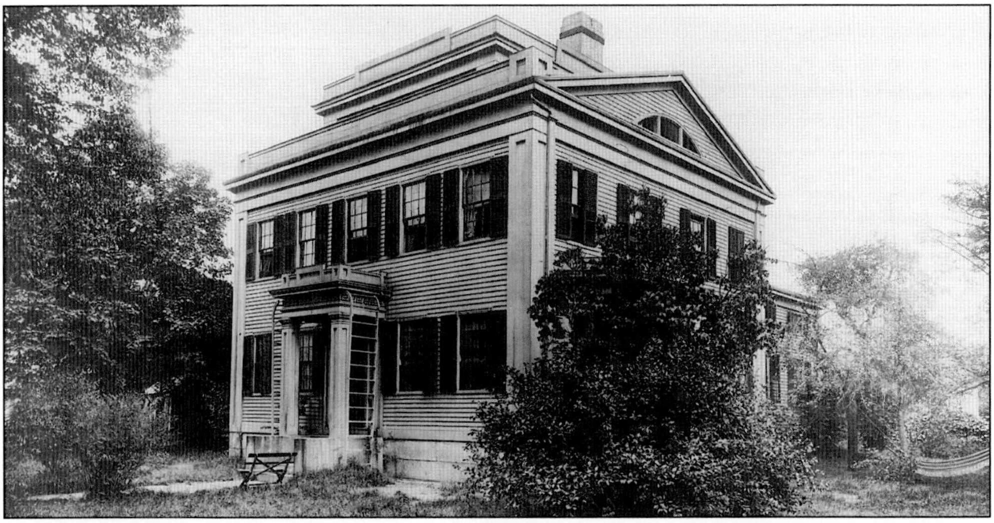

Samuel Ward King (1786–1851) was the only Johnston resident ever elected governor of Rhode Island, serving in that post from 1840 to 1843; before that he served many years on the town council and as town clerk. A physician and surgeon, he served in that capacity in the Navy during the War of 1812. After returning from the service he resided in the Olneyville section of what was then Johnston. This picture shows his residence on the south side of Plainfield Street in Olneyville. (Photograph courtesy of the R.I. State Archives.)

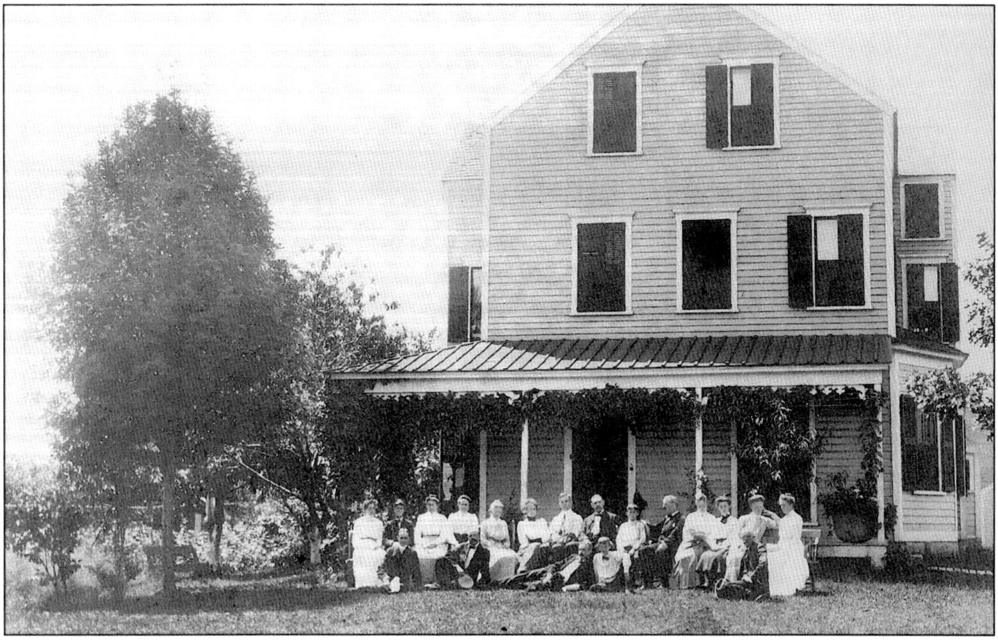

At the turn of the century this was a boardinghouse, located at 22 Milton Street off George Waterman Road. It was run by Nellie (Sweet) Harris. Frank Mitchell and his future wife, Harriet, met here; they were married in 1916, and later bought the house, which they were forced to sell during the Depression. The Savage family later owned the property. The house still stands. (Photograph courtesy of James E. Mitchell.)

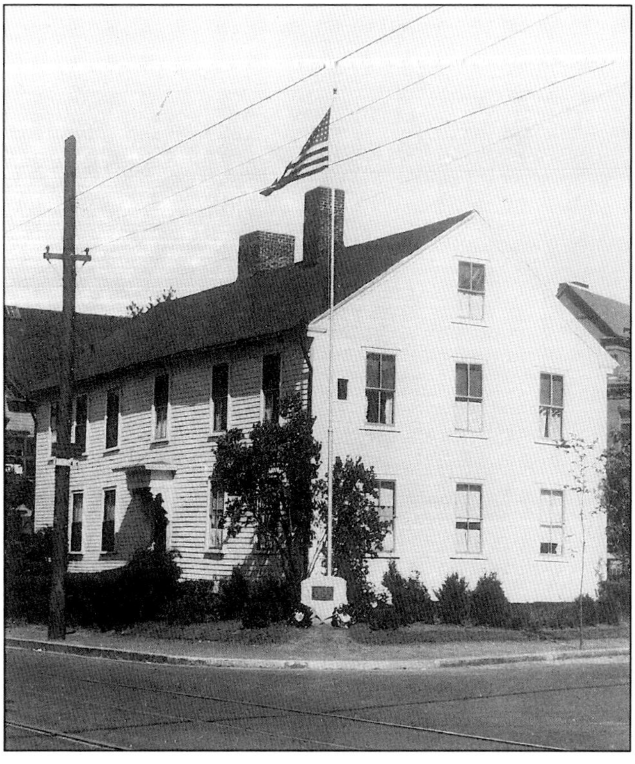

This house, situated at the corner of Plainfield and Killingly Streets, was the Nehemiah Sheldon House. Mr. Sheldon lived in the house from 1763 to 1814, at a time when this section of Olneyville was part of Johnston. Many Johnston Town Council meetings were held here during this period. It is thought that the house was built in the early 1700s. In the upper right can be seen the roof of Johnston's first high school building. An auto body shop now stands on the site of the Sheldon House. (Photograph courtesy of Bob Whittaker.)

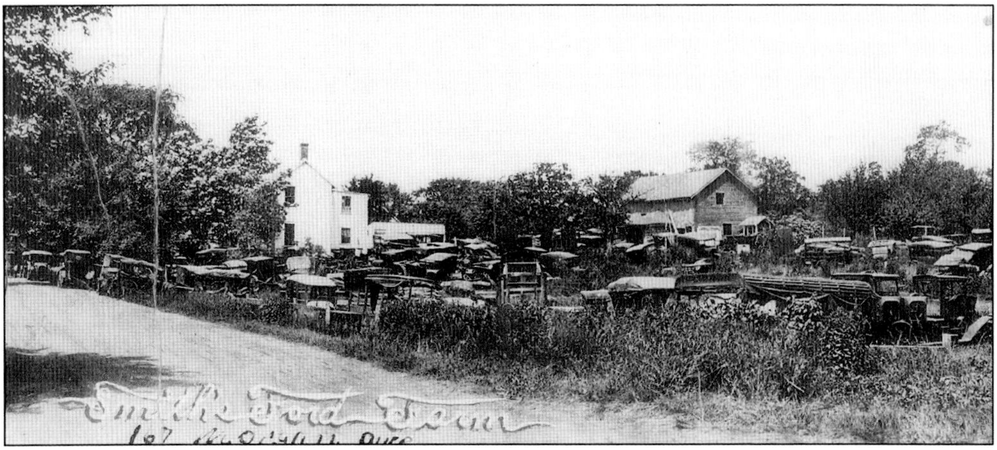

The Smith Ford Farm is shown in 1924 at 167 Morgan Avenue. Abraham Lincoln Smith, Pete's father, bought and sold junk Fords and also owned a new car dealership on Plainfield Street. His wife, Susan Collins, was a maid at Leander Peckham's house down the road. (Photograph courtesy of Bob Whittaker.)

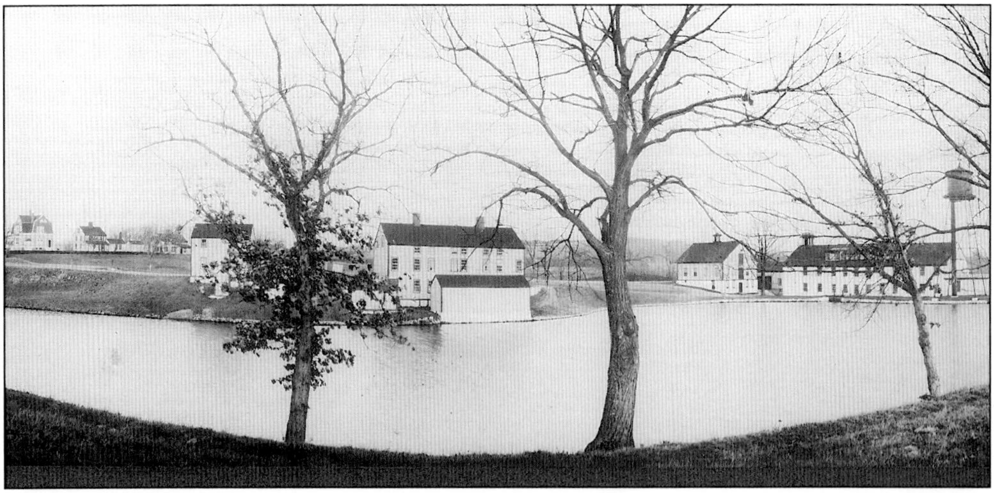

The Morgan Mill Pond, created by damming the Pocasset River, is shown here in the early 20th century. Early industrial views in rural settings such as this were almost pastoral in appearance. The 1817 mill is on the right, worker housing is in the center, and the mill owner's house looms highest in the distance among the area farms. (Photograph courtesy of Harold & Judy Beaudoin.)

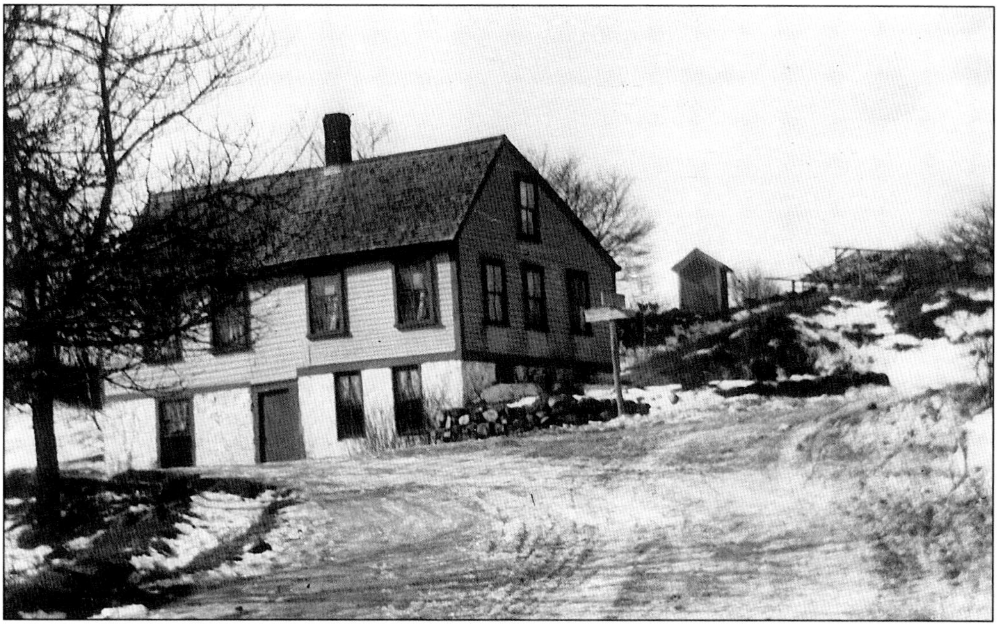

Local men gathered in the basement of the early home on the left, known by old-timers as the "Crotch Hotel," to drink after the day's work was done. The building, owned by Jim Vanner, once stood at the Simmonsville Avenue-Scituate Avenue junction. Simmonsville Avenue trails off to the left. (Photograph courtesy of Mabel Sprague.)

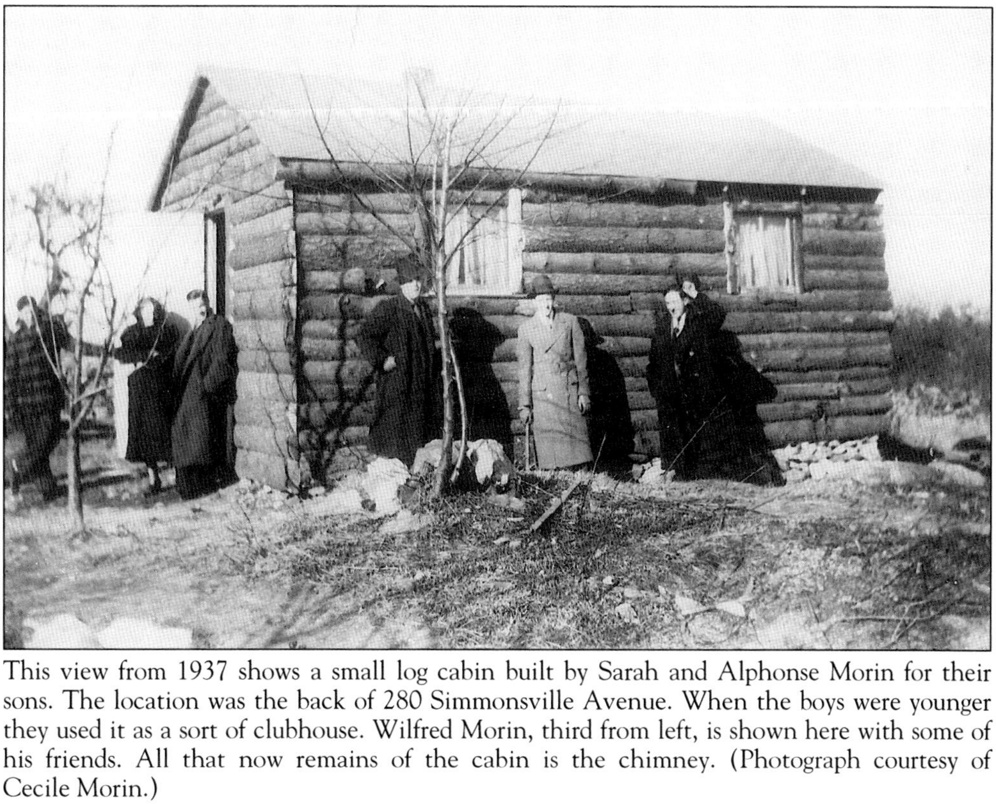

This view from 1937 shows a small log cabin built by Sarah and Alphonse Morin for their sons. The location was the back of 280 Simmonsville Avenue. When the boys were younger they used it as a sort of clubhouse. Wilfred Morin, third from left, is shown here with some of his friends. All that now remains of the cabin is the chimney. (Photograph courtesy of Cecile Morin.)

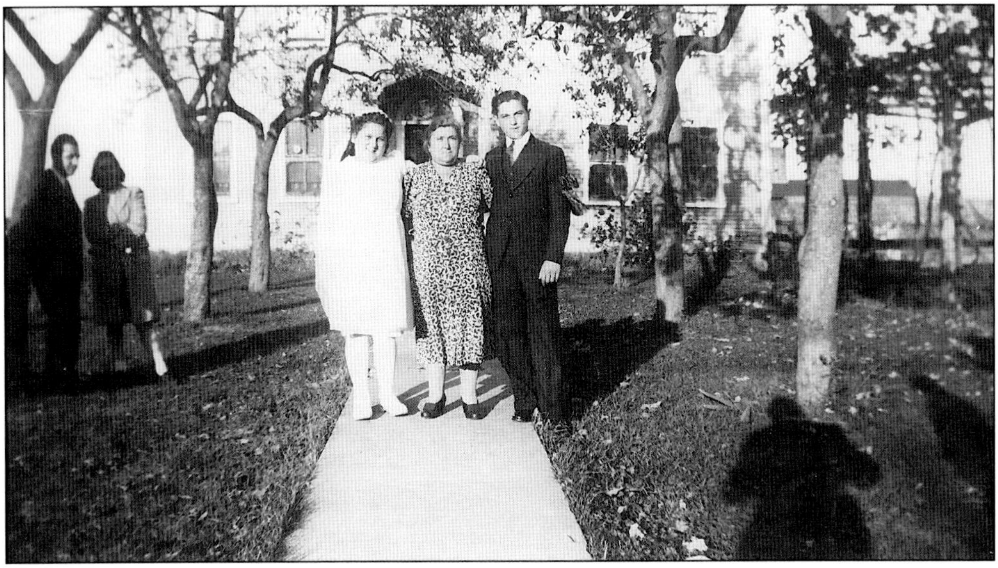

Standing on either side of their mother, Alfonsina, are Kay and Joseph D'Acchioli, celebrating their Confirmation in 1942. In the background is their house on Atwood Avenue, which was built by Dr. Harding Harris around 1799. Now an empty lot, this was once the site of the B & B Nightclub. (Photograph courtesy of Kay D'Acchioli.)

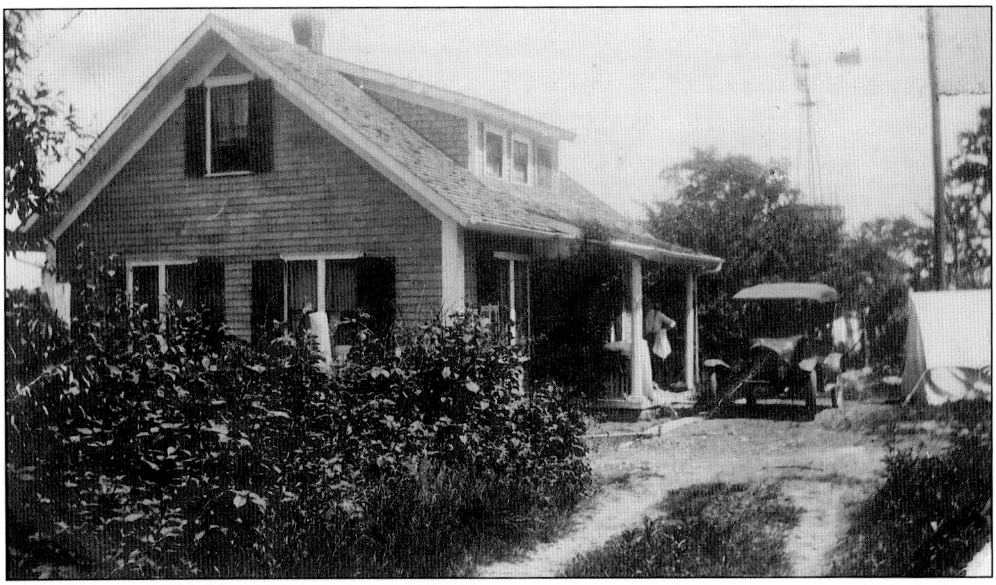

This home at 41 Harris Avenue is now owned by Dot and Al Baxter. In the background can be seen the windmill for the private Graniteville water company that supplied the village with fresh water. (Photograph courtesy of Dot Baxter.)

This picture of the Victoria Mill in Thornton was taken soon after the devastating 1938 Hurricane. The top portion of the mill shows damage caused by the high winds accompanying the storm. The mill, which was built in 1898 by Charles Fletcher, was repaired and is still in use today. Fletcher was born in England and named the mill after Queen Victoria. (Photograph courtesy of Carl Rainone.)

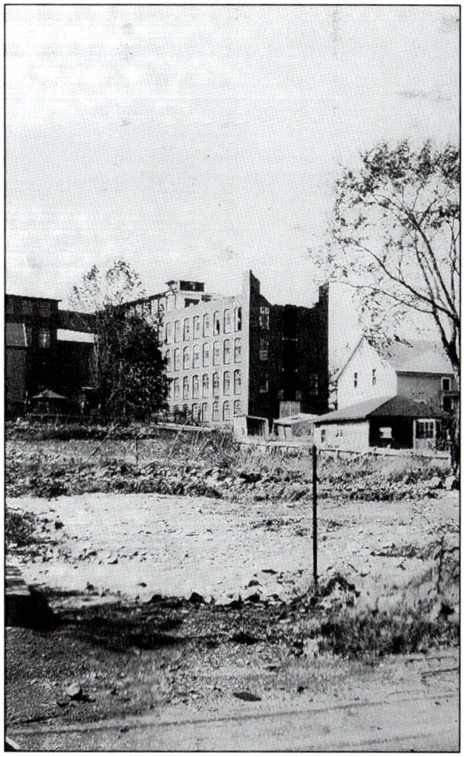

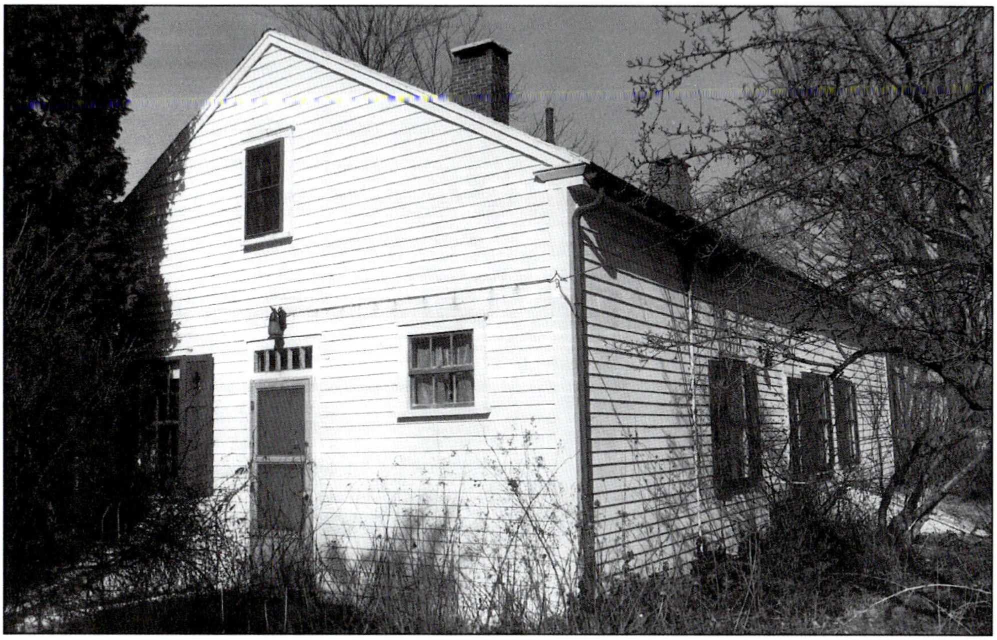

This small house stood just off Putnam Pike on the west side of Angell Avenue. It was torn down in 1997, and appears to have always been in the Angell family. Professor Howard Shawcross of Brown University, a relative, lived here in the 20th century. Next to the front door was a covered well enclosure, and inside were numerous early-19th-century architectural features. (Photograph courtesy of Walter Nebiker, RIH&HPC.)

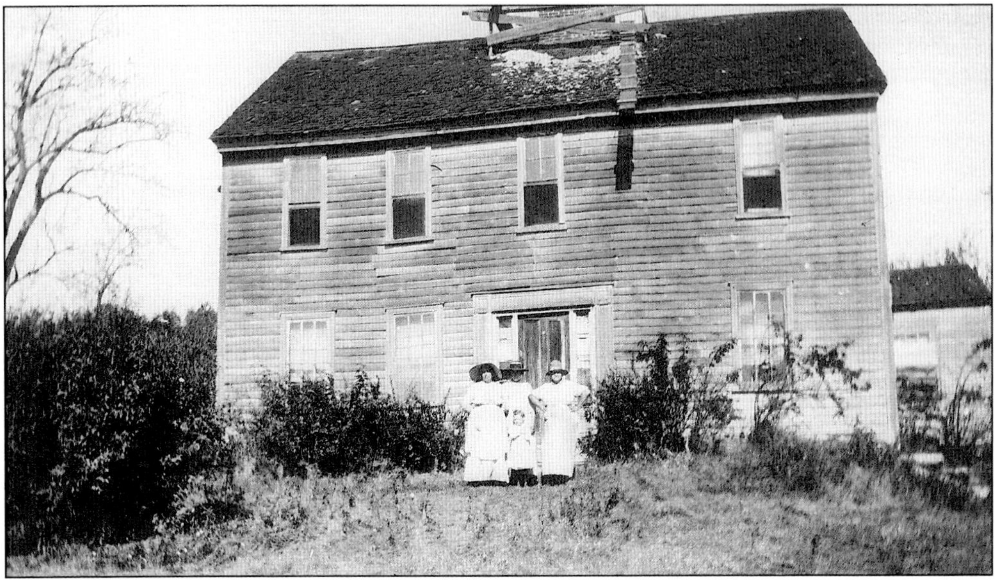

This house has been identified as the William Brown House (as on an 1895 map) on Brown Avenue, about 1/8 mile west of the site of the Belknap Chapel and one farm south of the Whipple Farm. Sisters Ida and Isabelle Brown used to live here along with Ida's husband, Edward Whipple. The sisters' nephew, Herbert "Bunny" Brown, and his family live here now. As far as is known, it has always been in the Brown family. (Photograph courtesy of Susie Brown.)

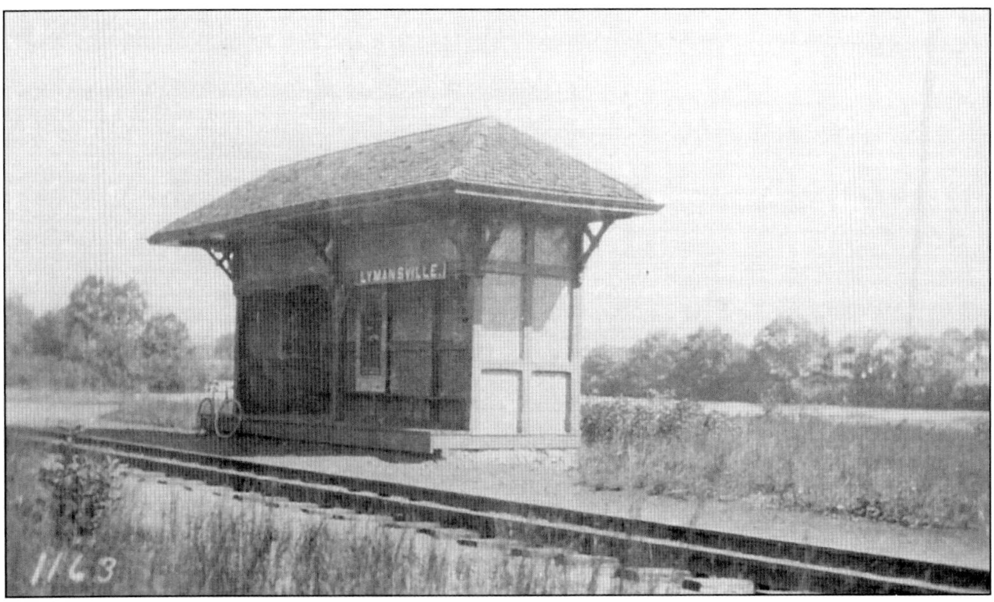

The Lymansville Train Station on the old Providence & Springfield Railroad was named for the North Providence village of Lymansville. The station and the tracks were actually on the Johnston side. The railroad was later taken over by the New York, New Haven and Hartford Railroad. (Photograph courtesy of Joe Coduri.)

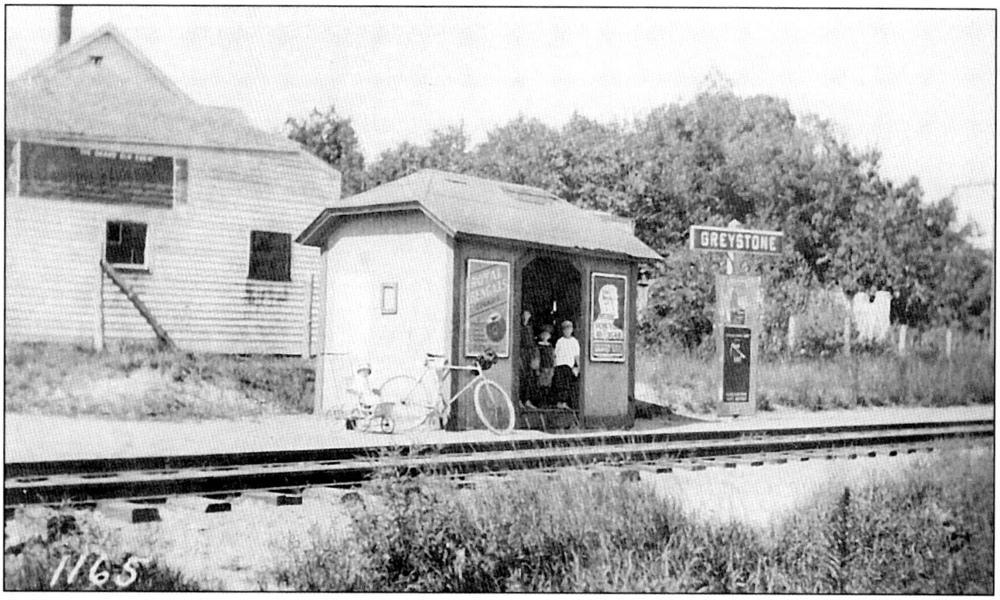

The Greystone station on the Providence & Springfield Railroad line was located at the bottom of Angell Avenue in Graniteville. At Centredale, Allendale, and Lymansville the stations were named after the nearby North Providence villages, but all were actually in Johnston, as was all the trackage. (Photograph courtesy of Joe Coduri.)

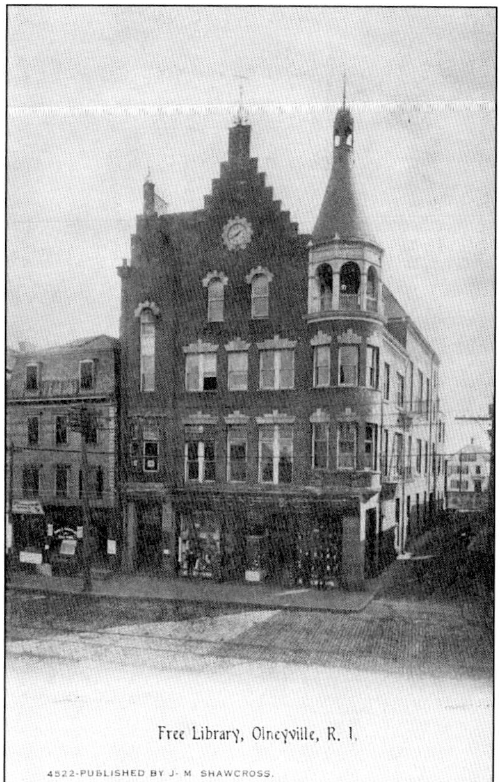

This Flemish-style building housing the Olneyville Free Library was built in 1891 in the part of Olneyville Square that was then in Johnston. The opulence of this building reflected the wealth of this part of our town. Johnston lost this great building in 1898 when this section of the town was annexed to Providence. The free library, organized in 1875, was housed first at 12 Hartford Avenue and later in the Irons Block. (Photograph courtesy of Louis McGowan.)

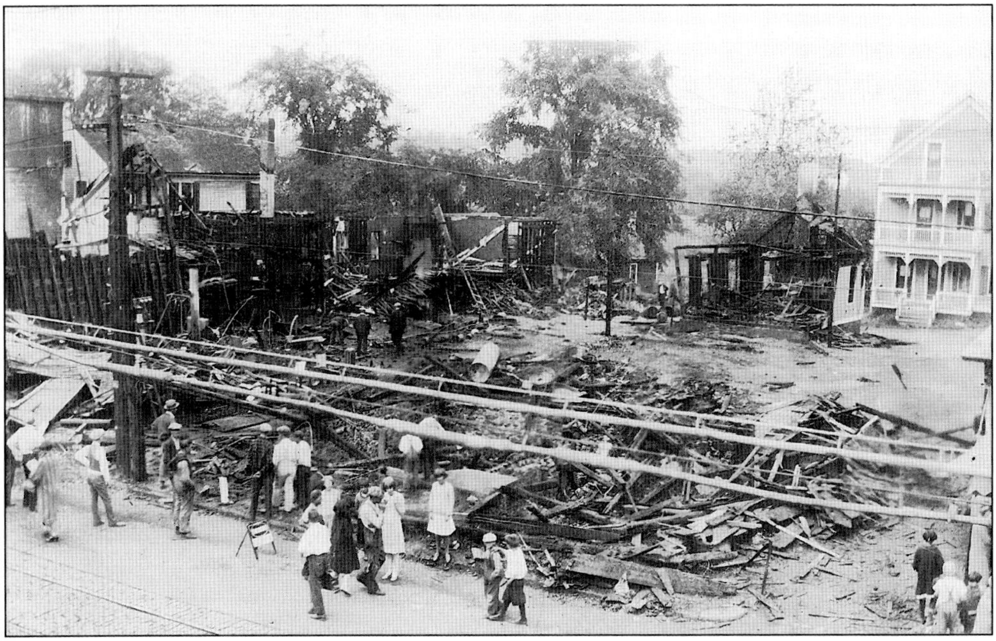

This photograph shows the devastation from a fire on July 5, 1926, in Thornton, which started in the dry goods store of John Saar at 1377 Plainfield Street. The total loss was $75,000. Five buildings were destroyed, five were badly damaged, and a dozen volunteer firemen were injured. Buildings belonging to the Aitchison and Ferri families were destroyed. (Photograph courtesy of Carl Rainone.)

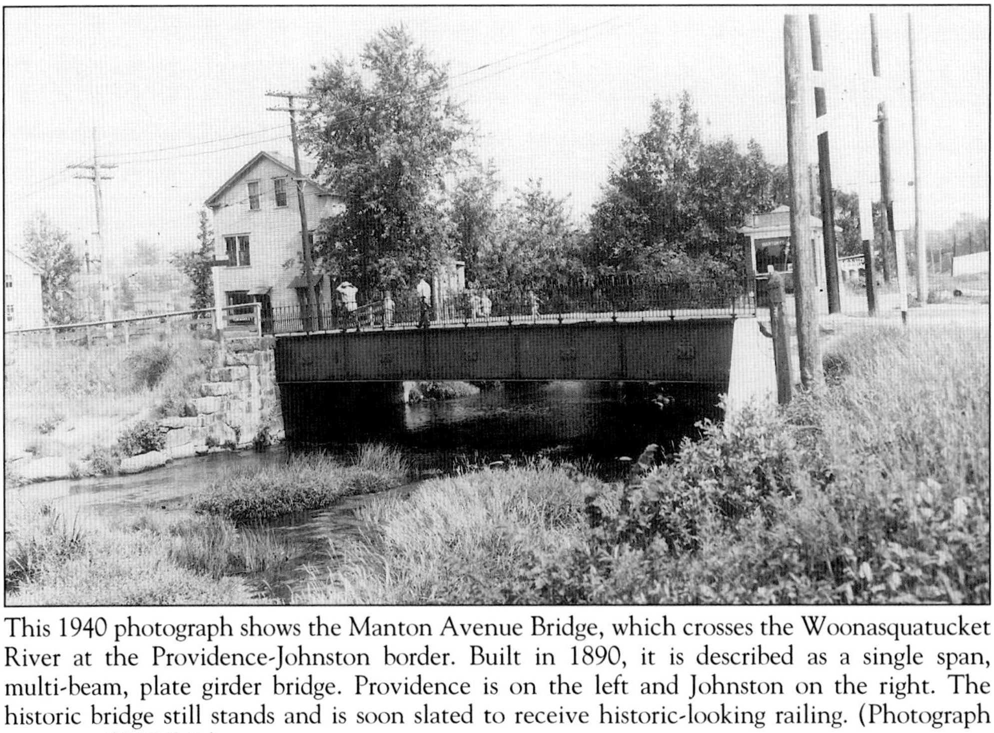

This 1940 photograph shows the Manton Avenue Bridge, which crosses the Woonasquatucket River at the Providence-Johnston border. Built in 1890, it is described as a single span, multi-beam, plate girder bridge. Providence is on the left and Johnston on the right. The historic bridge still stands and is soon slated to receive historic-looking railing. (Photograph courtesy of RIDOT.)

Two

Small Businesses and Big Mills

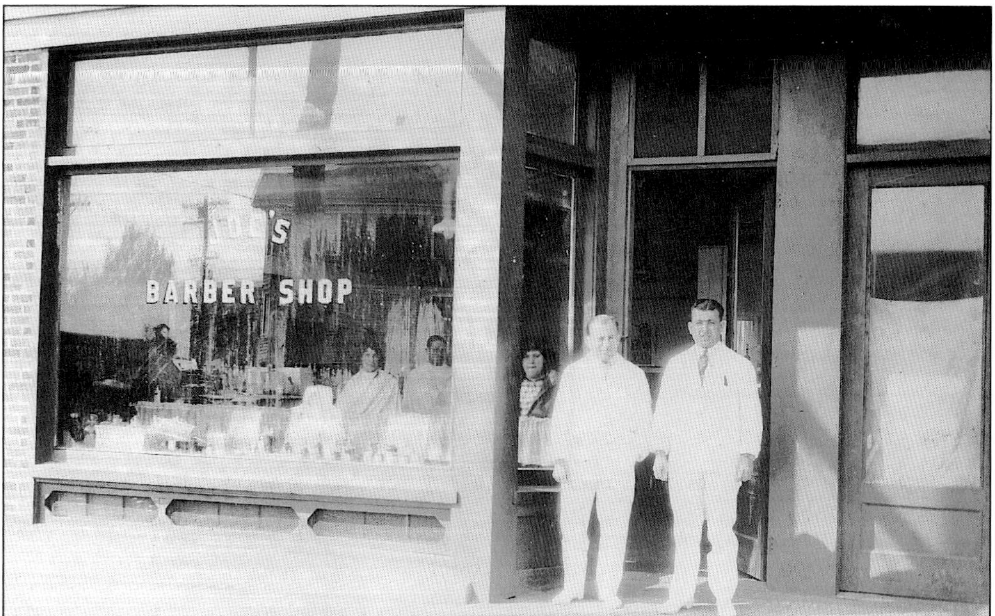

Joe Croce's barbershop was in the Ferri Block in Thornton between Ferri's Spa and Mike Leo's pool room. Joe (left) sold out to Anthony "Handsome" Ferri (right). There were barber shops in at least four locations in Thornton during this period, the 1920s. (Photograph courtesy of Carl Rainone.)

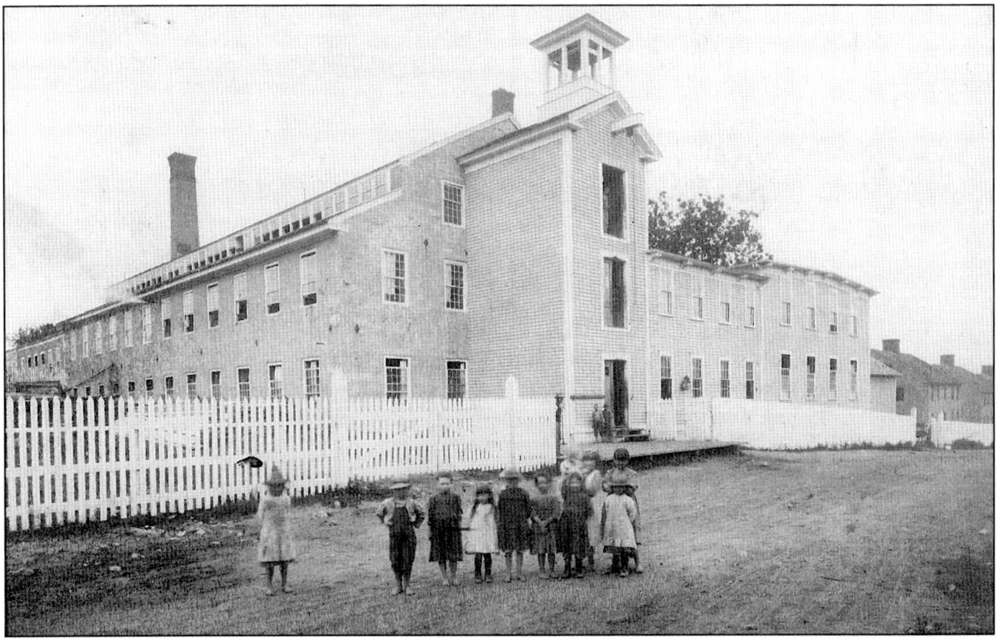

Thornton Worsted Mill was totally destroyed by fire on September 2, 1893. At that time William A. Shaw was president and owner, and William J. Shaw was superintendent. The main stone structure with the through-going monitor, which stood just west of the British Hosiery Mill on Mill Street, dates to the 1830s or 1840s. In 1869 the Providence Thread Company was using the site. In the 1880s Charles Fletcher owned the property, and in 1885 his son Joseph took charge of the business and it became known as Thornton Worsted. Three stone mill houses can just be seen on the right. (Photograph courtesy of Harold & Judy Beaudoin.)

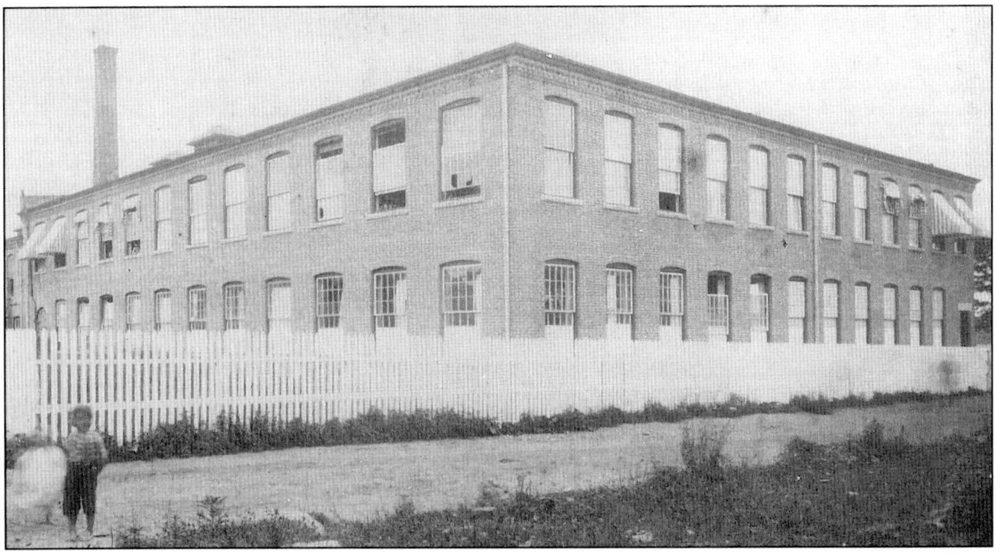

The British Hosiery Mill, pictured here c. 1890, was constructed in 1884 by Charles Fletcher. He built it for Robert W. Cooper, who came over from England with his own equipment and work force to manufacture fancy men's hosiery. Later firms in this complex were the Priscilla Worsted Mill and the Barker Chadsey Company. The building still stands but is vacant. (Photograph courtesy of Harold & Judy Beaudoin.)

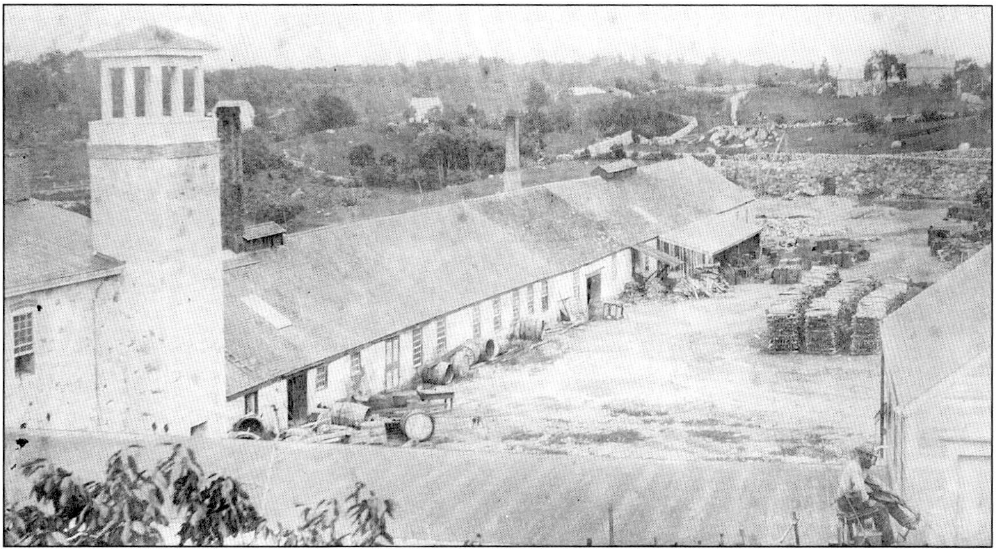

This turn-of-the-century view shows part of the Hughesdale Company Chemical Works on Central Avenue in Hughesdale. Theodore Hughes took over the business after his father, Thomas Hughes, passed away in 1884. The company made chemicals for the textile industry. At other times soap for the same industry was manufactured here as well as textiles themselves. (Photograph courtesy of Jean Spina.)

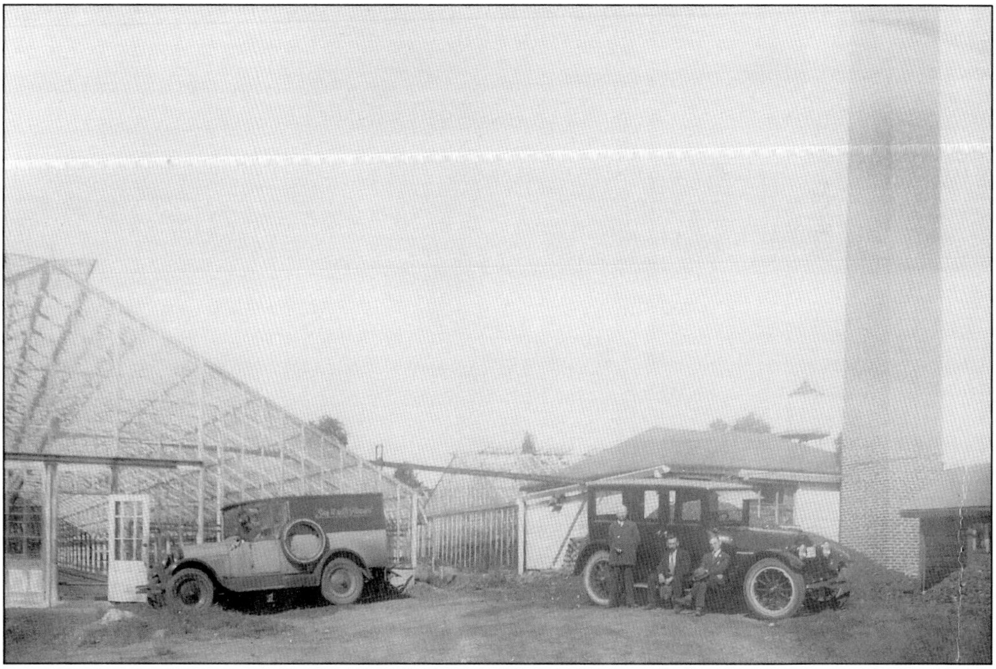

Holscher's Greenhouse is pictured here around 1929. After Herman Rudolf Holscher immigrated to America from Holland, he opened a greenhouse on 1447 Hartford Avenue in the early 1900s. His main business was selling cut flowers wholesale. In the picture, Herman is on the right; his cousin, Jan Jansen, is in the middle; and his father, Johan Friedrich Holscher, is on the left. Johan happened to be visiting from the old country. The greenhouse closed around 1990 and is now the site of a Shaws supermarket. (Photograph courtesy of the Holscher family.)

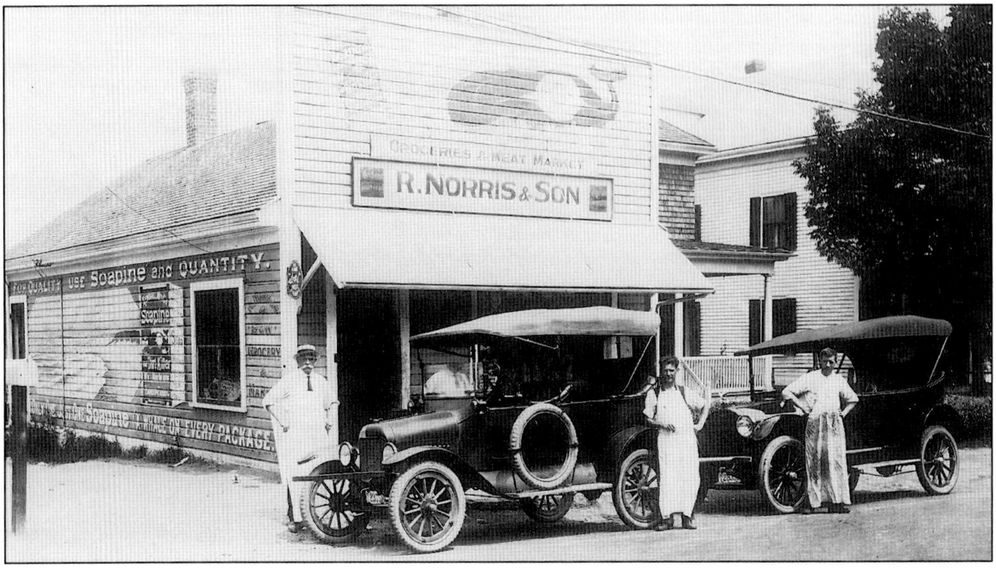

The R. Norris & Son Market was located at 117 Putnam Pike on the corner of Cottage Avenue. Locals remember sawdust on the floors, well-stocked shelves filled with groceries, and plenty of penny candy. The market was in business from the teens through the 1930s. (Photograph courtesy of Nellie Dahlin.)

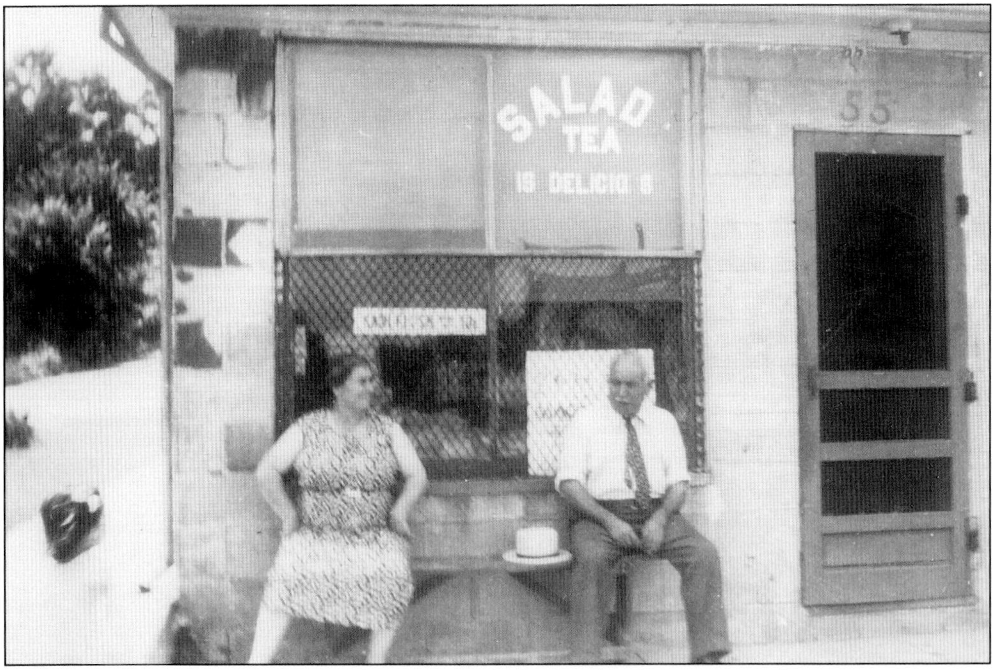

Rotondo's Grocery Store was at the corner of Rhode Island Avenue and George Waterman Road. Frank Rotondo built it about 1921 and ran it with his wife, Carmina. In the same building was the Royal Social Club and Grape's Barber Shop (run by Aggrapino Rotondo). The store was operated until around 1950 by the Rotondo family. A Mr. Dolbey then ran it until Highland Memorial Cemetery bought the property and tore the building down. (Photograph courtesy of Tina Russo.)

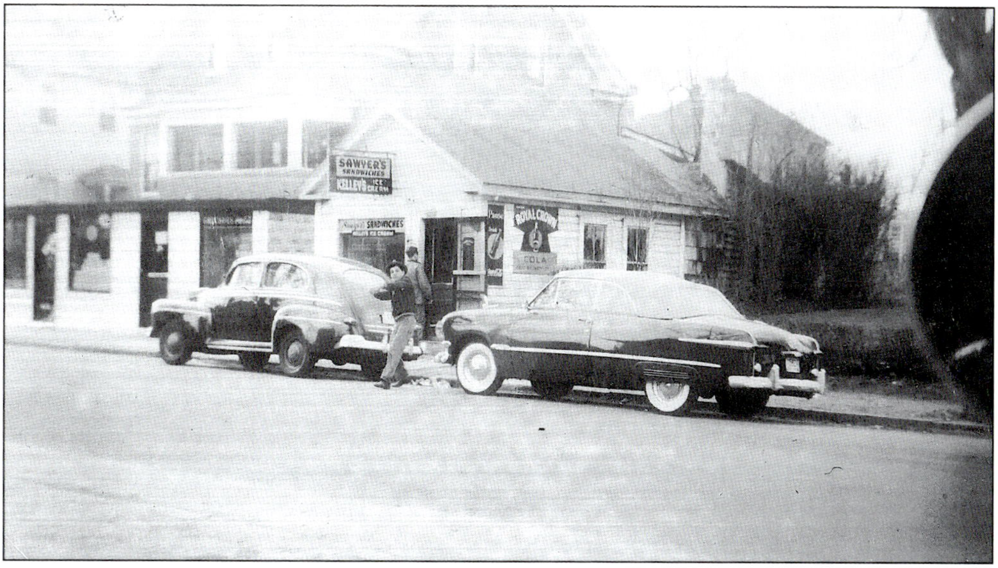

Sawyer's Snack Bar, in the center, was torn down in the 1950s to make way for the present brick structure at the corner of Plainfield and Walnut Streets. Pezza's Market is on the left. The 1950 Ford on the right belonged to Herbie Brooks, a teacher in town. Tommy Cappelli, also a teacher and principal in Johnston, stands between the cars. (Photograph courtesy of Bob Whittaker.)

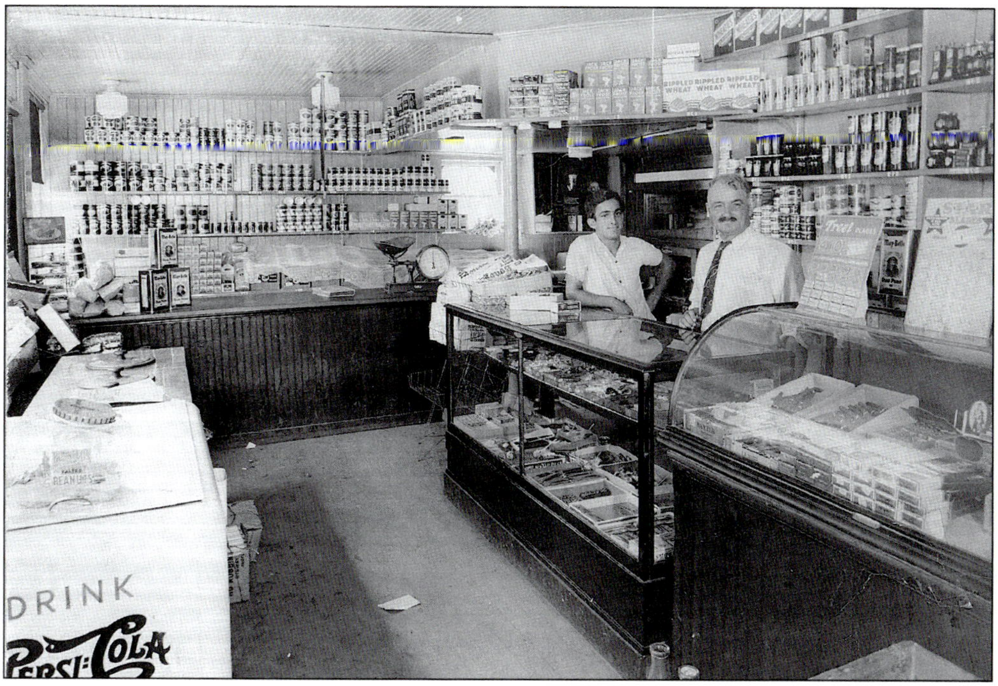

Vincent Pezza (right) emigrated from Italy to New York. In 1919 he moved to Johnston, where he ran Pezza's Market on Plainfield Street (pictured here in the 1930s). His son Lawrence (left) took over the business in 1947 and ran it until 1989. It was a typical, small neighborhood market where friendly service and good meats brought people in even though the big markets had come to dominate the scene. (Photograph courtesy of Lawrence Pezza.)

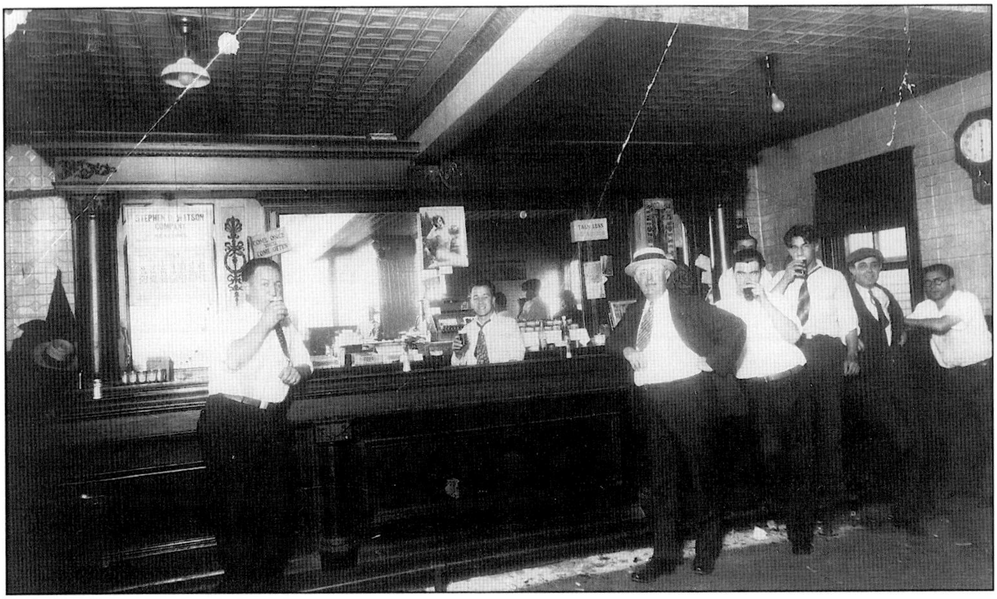

Ferri's Tavern, located on Plainfield Street in Thornton, is shown here in 1930 before the bar stools were put in. Andrew "Buzzi" Ferri is the bartender and Mike "Butch" Ferri is on the left drinking a glass of beer. Third from the left in front of the bar is Andrew Tobin, then Nicky Ferri, Joe Golini, and Mike Rainone. The dining and dancing area in back had not yet been added. The Ferris took over the tavern, originally known as Hartshorn's Bar, in the teens. (Photograph courtesy of Nikki Ferri Gizzarelli.)

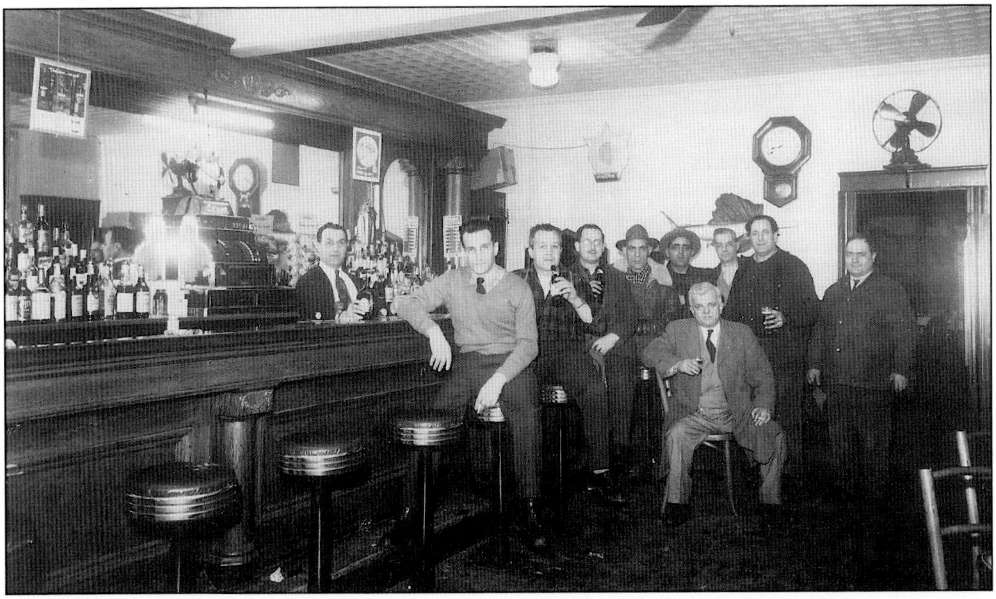

Ferri's Tavern, with Louis "House" Ferri behind the bar, is shown here in 1948. Freddie Ferri is seated on the first stool with Buzzi Ferri behind him. Joe Golini is seated on the chair to their left. Behind Golini with the hat is Thomas "30 days" Ricci, then from left to right are, Al Iannotti, unidentified, and Tom Butmarc. Through the door was the dining and dancing area. For another view of this bar see the bottom of p. 12 in *Johnston, Volume I*. (Photograph courtesy of Nicky Ferri Gizzarelli.)

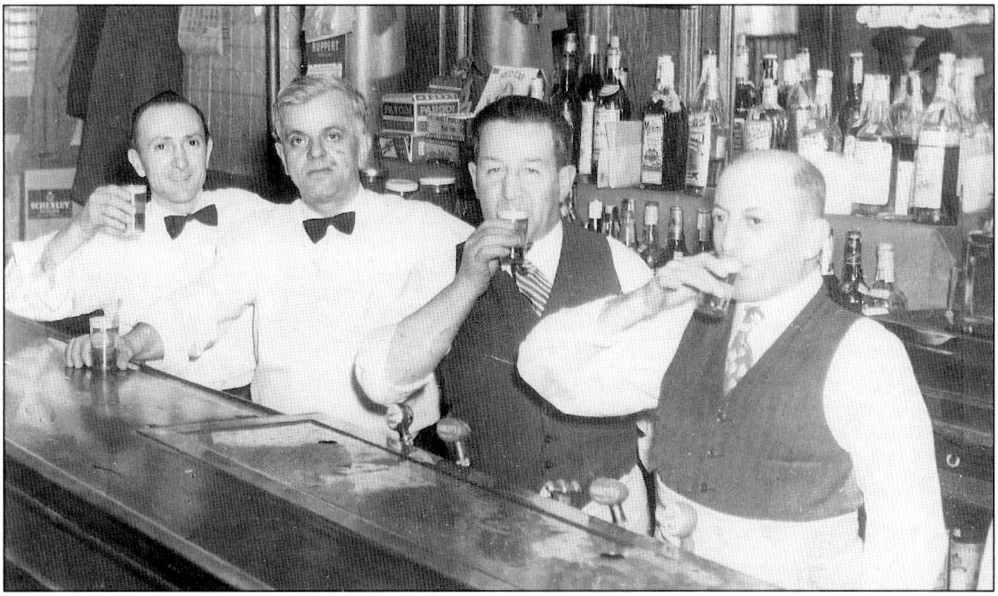

Behind the bar at Ferri's Tavern are, from left to right, Buddy ?, Joe Golini, Butch Ferri, and Joe Croce. The scene looks to be in the 1940s. A 1926 fire destroyed the original Ferri's Tavern, but it was rebuilt on the site. Nicolina Ferri and her family lived upstairs. (Photograph courtesy of Nicky Ferri Gizzarelli.)

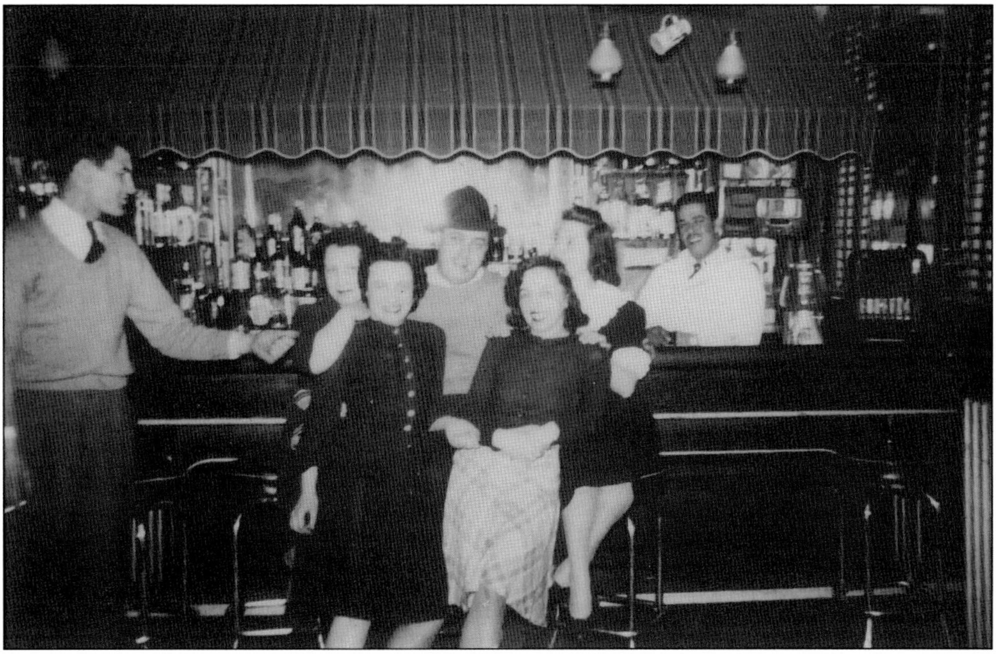

Inside the bar at the Cypress Cafe on Greenville Avenue are a group of friends in the 1940s. The building is still there but is now used for a flower business. Adolf Guidone is the lucky man in the middle. Mike Fandetti is on the left and Paul Deluca is on the right. DeLuca owned the Yellow Jacket Motel on Hartford Avenue. The State of Rhode Island took his motel property for Route 295 and, ironically, also took his house property on Greenville Avenue for the same project. (Photograph courtesy of Louis "Smokey" Ullucci.)

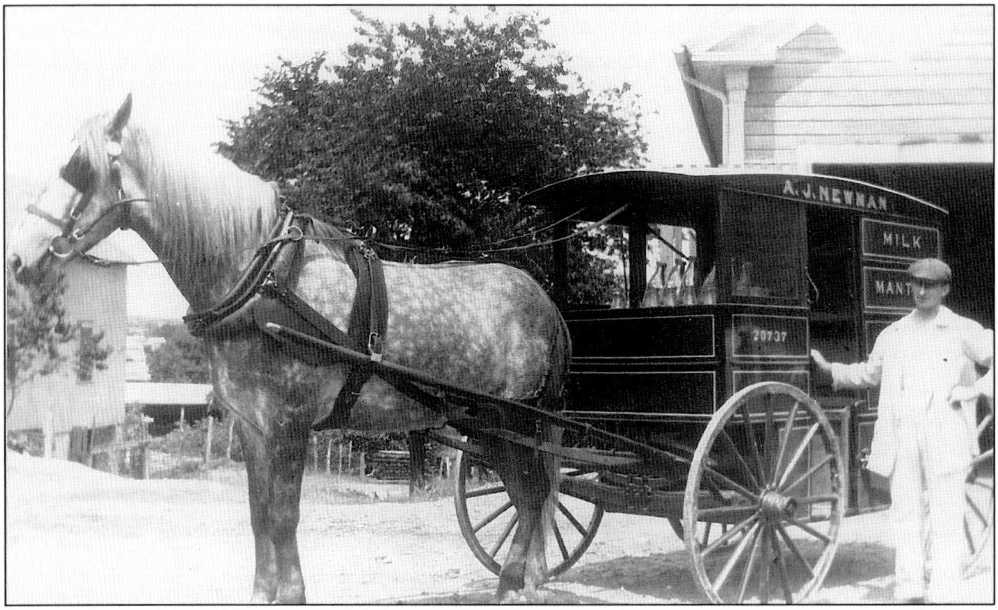

Arthur J. Newman delivers milk on Greenville Avenue for the A.J. Newman Dairy, located in Manton, before World War I. The dairy was formerly part of the original Newman Dairy, which was started by his father, Joseph Newman, in 1879. Arthur, who received the business from his mother, later sold it to his uncle, John F. Newman, and went to work for his brother Walter at the W.C. Newman Dairy. (Photograph courtesy of Earl Newman.)

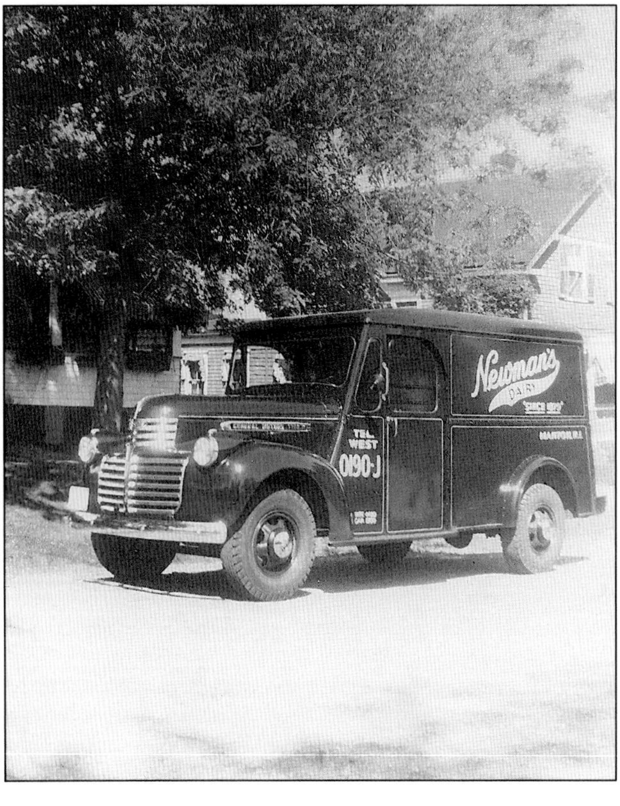

This *c.* 1940 photograph shows a General Motors delivery truck, one of the first enclosed milk delivery trucks, owned by the W.C. Newman Dairy. Walter C. Newman started the business, located in Manton, in the early teens when he was given one of his father's delivery routes. Walter's son Earl later took over the business, finally selling out to the Pippin Orchard Dairy in 1961. (Photograph courtesy of Earl Newman.)

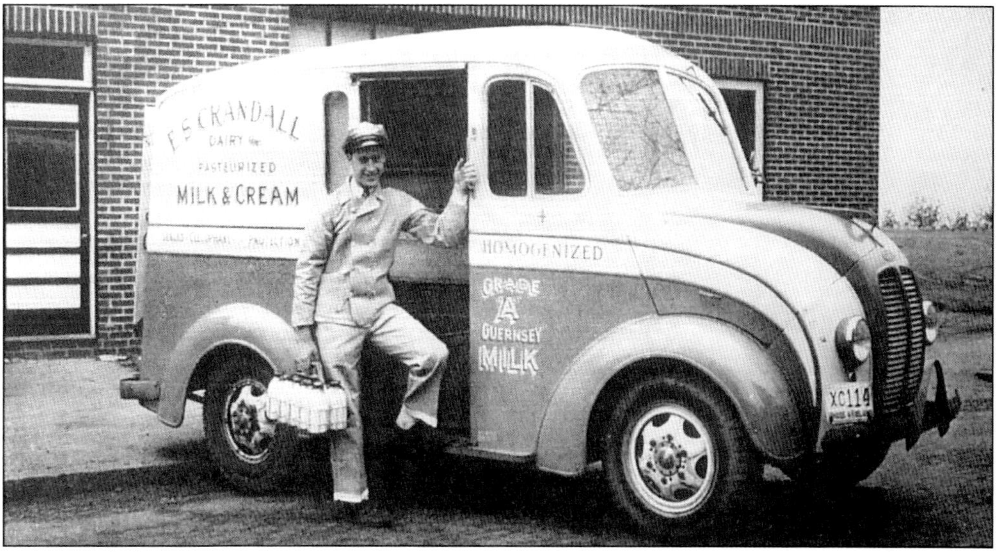

Ray Crandall poses next to his delivery truck for the dairy that was started by his grandfather, Edward Sweet Crandall, in Providence. The dairy later moved to 12 Lowell Avenue, also in Providence, before Edward bought the former Tillinghast farm on Morgan Avenue in 1938 and built a new barn for his cows. He soon gave the business to his son, E. Thomas Crandall. The processing plant remained in Providence until 1955, when they built their new plant in Johnston. The dairy closed in 1971. (Photograph courtesy of Mabel Sprague.)

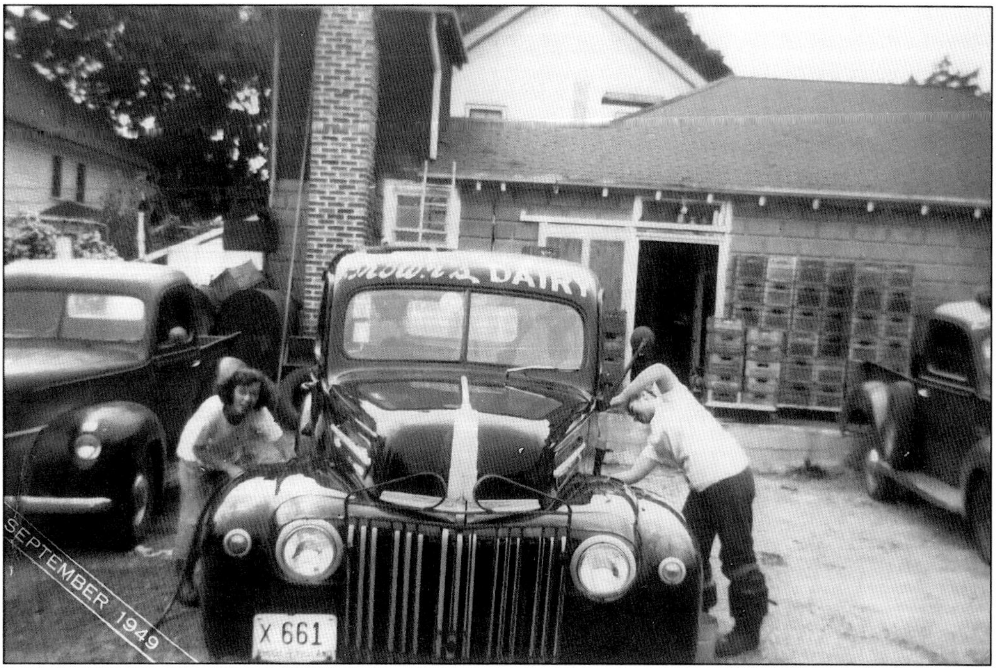

Shirley Dove (left) and Millicent (Brown) Newsham wash one of the delivery trucks for the J.O. Brown Dairy on Walnut Street in Thornton. John and Lillian Brown, Millicent's parents, ran the small dairy, which processed milk from area farms. The building remains, although the dairy is long gone, a victim of the large out-of-state milk processors. (Photograph courtesy of Millicent Newsham.)

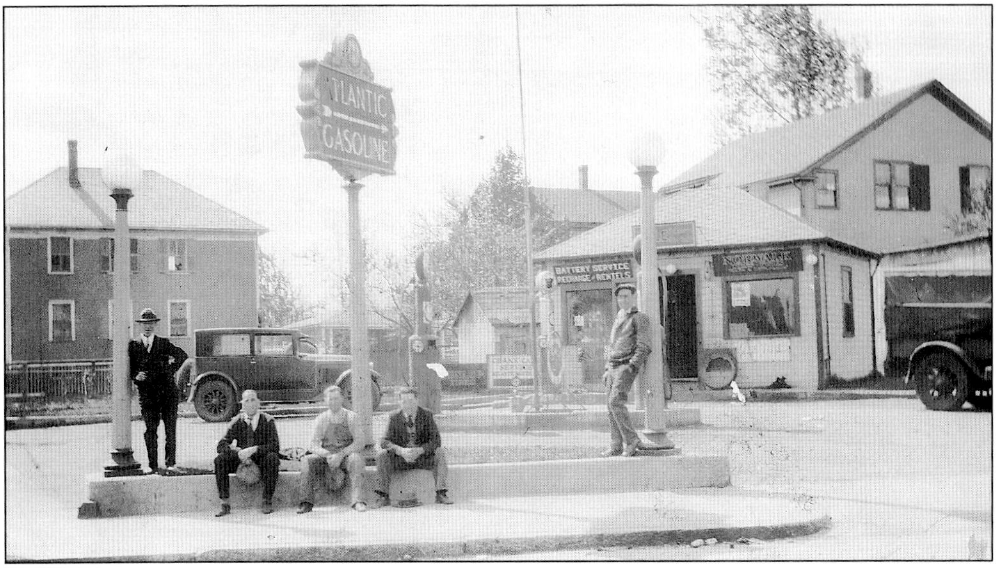

"Atlantic keeps your car on the go," a jingle from the 1950s told us. Here we see an Atlantic station in the late 1920s or early '30s at the corner of Atwood Avenue and Plainfield Street. John Parillo built the station in 1923 or 1924 and ran it until his brother Rocco took over the business. Rocco later sold out to Vincent "China" Salzillo. (Photograph courtesy of Carl Rainone.)

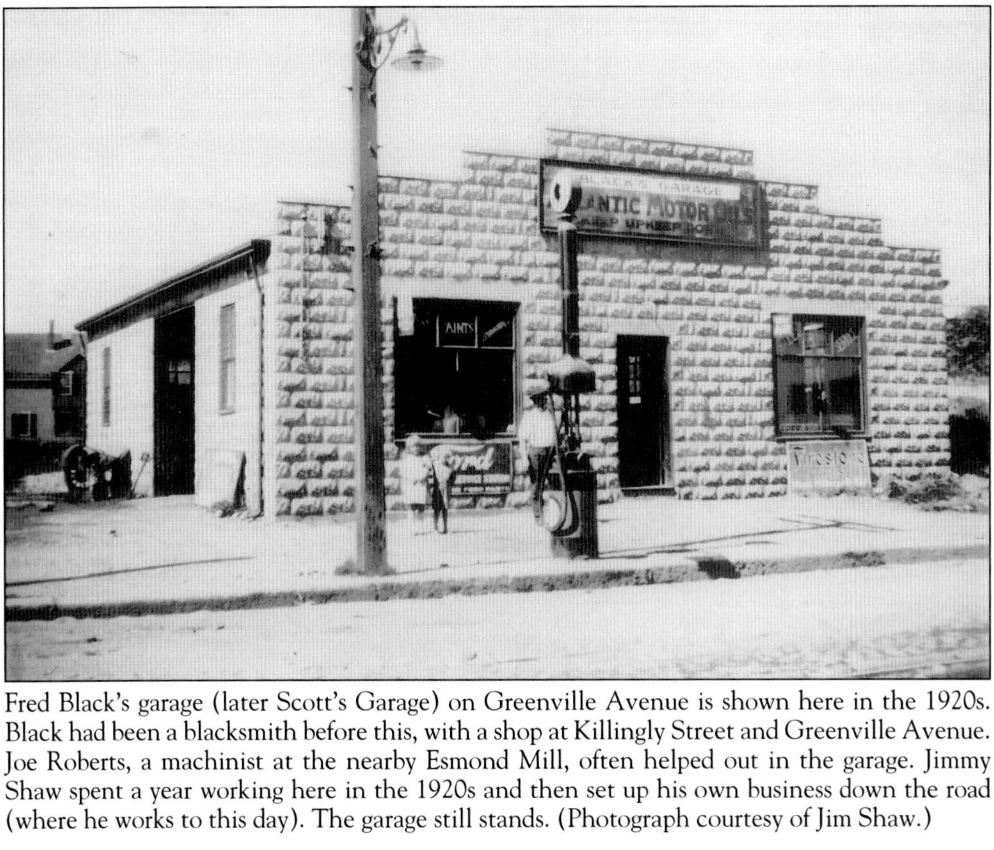

Fred Black's garage (later Scott's Garage) on Greenville Avenue is shown here in the 1920s. Black had been a blacksmith before this, with a shop at Killingly Street and Greenville Avenue. Joe Roberts, a machinist at the nearby Esmond Mill, often helped out in the garage. Jimmy Shaw spent a year working here in the 1920s and then set up his own business down the road (where he works to this day). The garage still stands. (Photograph courtesy of Jim Shaw.)

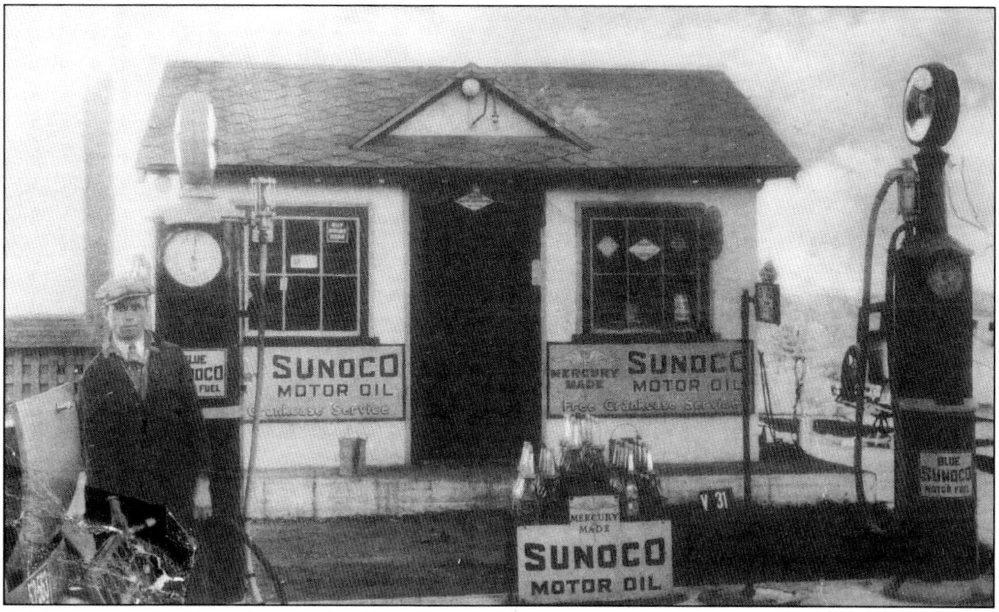

The B & R Filling Station at 54 George Waterman Road was started by Salvatore "Sam" Butera and John Rotondo. The building still stands although it has been much changed. Salvatore Butera Jr. rents the building to an auto body shop. (Photograph courtesy of Tina Russo.)

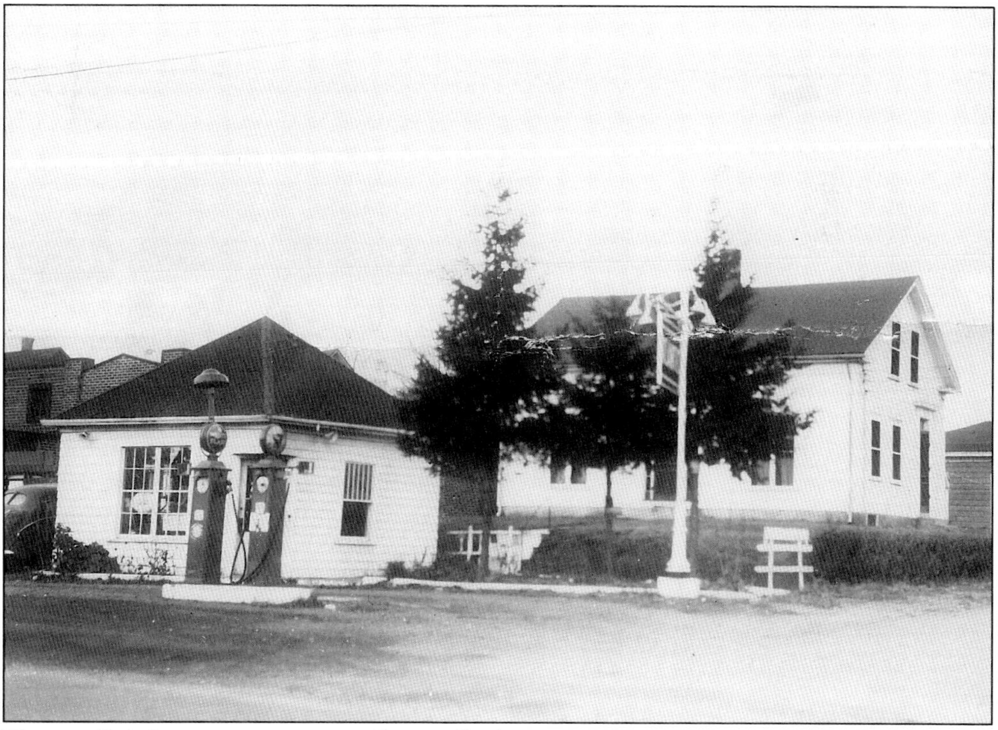
This small Atlantic gas station on Greenville Avenue in Manton was torn down mid-century to make room for expansions at Shaw's Garage next door. The station was run by Henry Carson until he died. Carson lived in the house out back, which was torn down at the same time the station was. (Photograph courtesy of Jim Shaw.)

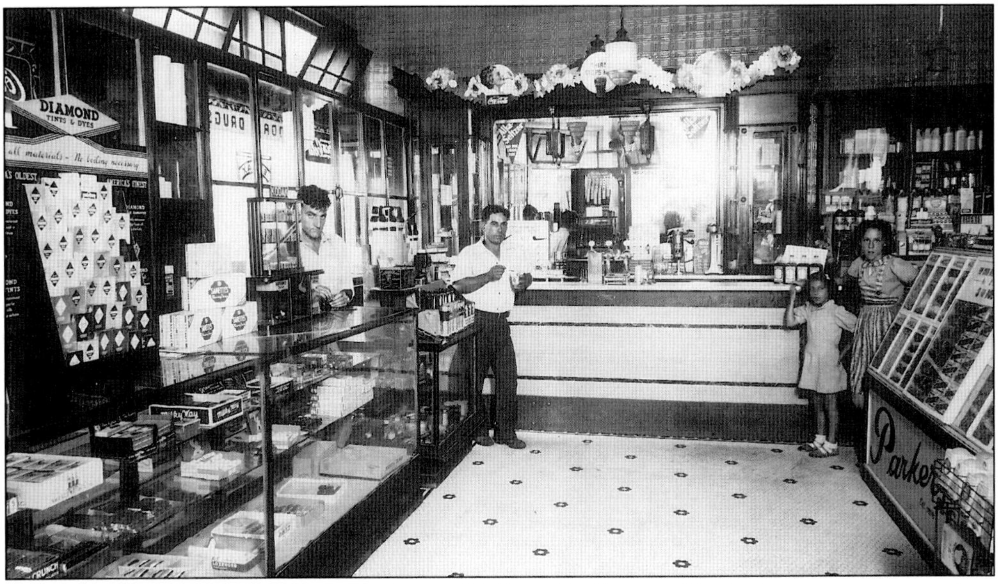

Golini's Drugstore was built in 1921 by William J. Golini. He had previously served as pharmacist at Victoria Pharmacy across the street in Johnston. William's son Joseph (left) took over the business and ran it until the mid-1980s. Second from the left is Americo Tortolani. His grandson Robert bought the business from Joseph in the 1980s. The two girls were children of Carmella Disciulo. The store closed in 1997. (Photograph courtesy of Al Forte.)

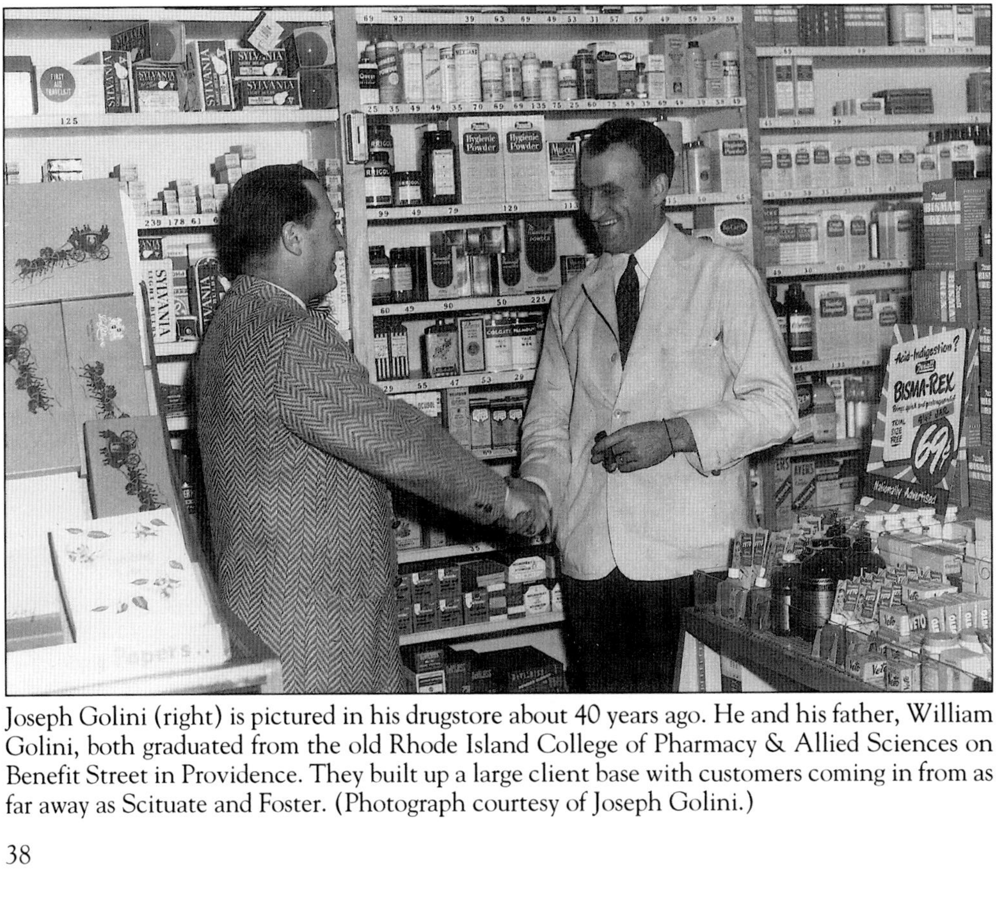

Joseph Golini (right) is pictured in his drugstore about 40 years ago. He and his father, William Golini, both graduated from the old Rhode Island College of Pharmacy & Allied Sciences on Benefit Street in Providence. They built up a large client base with customers coming in from as far away as Scituate and Foster. (Photograph courtesy of Joseph Golini.)

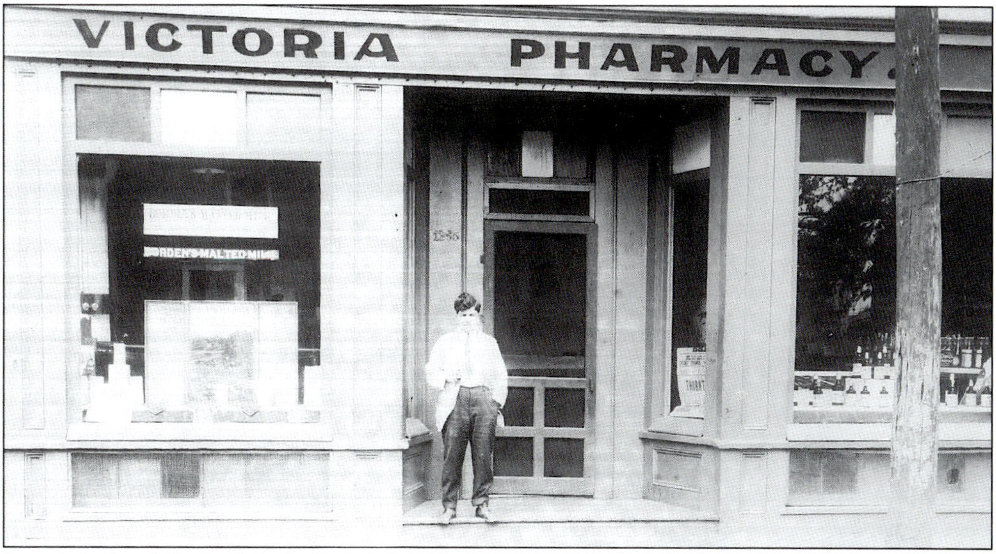

Joseph Judge (changed from Del Guidice) stands in front of the Victoria Pharmacy at 1365 Plainfield Street in the Myrtle Hall building. He was a partner here for a few years in the teens with William J. Golini. Judge later worked for Almond O. Smith in Thornton and for Liggett's Drugstore in Providence. A son of Filippi and Rosaria (Angelotti) Del Guidice, he married Jane Ann Shaw. (Photograph courtesy of Sam Coupe.)

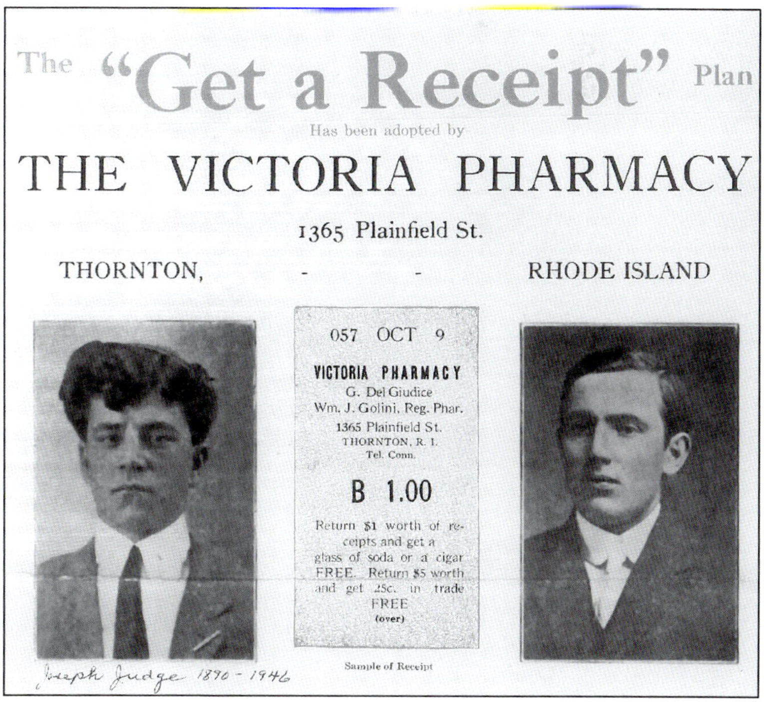

At the Victoria Pharmacy in the late teens, Joseph Judge and his partner, William J. Golini, learned the benefits of advertising and of the use of receipts to get people into their drugstore. The message cut off at right is repeated below in Italian to appeal to the large Italian population in the village. (Photograph courtesy of Sam Coupe.)

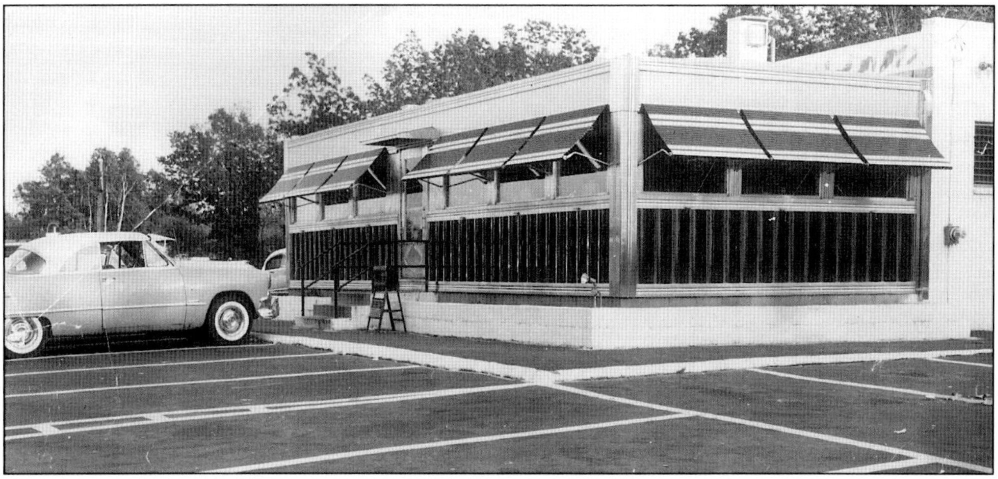

Lloyd's Diner on Hartford Avenue was owned and run by Lloyd and Lorraine Hopkins. They bought the diner in 1957 and ran it until 1980, when their daughter, Jean Arcand, took it over. She operated it until 1987. Standing empty for a couple of years, the diner was moved to New Hampton, NH, after sitting vacant in Long Island for three years. It was the last Worcester Diner ever built, number 850. (Photograph courtesy of Jean Arcand.)

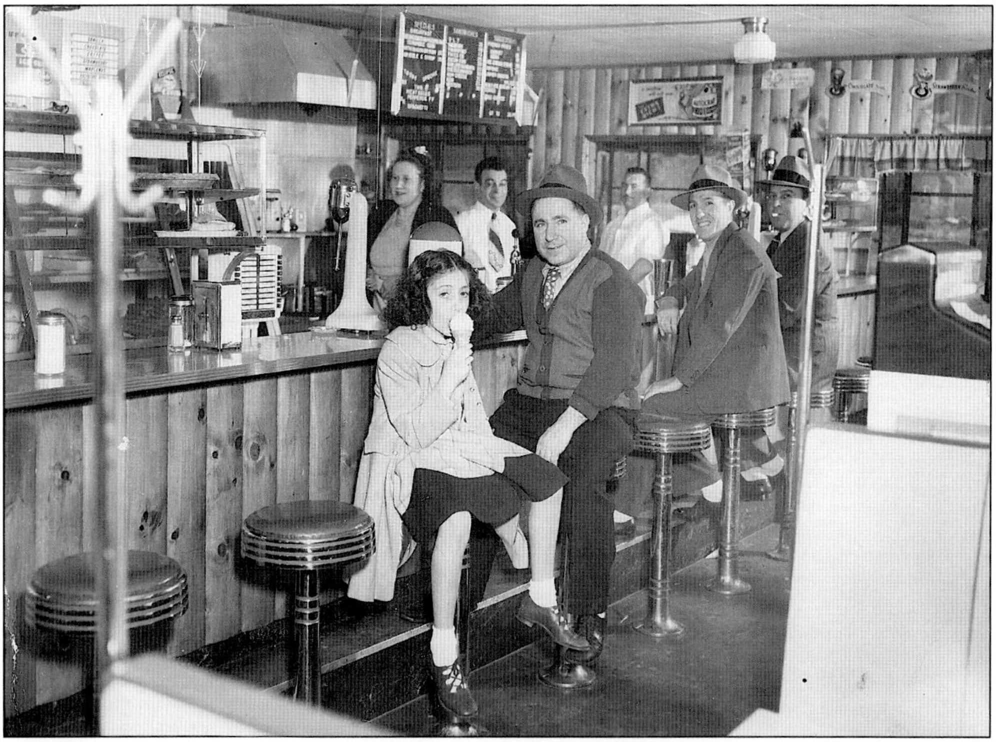

The Moosehead Diner on Hartford Avenue was built in 1939 by Tony Petrucci, who also built the Pike Drive-in. He ran it until about 1975, when McDonald's built on the spot. It featured log cabin styling on the exterior. Behind the counter are, from left to right, Marion Petrucci; her husband, Tony; and Pat, the chef. In front of the counter is Angelo Dedora with his daughter. Next down the counter is Vincent Furia and then Louis Furia. (Photograph courtesy of Tony Petrucci.)

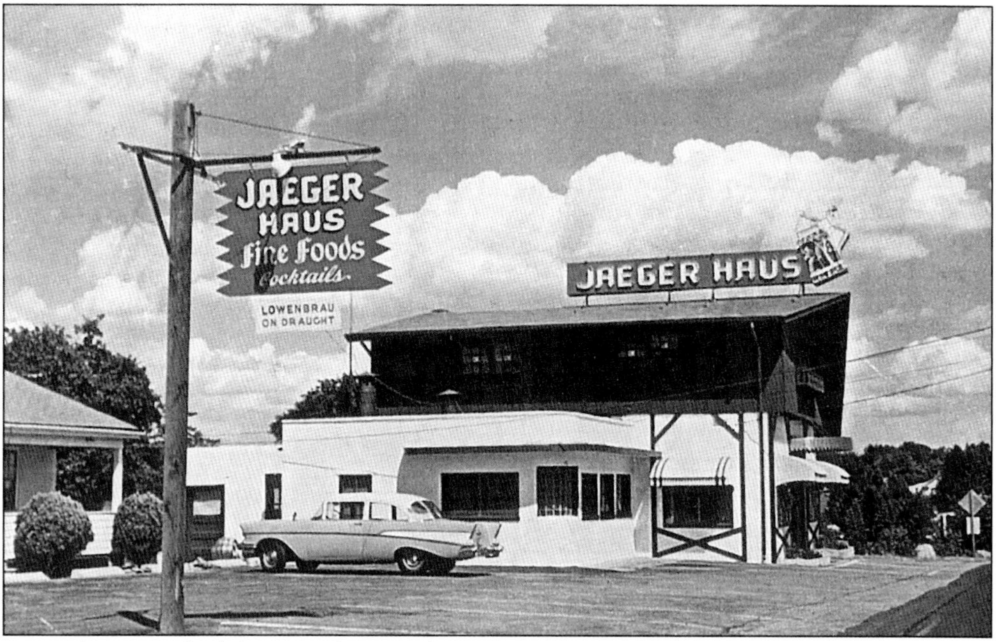

Located on Hartford Avenue close to the Scituate border, the Jaeger Haus restaurant was a popular dining spot for locals and passers-by. William Jaegar Sr., a councilman in town, bought the property in 1945 and started Jaeger's Ice Cream. In 1951 the name was changed to Jaeger Haus. William Sr. ran the business until 1968, when he sold it to his son, William Jr. In 1977 Norman Green bought the business and ran it under the same name. Green sold out, and for a while it was a Beef & Bun. The building burned in 1995. (Photograph courtesy of Joe Coduri.)

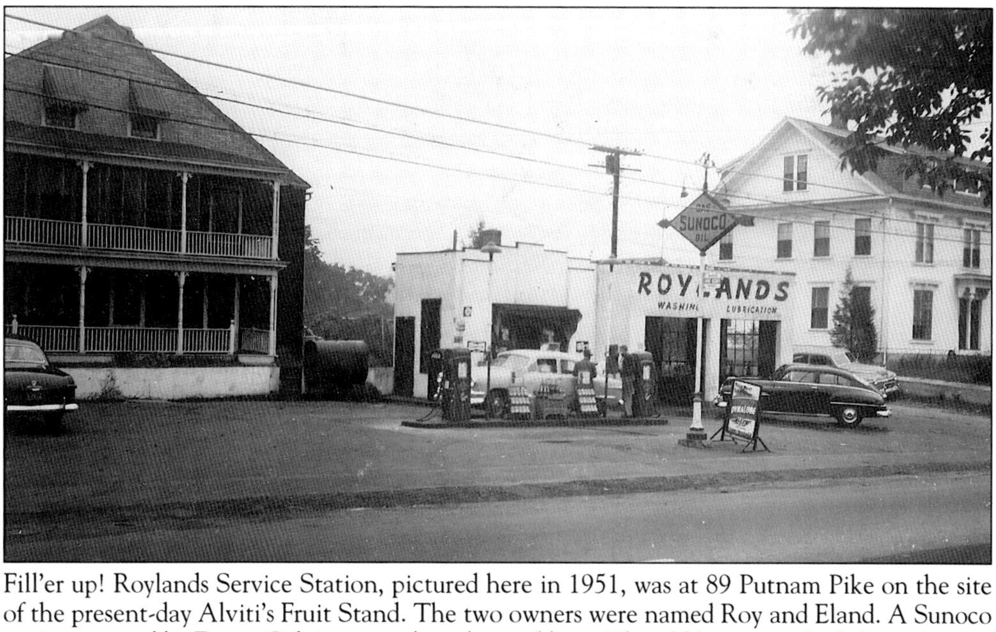

Fill'er up! Roylands Service Station, pictured here in 1951, was at 89 Putnam Pike on the site of the present-day Alviti's Fruit Stand. The two owners were named Roy and Eland. A Sunoco station, owned by Ernest Calciura, was later located here. The old house on the left was known as the Barn House. In the 19th century, stagecoaches would stop here to change horses on the way to Chepachet. (Photograph courtesy of Ernest Caloura.)

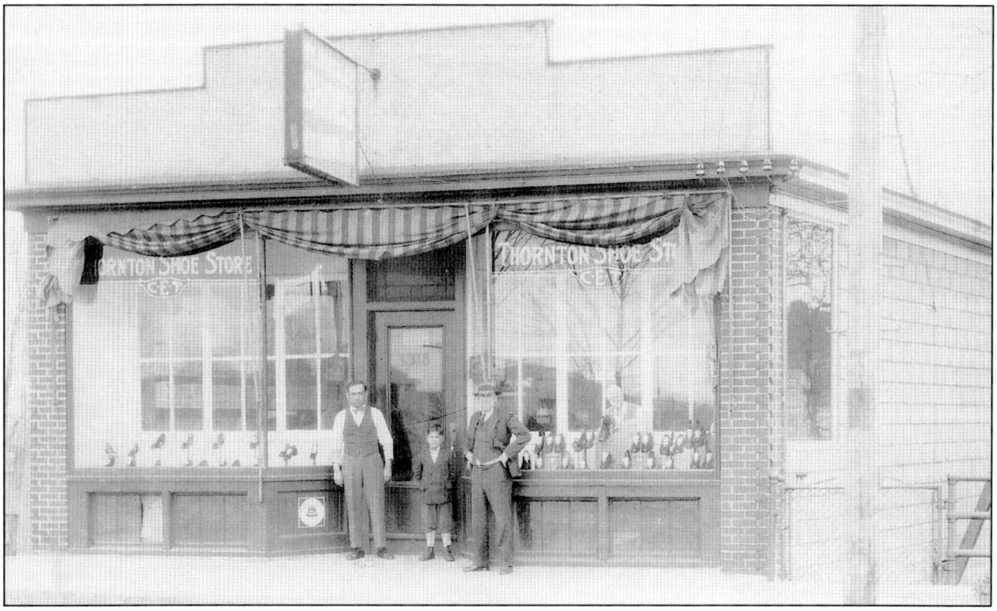

The Thornton Shoe Store, 1318 Plainfield Street, was operated by Claudio E. Tortolani. His wares are proudly displayed in the windows. The building still stands, having undergone some changes and a large addition. It later became Little Rhody's Hardware & Gift Shop, run by the Mendozzis. Today it is the home of Johnston Lawnmower. (Photograph courtesy of John Ricci.)

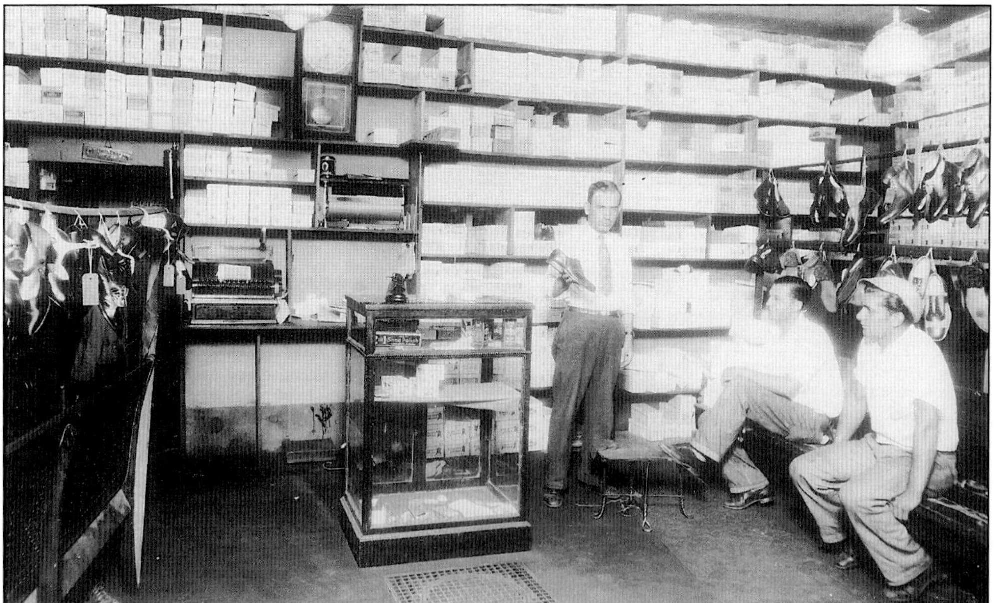

The interior of the Thornton Shoe Store is shown here in the late 1920s. Claudio "Vic" E. Tortolani sold new shoes and repaired old ones. Sam Coupe from Simmonsville Avenue remembers decorating his windows in the 1920s. Being very good at his trade, the federal government paid Claudio to repair shoes for the Army during World War II, which he did at another site. (Photograph courtesy of John Ricci.)

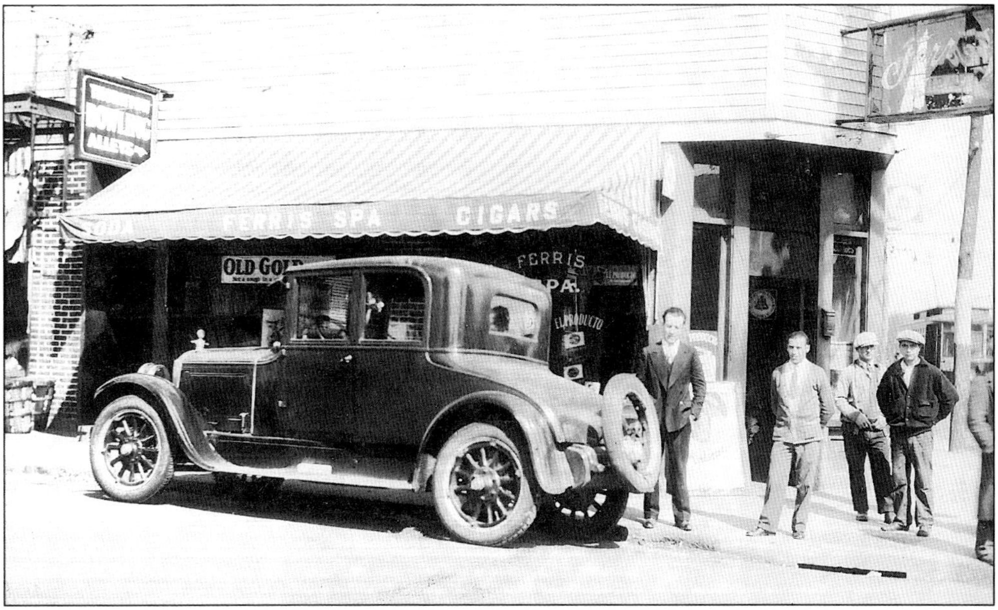

Ferri's Spa, photographed here in 1928, was located in the Ferri Block, which was built in 1920 by Vincent Ferri at the northwest corner of the intersection of Plainfield Street and Atwood Avenue. The original business at that location was Vincent Ferri's drugstore, followed by a cigar shop run by Frank Barbato. Emil Fuoco ran his spa here for 31 years. The entrance to the Thornton Bowling Alleys is on the left, and the Hughesdale trolley can be seen on the right. (Photograph courtesy of Carl Rainone.)

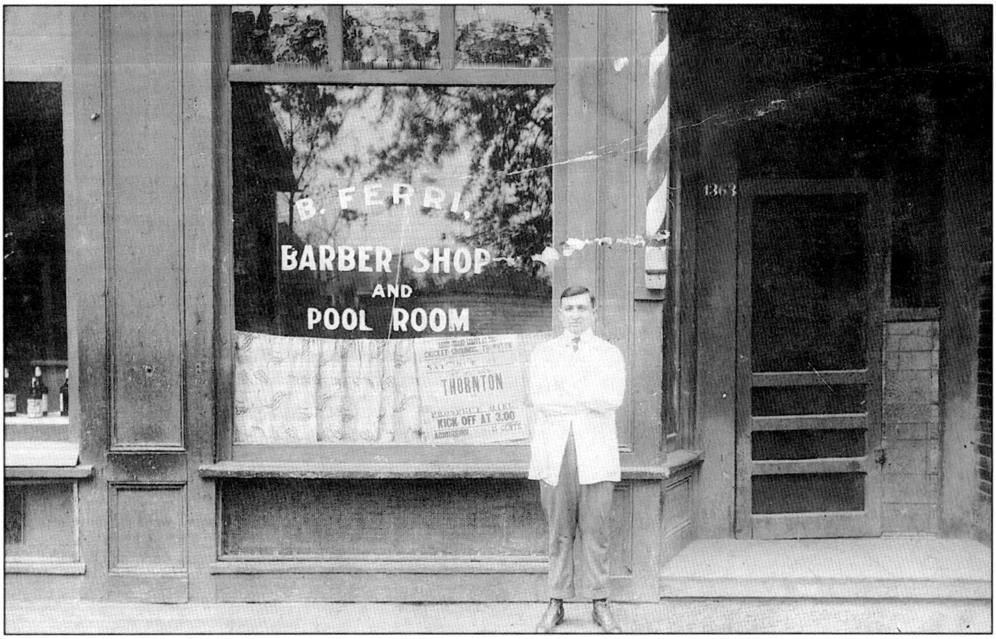

Basil Ferri's Barbershop & Pool Room is shown at 1363 Plainfield Street, in Myrtle Hall in the early 20th century. His sister Margaret was married to Gilbert Hartley, who ran a newspaper business a few buildings west of the Myrtle Hall building. Jim McDonough ran a barbershop here before Basil. (Photograph courtesy of Carl Rainone.)

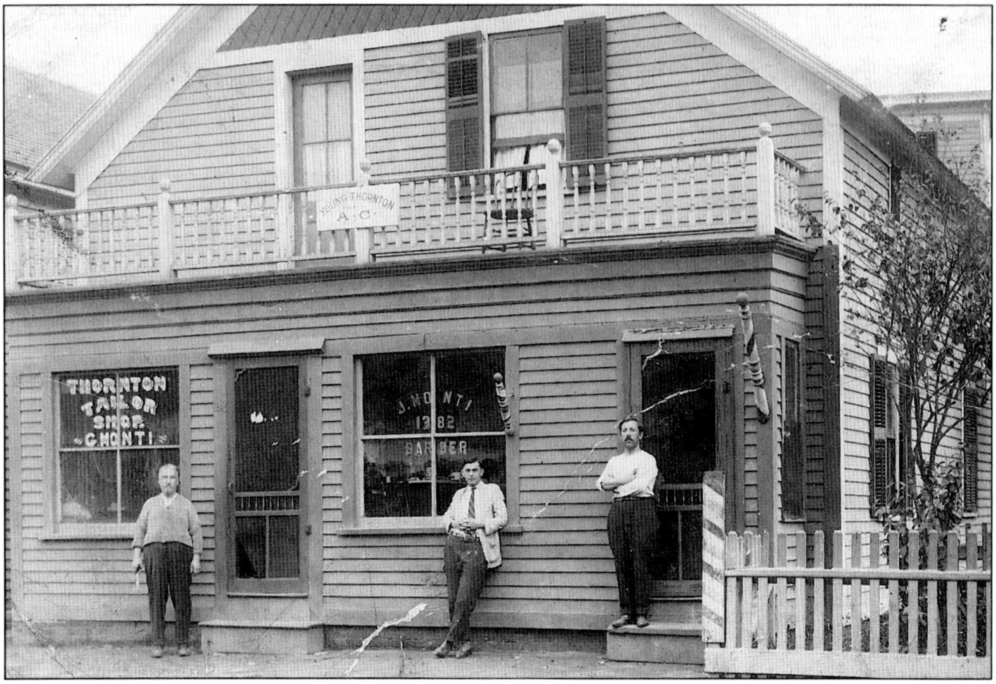

This building at 1382 Plainfield Street in Thornton housed three businesses and groups. The Young Thornton Athletic Club was upstairs, G. Monti's Thornton Tailor Shop was on the left on the first floor, and Joe Monti's barbershop was on the right. The building burned in the winter of 1919–20, and the present building, formerly Golini's Drugstore, replaced it. (Photograph courtesy of Carl Rainone.)

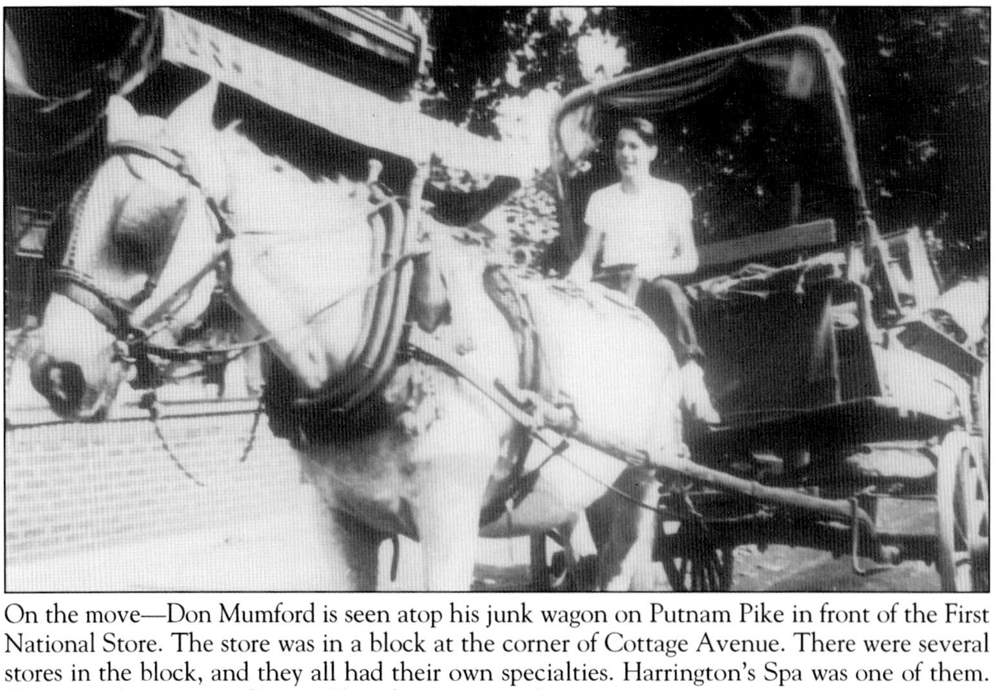

On the move—Don Mumford is seen atop his junk wagon on Putnam Pike in front of the First National Store. The store was in a block at the corner of Cottage Avenue. There were several stores in the block, and they all had their own specialties. Harrington's Spa was one of them. (Photograph courtesy of Laura Charnley Panicucci.)

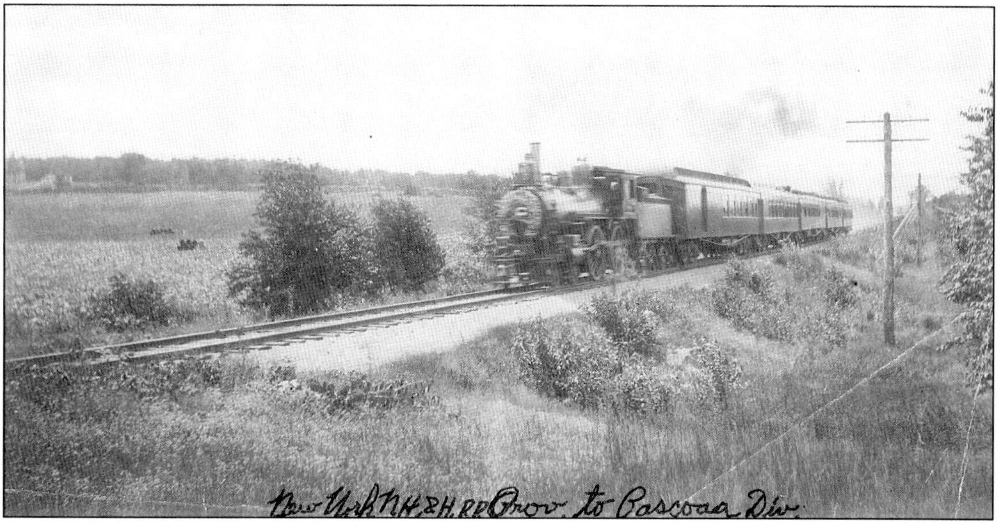

The railroad was a necessity for local businesses in the days before trucks carried most freight. The Providence & Springfield line also carried passengers, as this 1920s photograph taken near Allendale shows. The scene is actually in Johnston, as the rail line was built on the Johnston side of the Woonasquatucket River. The New York, New Haven and Hartford Railroad terminated passenger service on this run in the 1930s. Freight service ended in 1962. (Photograph courtesy of Thomas E. Greene.)

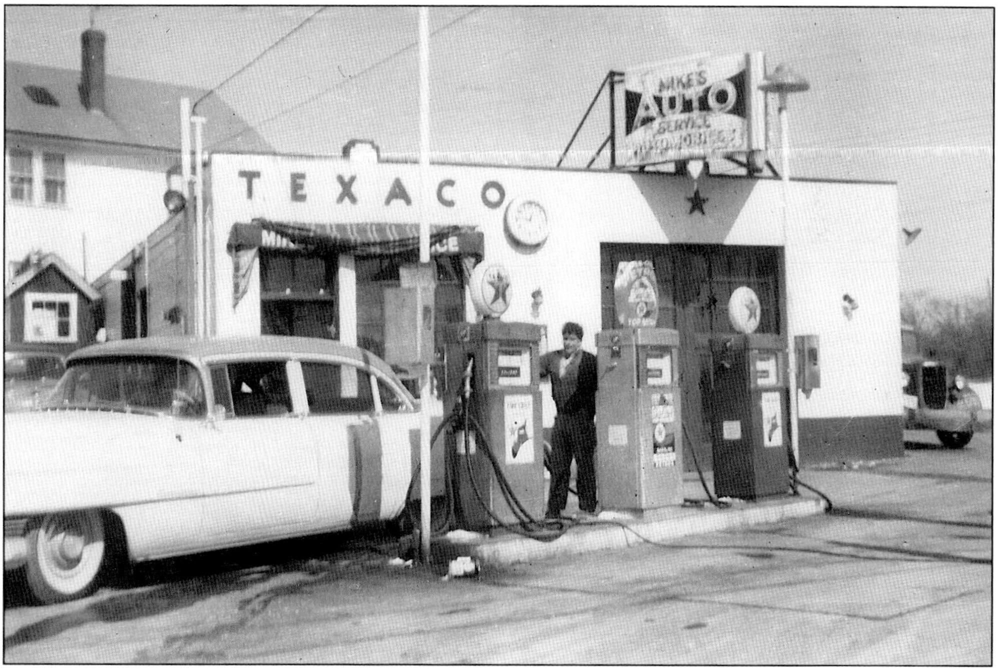

Mike's Auto Service and Sales was a Texaco station that did business from the 1930s to the early 1960s on Hartford Avenue at Atwood Avenue. It was owned by Mike Ferrante. His sons Vincent (pictured here) and Mike helped him with the work. Mike's father, Vincenzo, owned the land on both sides of Atwood Avenue from Hartford Avenue to the Central Fire Station. The gas station was torn down in the early 1960s to make way for a Burger Chef. (Photograph courtesy of Vincent Ferrante.)

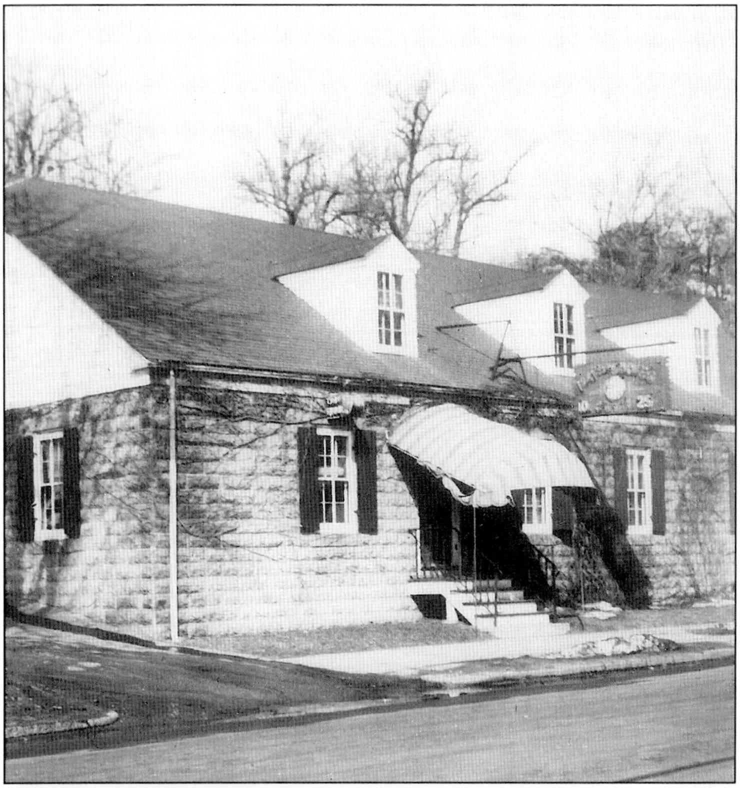

The 1025 Club on Plainfield Street, shown here in 1948, was built on the site of the Fenner Stand, which burned about 1939. When re-opened by McGarry and McCourt, it was re-named the 1025 Club. The building is still there although many additions have been made. Few Rhode Islanders have not attended at least one wedding reception, sports banquet, or political function here. (Photograph courtesy of Bob Whittaker.)

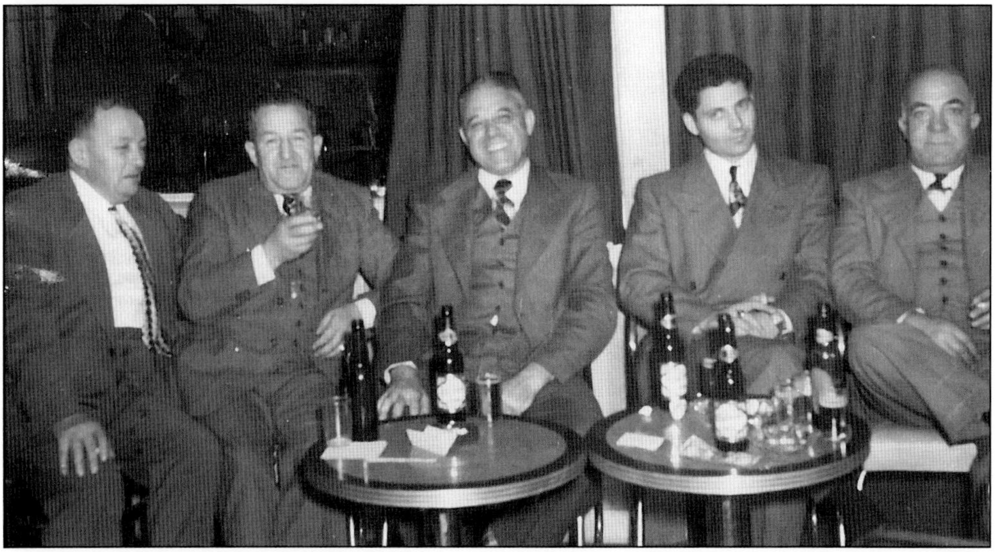

Enjoying a beer at the B & B Nightclub are five members of the Johnston Town Council in the mid-1950s. From left to right are William Jaeger, "Butch" Ferri, Leo Bouchard, Al Cappelli, and Vernon Whittaker. "Butch" Ferri owned the establishment along with his brother, "Buffy" Ferri. In the early 1950s the brothers purchased the former D'Acchioli house on Atwood Avenue. They then moved Jackavony's Pub from across the street, joined it to the old house, and the B & B was born. The site is now an empty lot. (Photograph courtesy of Dorothy Ferri Wilner.)

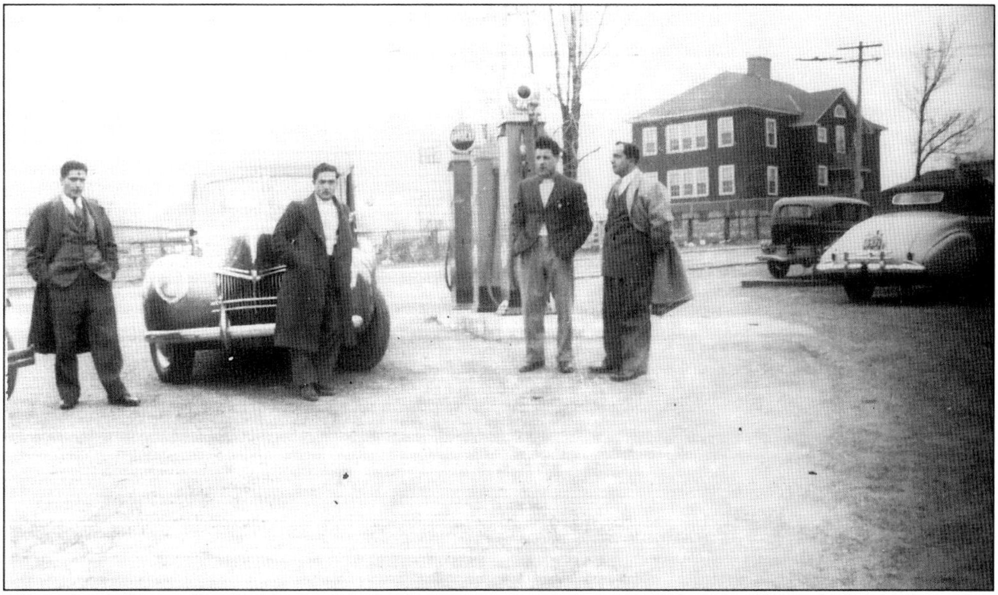

At the corner of Greenville and George Waterman Avenues once stood Chick's Filling Station, here seen in the 1940s. The Lincoln School is in the background. From left to right are Mike DiBennedetto, Christy Marino, Louis "Smokey" Ullucci, and George Montagano. George and his brother Joe later ran the station under the Amoco flag. (Photograph courtesy of Louis "Smokey" Ullucci.)

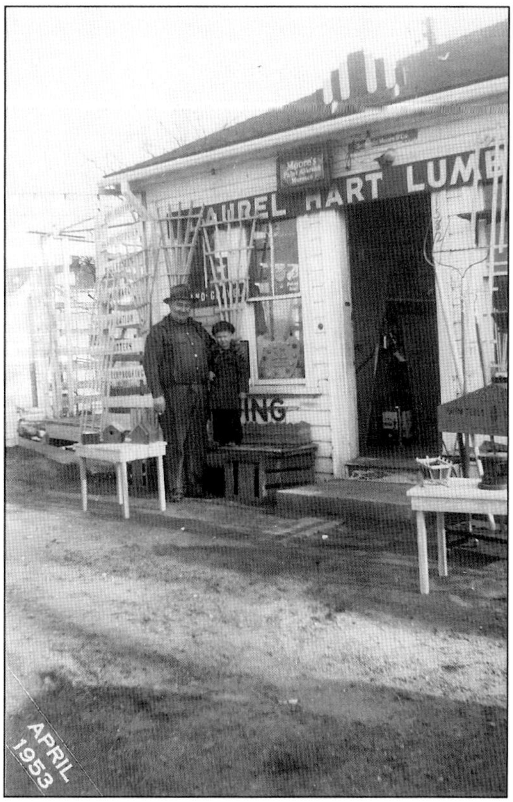

Laurel Hart Lumber sold building and garden products in the early 1950s at the corner of Hartford Avenue and Pocasset Road. Louis E. McGowan, the owner, and his grandson, Raymond McGowan, stand out front. See the top of p. 92 in *Johnston, Volume 1*, for a view of the building when it was a gas station. The building was moved to Scituate on the Dexter Bros. Oil property, where it still sits. (Photograph courtesy of Raymond McGowan.)

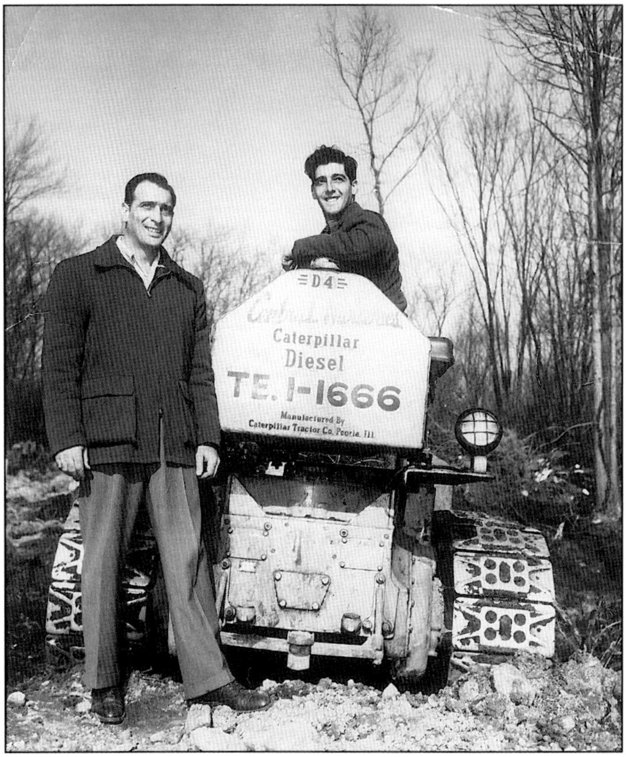

This picture from 1954 shows brothers Mario and Tom Pagliarini (sitting in the tractor) of Central Nurseries. The business was started by their father, Alessandro, in 1936 in Cranston. It moved to Central Avenue, Johnston, in 1946, and later opened at its present location, 1155 Atwood Avenue, in 1962. The Caterpillar tractor in the picture was one of the first hydraulically operated machines of its type in the state. (Photograph courtesy of Central Nurseries, Inc.)

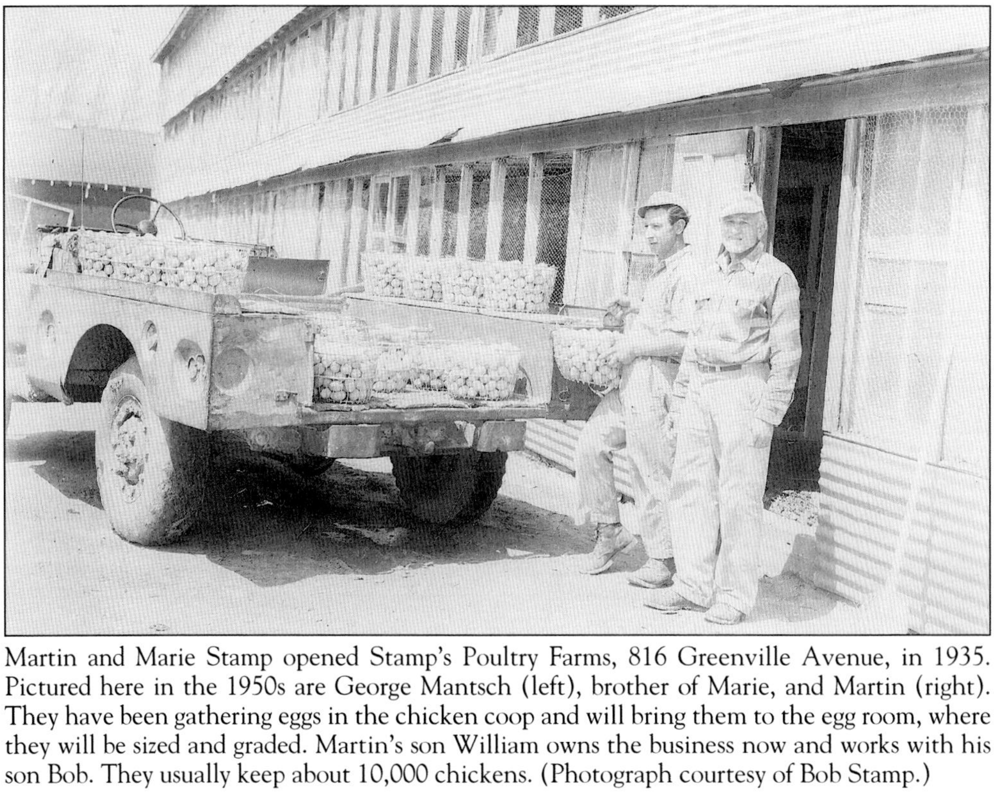

Martin and Marie Stamp opened Stamp's Poultry Farms, 816 Greenville Avenue, in 1935. Pictured here in the 1950s are George Mantsch (left), brother of Marie, and Martin (right). They have been gathering eggs in the chicken coop and will bring them to the egg room, where they will be sized and graded. Martin's son William owns the business now and works with his son Bob. They usually keep about 10,000 chickens. (Photograph courtesy of Bob Stamp.)

Three

SCHOOLS AND CHURCHES

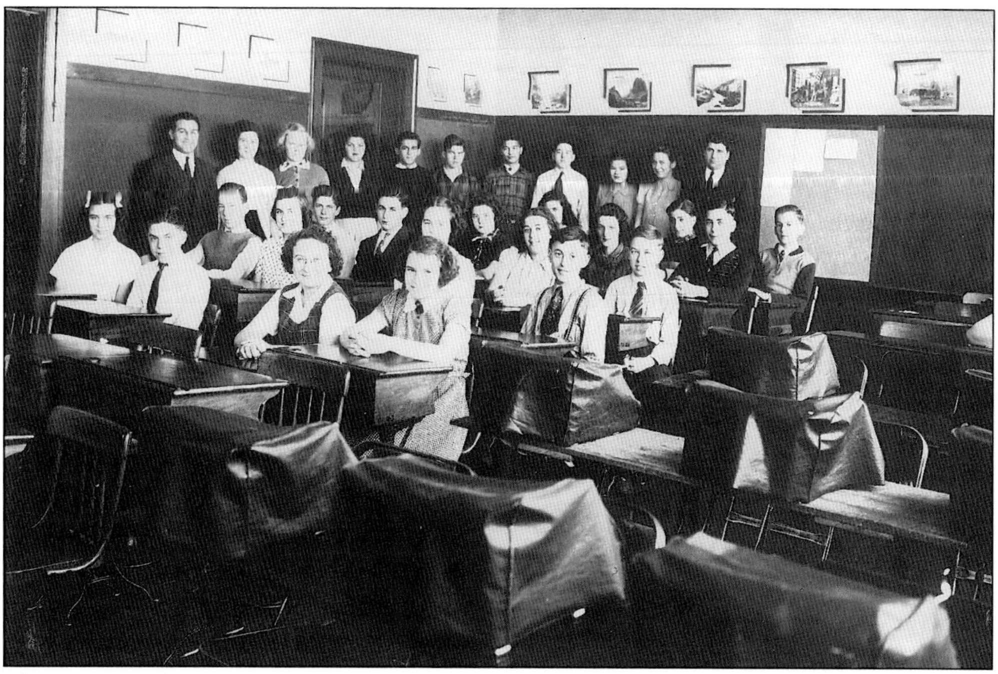

This *c.* 1940 classroom scene was taken in Thornton Junior High School. From left to right are as follows: (seated) Lilian Knott, Albert Pitocco, Rose Cenami, Dorothy Youde, Irving Youde, Jenny DiFazia, Mary Buckley, Galileo Dalmazzi, Robert Zoglio, Joseph Criscuolo, Anna Aurecchia, Sandra Devolve, Clara Barber, Rose Pezza, Domenic Merolla, Lena Jackavone, Gerald Lanni, and Howard Lane; (standing) Nicholas Ferri, Marie Desisto, Eva Stanley, Anna Chiarini, Nicholas Cerra, Joe Canterio, Peter Carpentier, Andrew Ferri, Concetta Russo, Dora Lusi, and Vincent Rampone. (Photograph courtesy of Olga & Joe Criscuolo.)

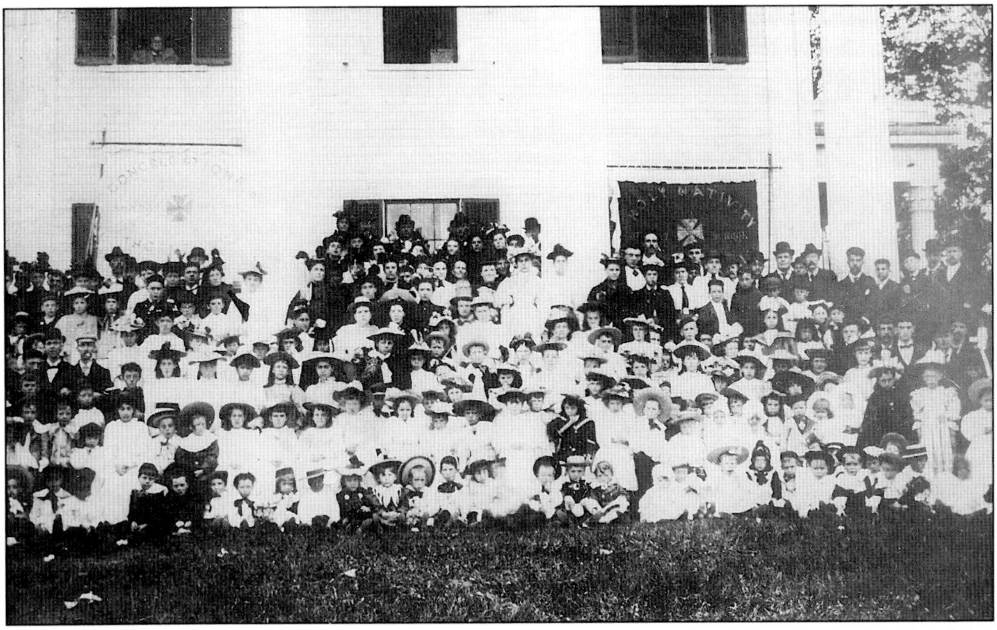

This *c*. 1900 photograph shows members of two area churches gathered on the west side of the James F. Simmons mansion in Thornton. The banner on the left tells us the Congregational Church Sunday School is pictured here; the one on the right is from the Holy Nativity Church Sunday School (Episcopal). (Photograph courtesy of Sam Coupe.)

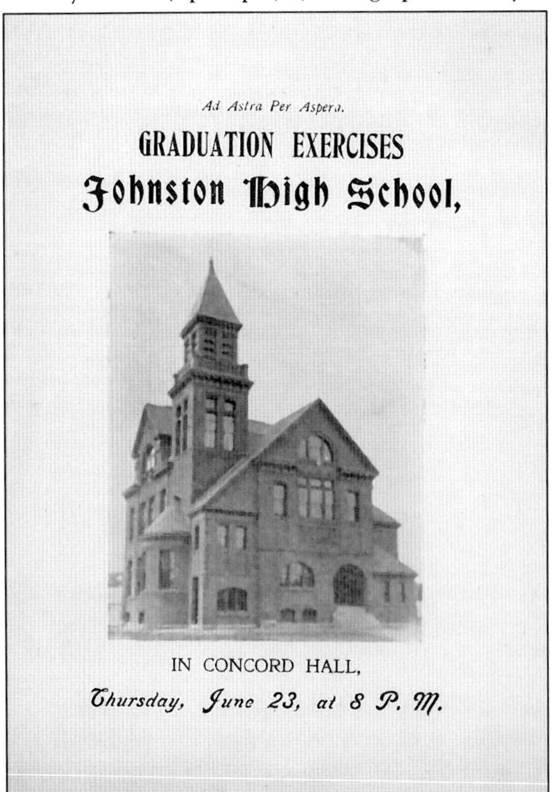

Ad Astra Per Aspera.

GRADUATION EXERCISES

Johnston High School,

IN CONCORD HALL,

Thursday, June 23, at 8 P. M.

Johnston's first high school building, shown here in 1926, opened in the fall of 1891 on Killingly Street near Plainfield Street. The high school opened in 1885 but operated until 1891 in rented rooms in the Odd Fellows Block in Olneyville. When the western Olneyville section was annexed to Providence in 1898, Johnston lost its high school and was without one for 60 years.

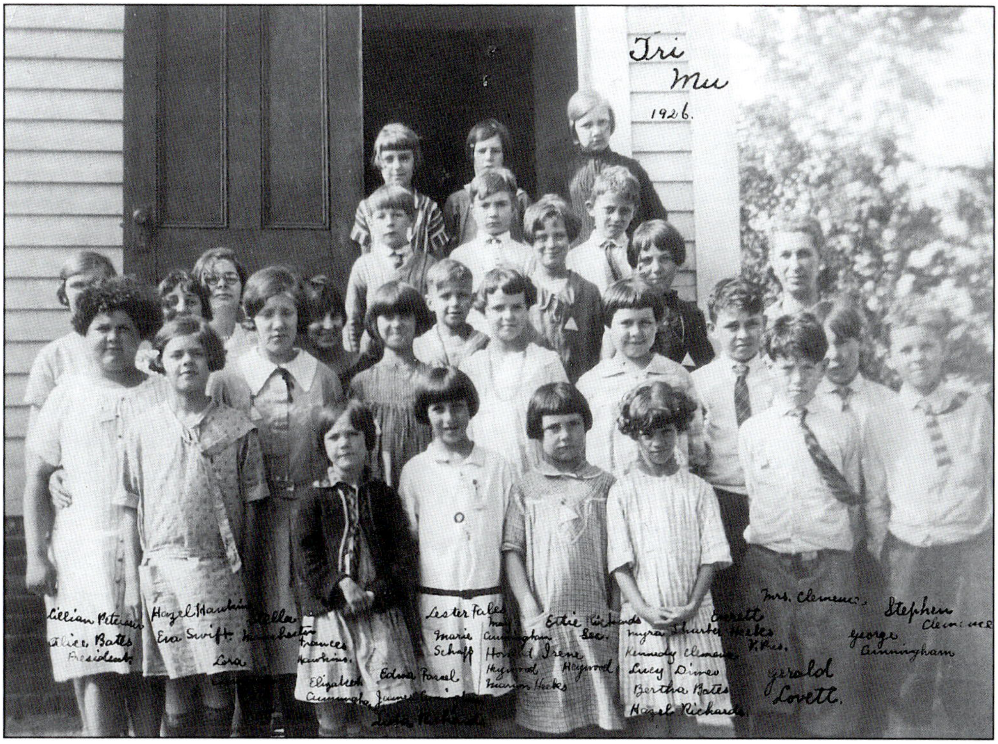

The local 4-H Club in Belknap, Tri Mu, was started by Lora E.O. Clemence and run by her and Ethel Fassel in the 1920s and 1930s. The group stands outside the Belknap School building, which still stands. (Photograph courtesy of Lora Clemence.)

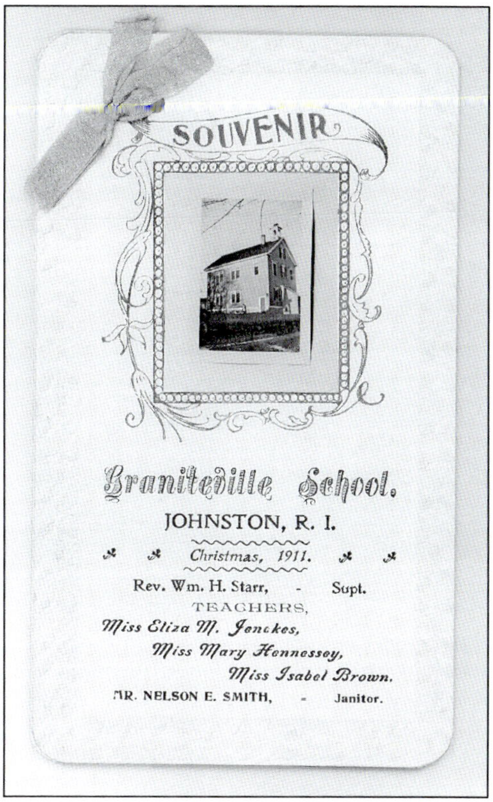

This little souvenir program for the old Graniteville School named all the pupils in its two rooms. Most of the students were English, with only a few Italian names present. The school, built in 1880, was used until 1931, when the present school was opened. (Photograph courtesy of Louis McGowan.)

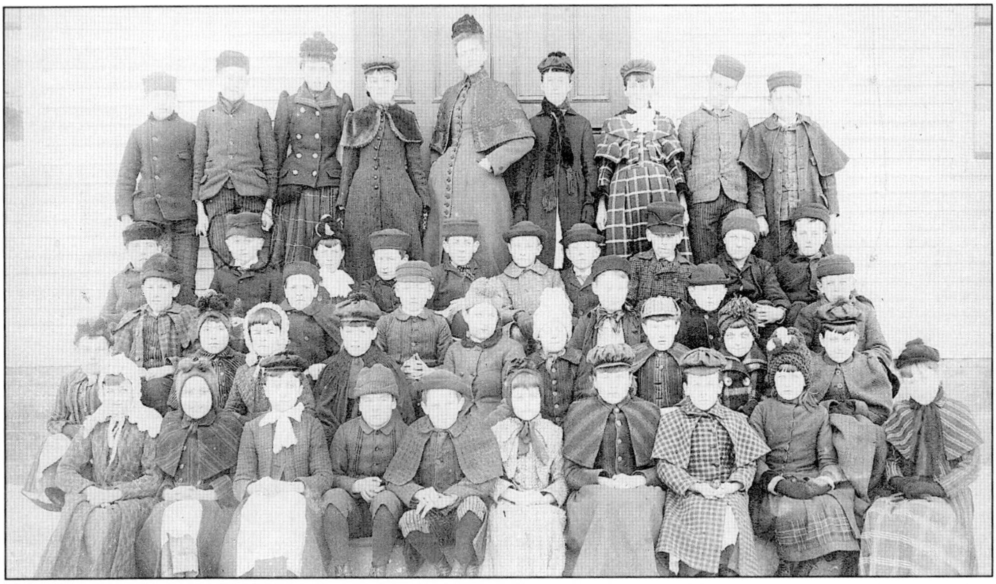

This very early school photo shows a school group in Thornton. The only person identified is George Crothers, who is second from the left in the third row back. He had a daughter, Ruth (Crothers) Stone, who in turn gave birth to Evelyn (Stone) Beaumier. Since Ruth was born in 1901 and her father was about ten or 12 years old in this photo, the picture is probably from the late 1890s. (Photograph courtesy of Evelyn Stone Beaumier.)

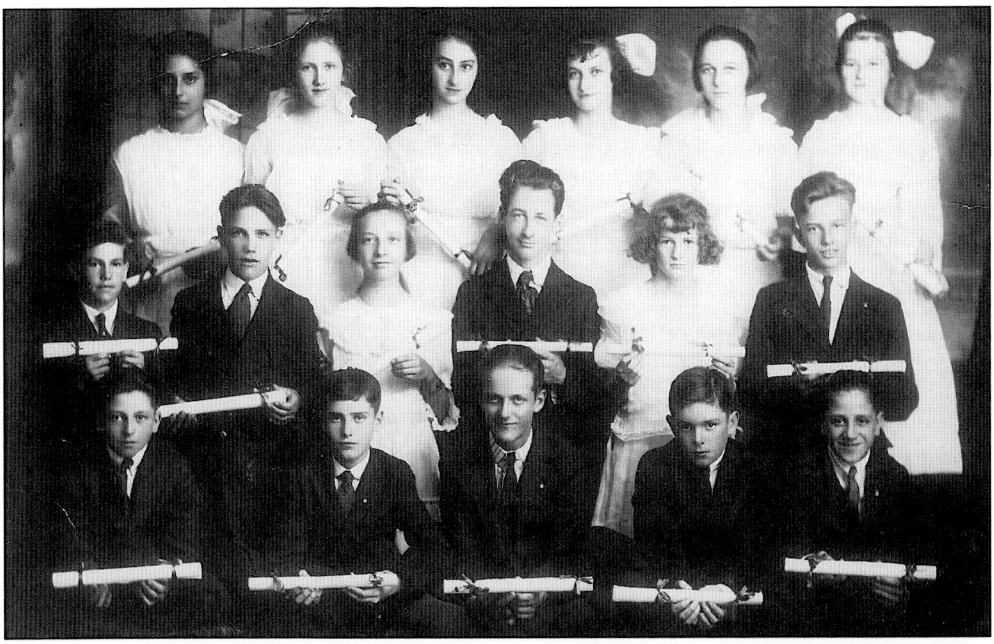

This is the 1921 graduating class from Manton Grammar School on Greenville Avenue. The building no longer stands. The students are, from left to right, as follows: (front row) T. Lombardi, A. Hinkley, C.O. Davies, J. Coughlin, and W. LaBlanca; (middle row) R. Wolsiewic, A. Hindle, Blanche ?, L.A. Rice, E. Armstrong, and A. Charlifour; (back row) A. Scorpio, Z. Cole, G. McRae, B. Pugh, E. Kardlaski, and C. Kulik. The ethnic mix of a textile village is clearly seen. (Photograph courtesy of Gert Newman Rice.)

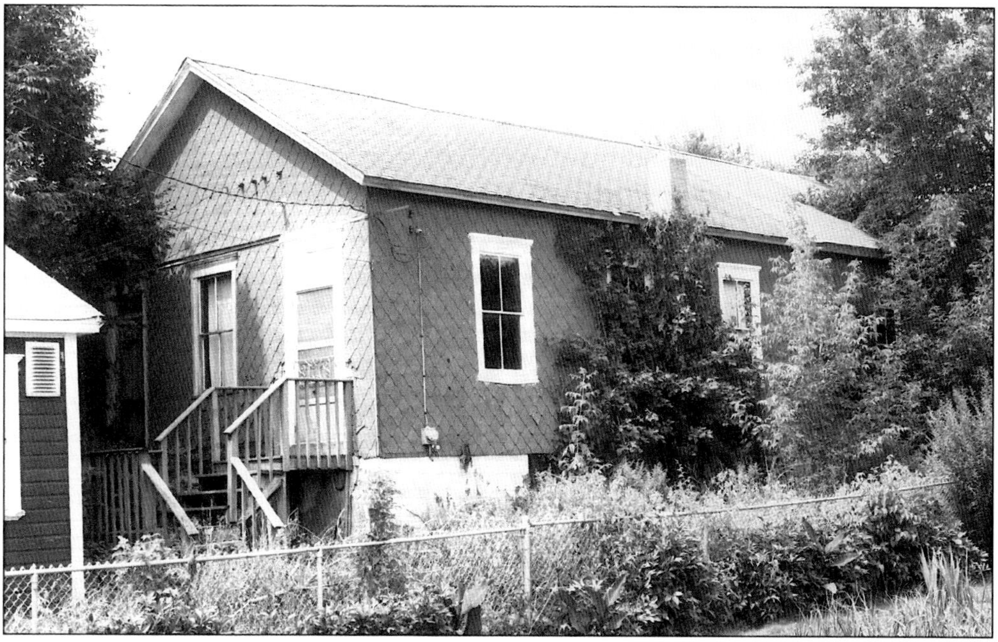

This photograph of the original Simmonsville School was taken in the 1980s. Since then it has been much altered. It was built in 1853 and served as the District 3 School for many years. After its days as a schoolhouse had ended, the building became host to a social club and barbershop. The barbershop was located in the rear of the building and the club featured a stage and piano.

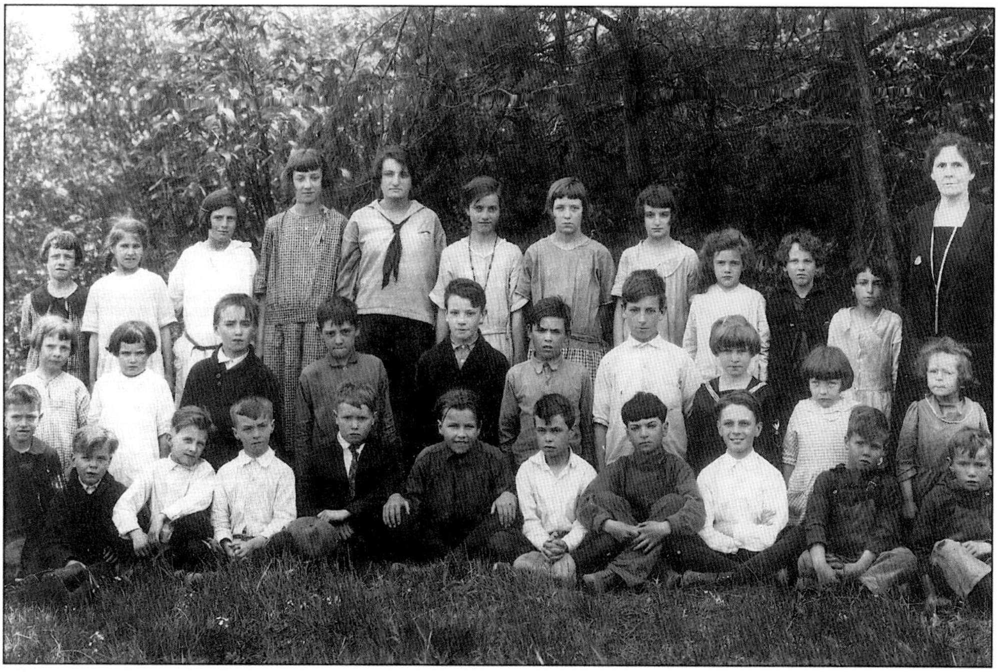

This picture of Brown Avenue School students was taken about 1924 or 1925. The school was a "portable" school, which could be moved if necessary. Susie Brown remembers a wood shed outside with a boys' outhouse at one end and a girls' at the other. Note the great disparity is the sizes of the students. (Photograph courtesy of Susie Brown.)

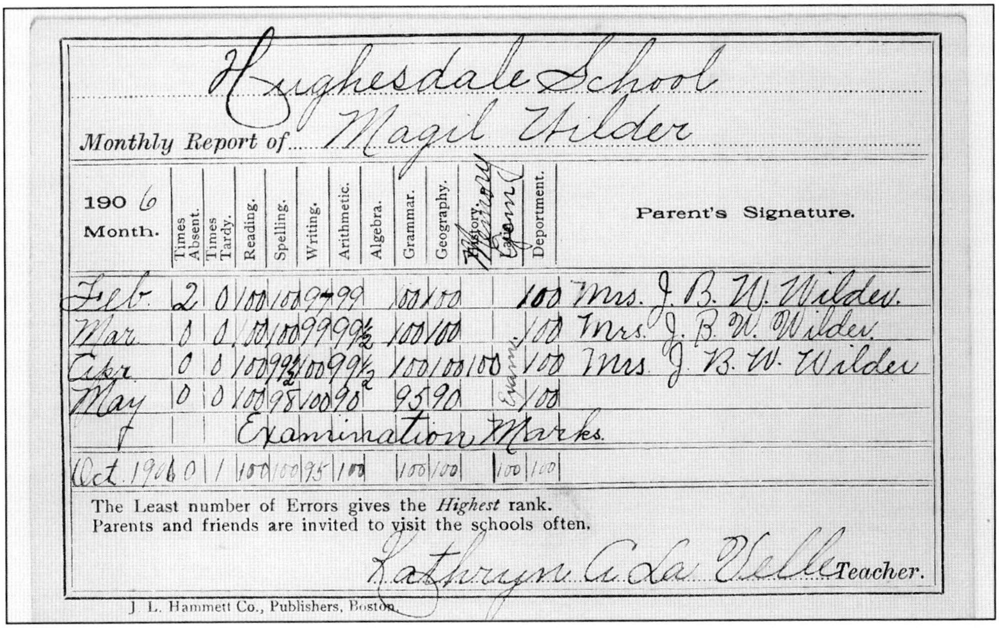

Hughesdale School

Monthly Report of Magil Wilder

1906 Month.	Times Absent.	Times Tardy.	Reading.	Spelling.	Writing.	Arithmetic.	Algebra.	Grammar.	Geography.	History. Exam.	Deportment.	Parent's Signature.
Feb.	2	0	100	100	97	99		100	100		100	Mrs. J. B. W. Wilder.
Mar.	0	0	100	100	99	99½		100	100		100	Mrs. J. B. W. Wilder
Apr.	0	0	100	99½	100	99½		100	100	100	100	Mrs. J. B. W. Wilder
May	0	0	100	98	100	98		95	90	Exam.	100	
Examination Marks.												
Oct. 1906	0	1	100	100	95	100		100	100	100	100	

The Least number of Errors gives the *Highest* rank.
Parents and friends are invited to visit the schools often.

Kathryn A. La Velle *Teacher.*

J. L. Hammett Co., Publishers, Boston.

Magel Wilder from Morgan Avenue was the daughter of Jacob B.W. Wilder. As can be seen by her grades, she was a good student. She continued in the same vein in future years, eventually receiving her doctorate in Biology from Cornell University. She later taught Biology at Brown University. (Photograph courtesy of Harold and Judy Beaudoin.)

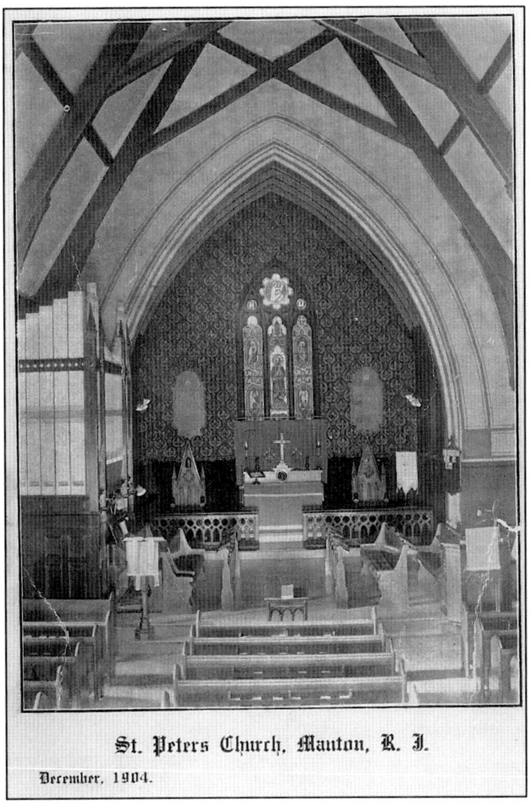

St. Peter's Church on Killingly Street was an Episcopal church dating back to 1846. It was probably designed by noted Rhode Island architect Thomas Tefft. The building burned in the early 1970s. The parish lives on in Providence. (Photograph courtesy of the Newman family.)

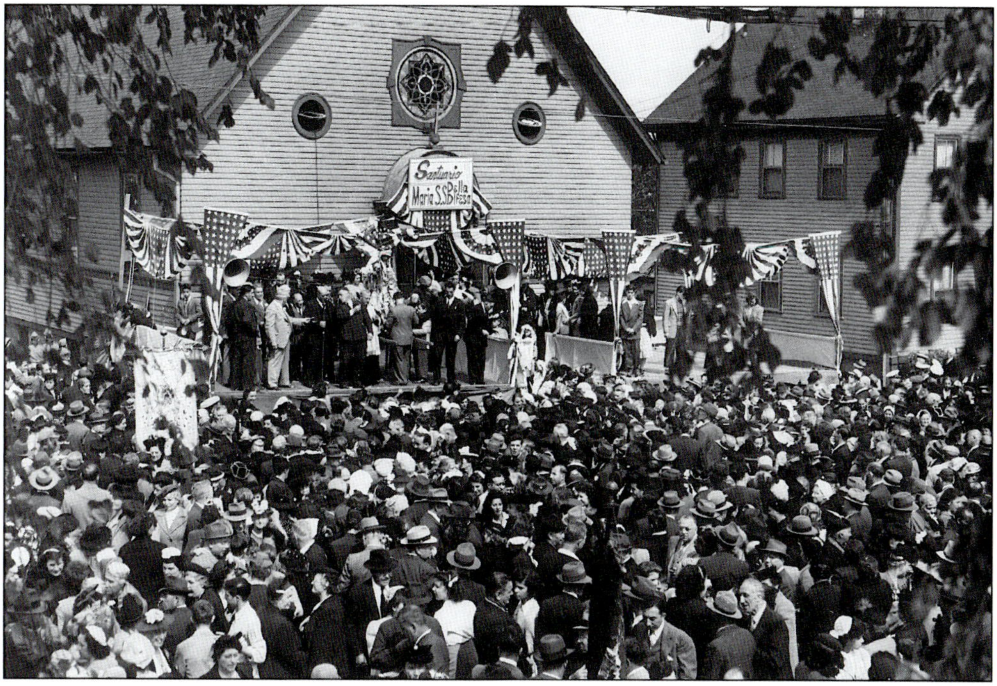

This 1940s photograph shows part of the huge crowd that gathered for the annual Madonna Della Difesa feast at the original Our Lady of Grace Church on George Waterman Road.

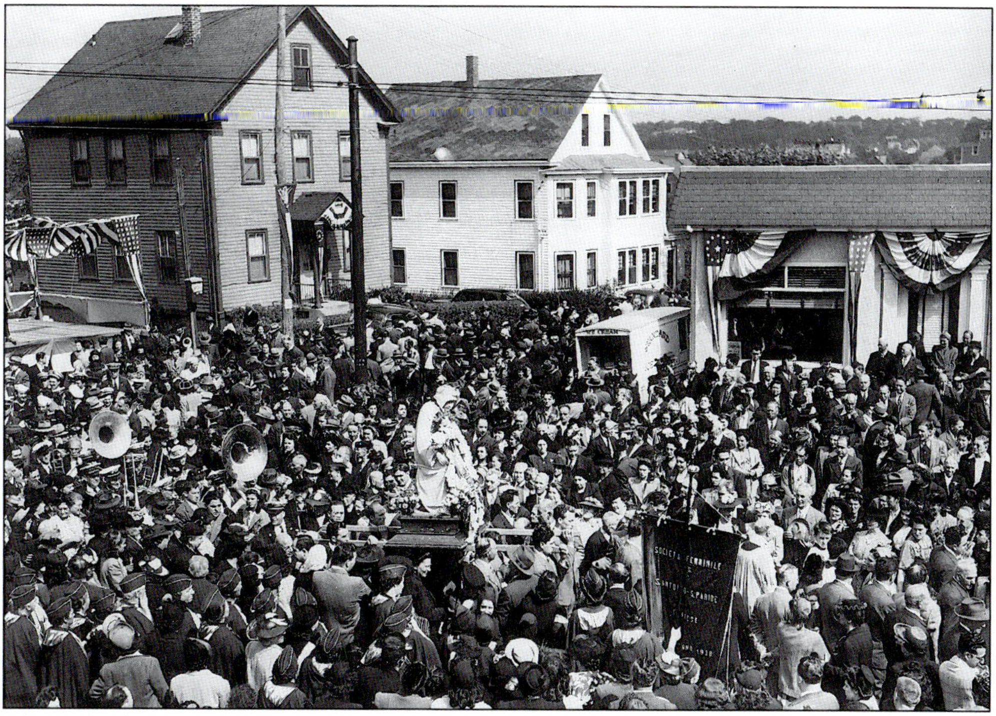

The multi-day Madonna Della Difesa feast at Our Lady of Grace attracted people from all over the Northeast and Canada. Here the statue of the Madonna is followed by a marching band. Local bands from Italian communities in the area entertained the feast-goers.

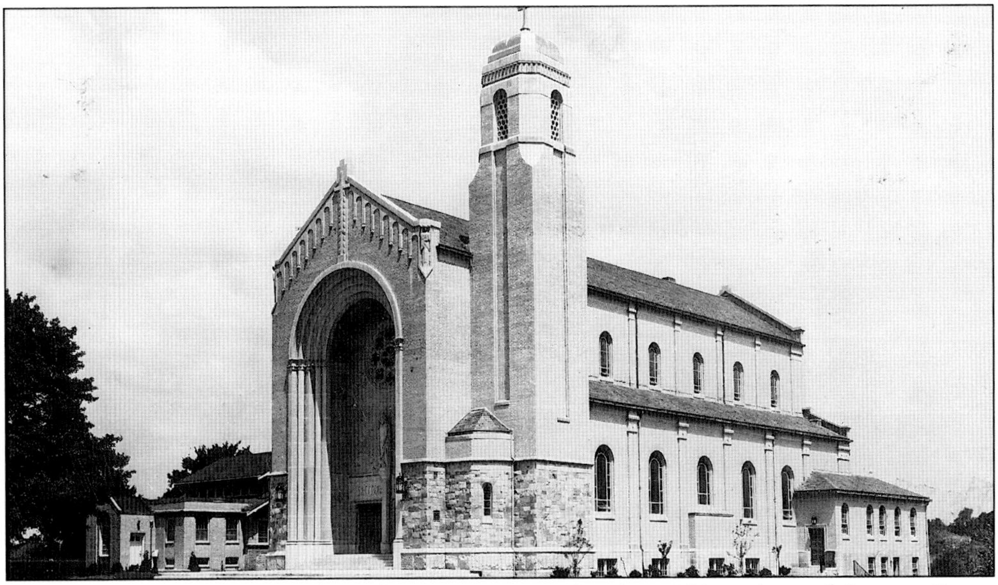

The second St. Rocco's Church in Thornton was completed in 1951 on Atwood Avenue. It was designed by Rhode Island architect Oresto Di Saia. The first church was built in 1903 on the Cranston side on Clemence Street. (Photograph courtesy of Carl Rainone.)

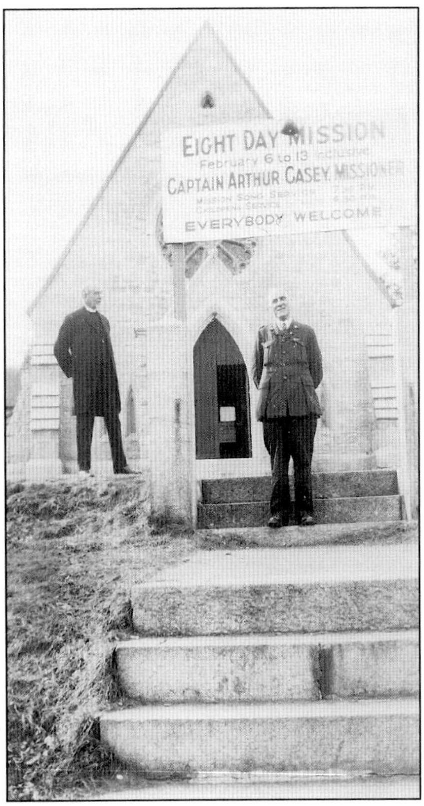

Captain Arthur Casey was the missioner for St. Peter's Church at their eight-day mission sometime in the 1940s. The building no longer stands. (Photograph courtesy of the Newman family.)

Four

POLICE, FIRE, AND POLITICS

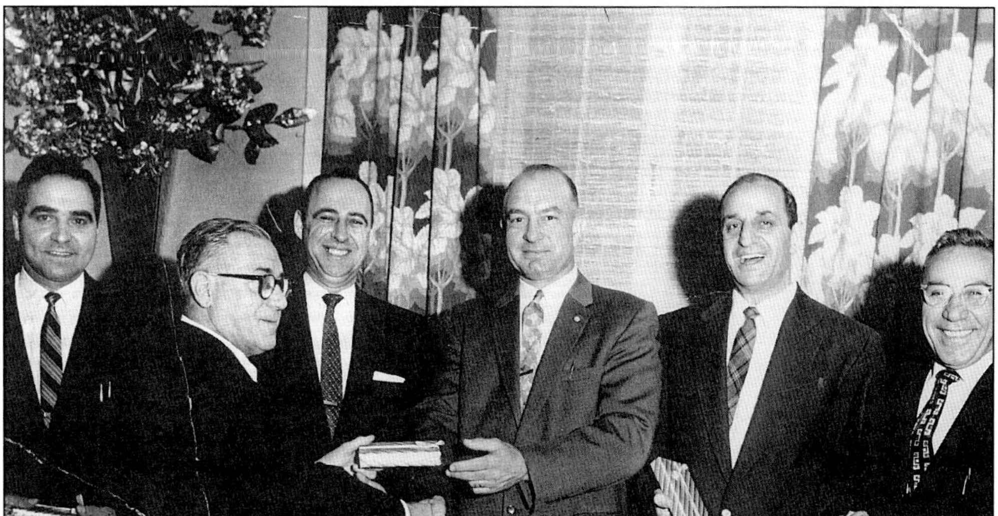

At a May 10, 1959 testimonial at Rhodes on the Pawtuxet, the elite of the Johnston Police Department were gathered. From left to right are Lt. Vincent Acciardo (chief in 1965 and 1966), Chief Anthony Rainone (chief from 1959 to 1965), Lt. Joseph Fleury, Dep. Chief Howard Heywood, Sgt. Angelo Riccitelli, and Capt. Joseph Rossi. Other chiefs were Chief Edwin Mendozzi (1966–1971) and Chief William P. Tocco (1971–1995). (Photograph courtesy of John Rossi.)

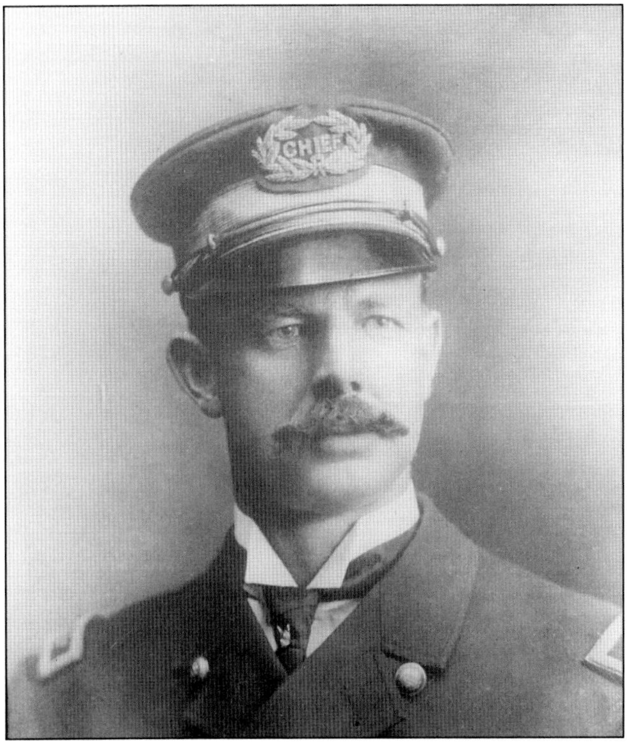

This impressive-looking gentleman was Hiram Kimball, who became police chief in 1898 and remained in that post until 1934, when Republicans were voted out of office. Hiram and his son, Hiram Jr., were basically the entire police force. In the early years he used a horse-drawn buggy in his police work, but in the late 1920s and early 1930s he used a Harley Davidson motorcycle. In 1933 a new REO Flying Cloud was purchased. (Photograph courtesy of Al Kimball.)

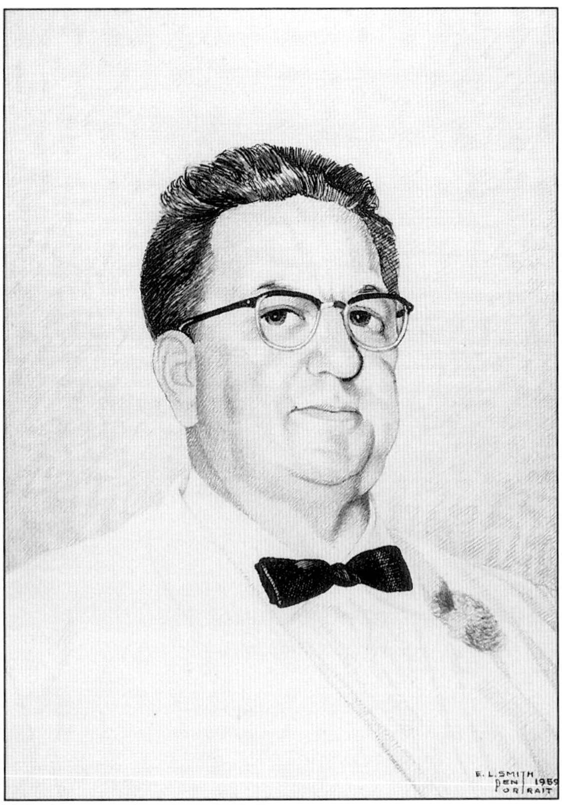

Pete Smith, an accomplished artist, made this drawing of Chester Colwell, who succeeded Hiram Kimball as police chief in 1934 and served until his death in 1959. Colwell, born in Johnston, was originally a farmer and butcher. Smith worked from his home at 167 Morgan Avenue as a freelance artist for Paramount Line. (Photograph courtesy of Bob Whittaker.)

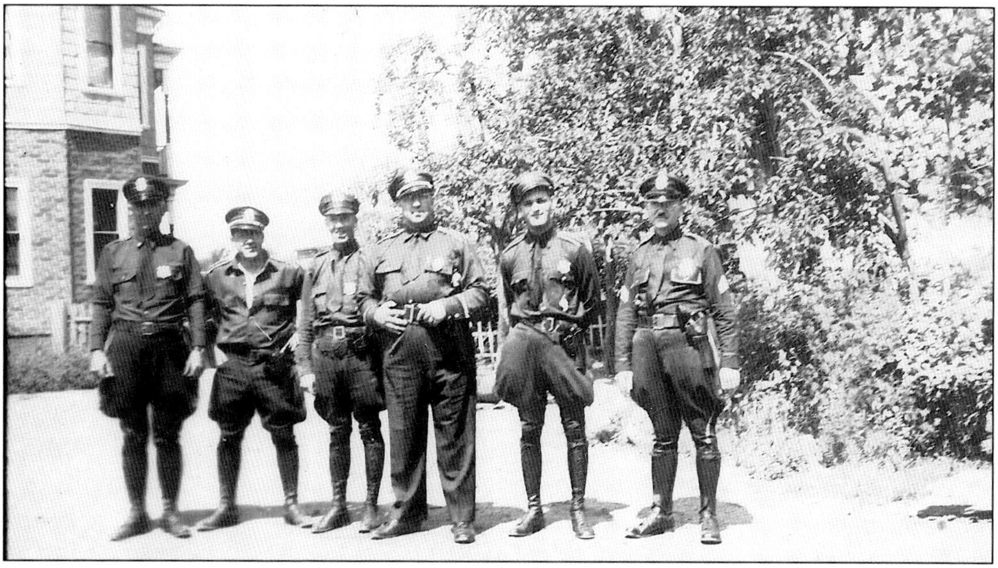

Chief Chester Colwell stands out from this group of police officers because of his impressive physical stature in this 1930s scene. Colwell was a controversial figure but was very popular with the voters. The others are, from left to right, Tom Kennedy, Anthony "Dep" Rainone, Jack Whalen, Colwell, Alfred Clapham, and Peter Jaswell. They constituted the police force at that time.

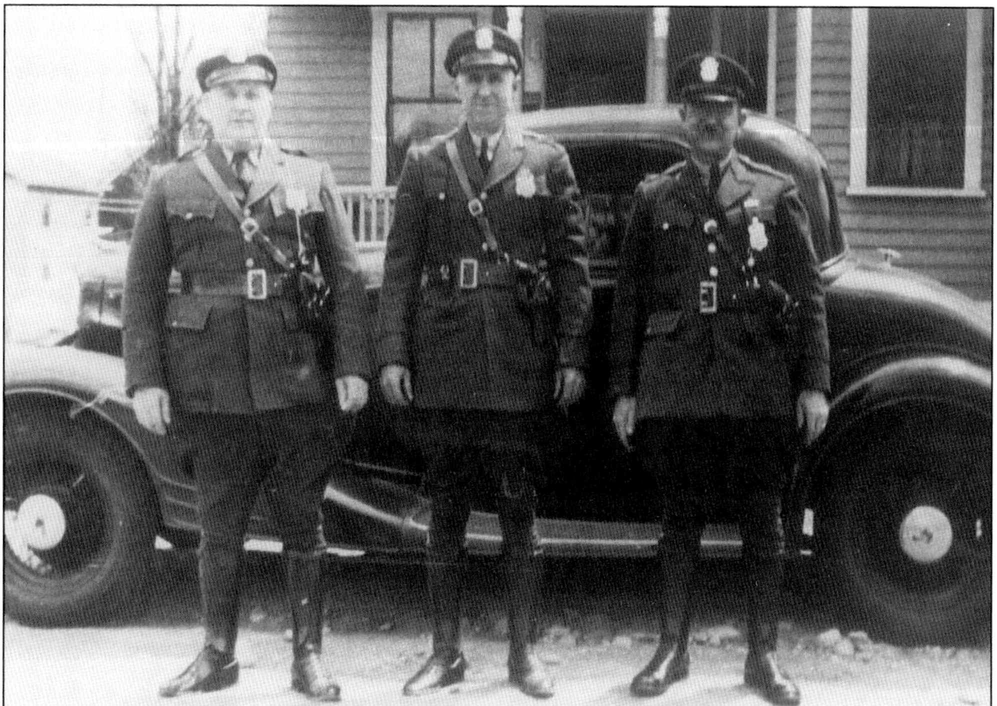

Three of Johnston's finest pose with the squad car about 1936. In the center is Tom Kennedy and on the right is Peter Jaswell, who was firearms instructor for the department. The car appears to be a 1932 or 1933 Ford. (Photograph courtesy of Al Forte.)

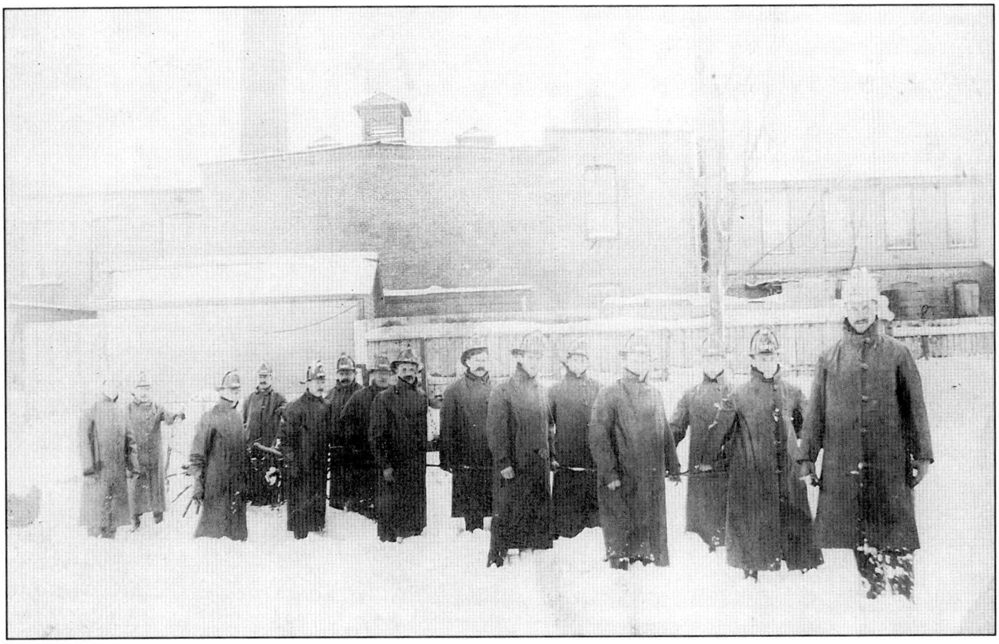

The British Hosiery Mill on Mill Street, Thornton, had its own firefighting crew, pictured here probably in the 1890s. They responded to fires in Thornton village, such as one in 1908 when Capt. John Shaw, pictured here in the white helmet on the right, was their leader. (Photograph courtesy of Sam Coupe.)

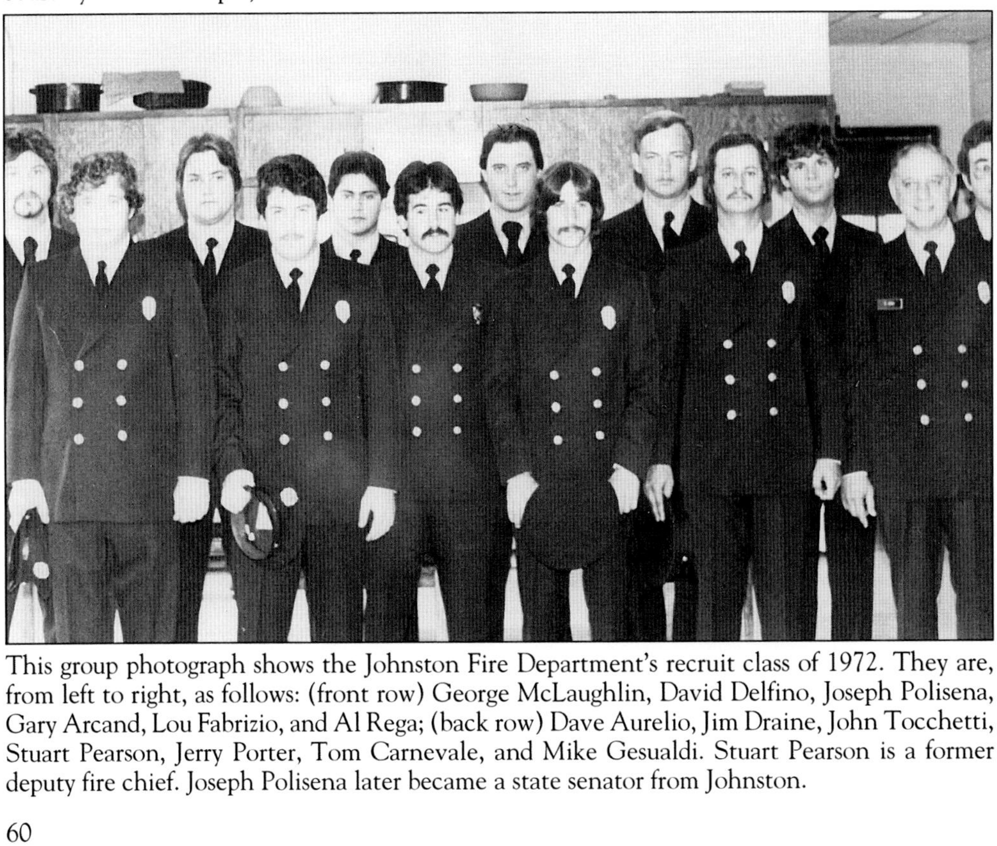

This group photograph shows the Johnston Fire Department's recruit class of 1972. They are, from left to right, as follows: (front row) George McLaughlin, David Delfino, Joseph Polisena, Gary Arcand, Lou Fabrizio, and Al Rega; (back row) Dave Aurelio, Jim Draine, John Tocchetti, Stuart Pearson, Jerry Porter, Tom Carnevale, and Mike Gesualdi. Stuart Pearson is a former deputy fire chief. Joseph Polisena later became a state senator from Johnston.

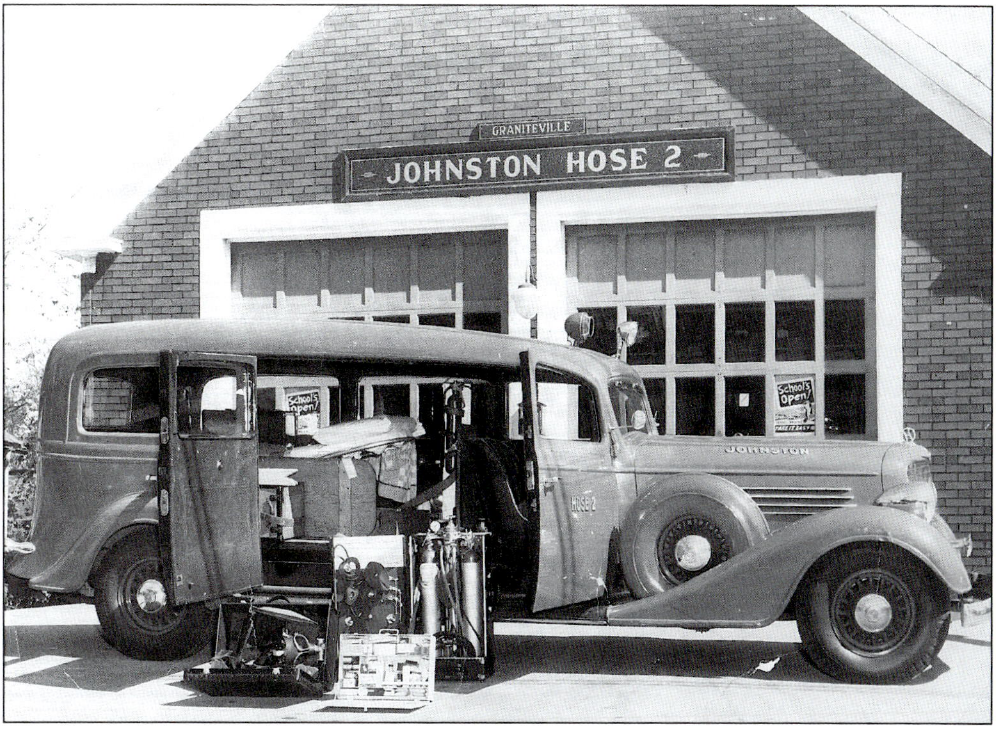

Johnston Hose #2, Graniteville, felt a lot of pride on the day their ambulance was delivered. It was a converted 1935 Buick hearse with a special Henney body, and was the first ambulance in town. The vehicle sits here in front of the station at Cottage Avenue and Putnam Pike. (Photograph courtesy of Francis Cox.)

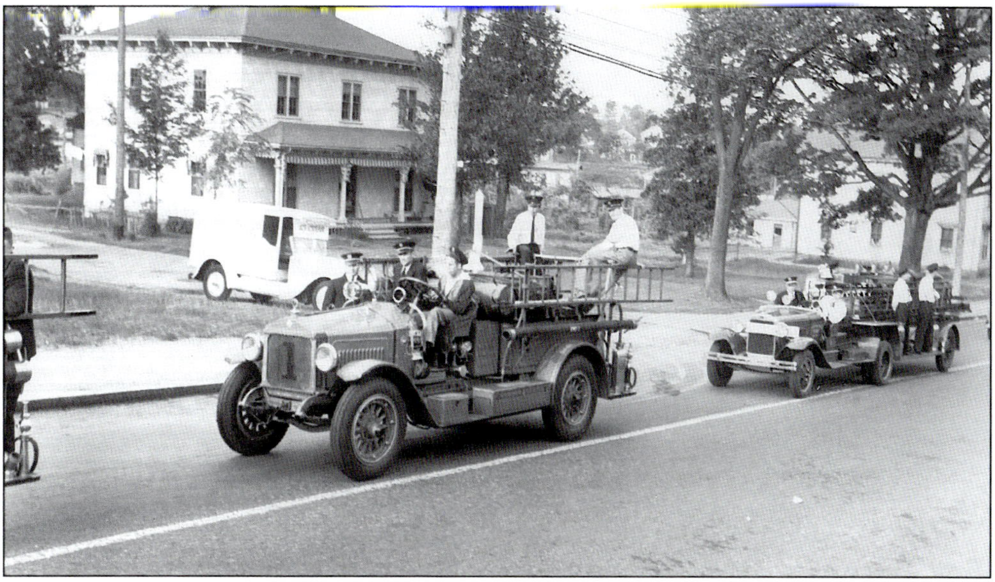

Town firetrucks are shown here parading on lower Greenville Avenue near Killingly Street. The ice-cream truck is there to soothe those parched throats. Firetrucks from the early days to the present have been a major part of local parades. Lee Street is on the left. The Ciarlo-LaPrade VFW Post building is on the right.

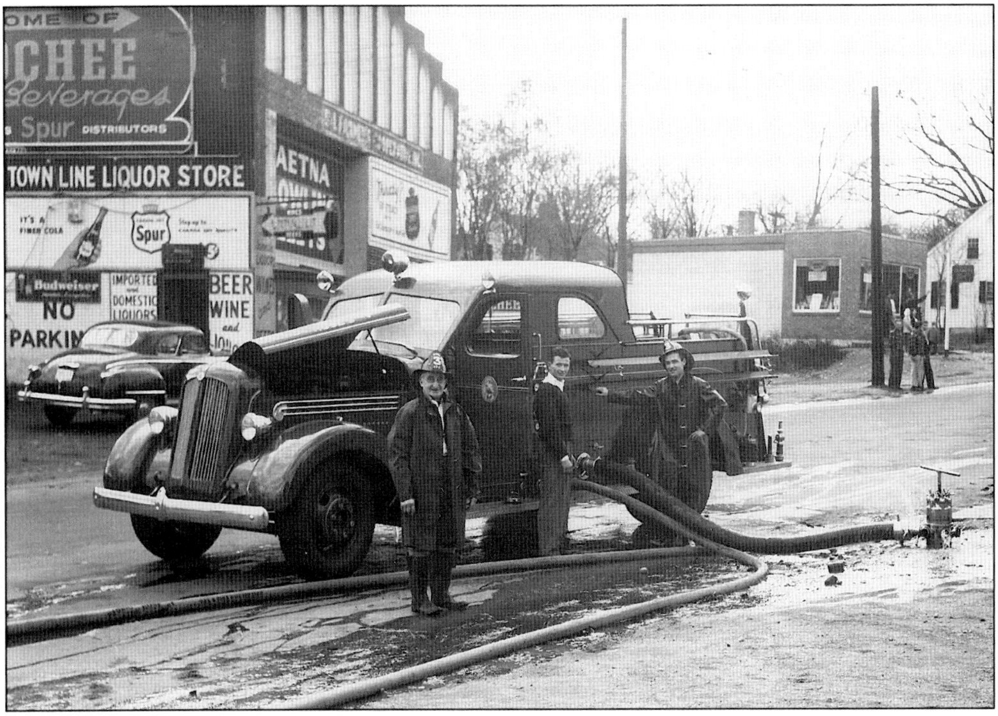

Johnston Hose 3 (Manton) had their hands full at the fire at the Ochee Springs Bottling Works in the late 1940s. The three firemen are Arthur Newman (left), Norman Finucane (center), and William F. Newman. The truck is a 1948 Seagraves. Volunteers from Graniteville and Thornton also responded. The building to the left is the old Providence & Danielson trolley barn. (Photograph courtesy of Adam Macari.)

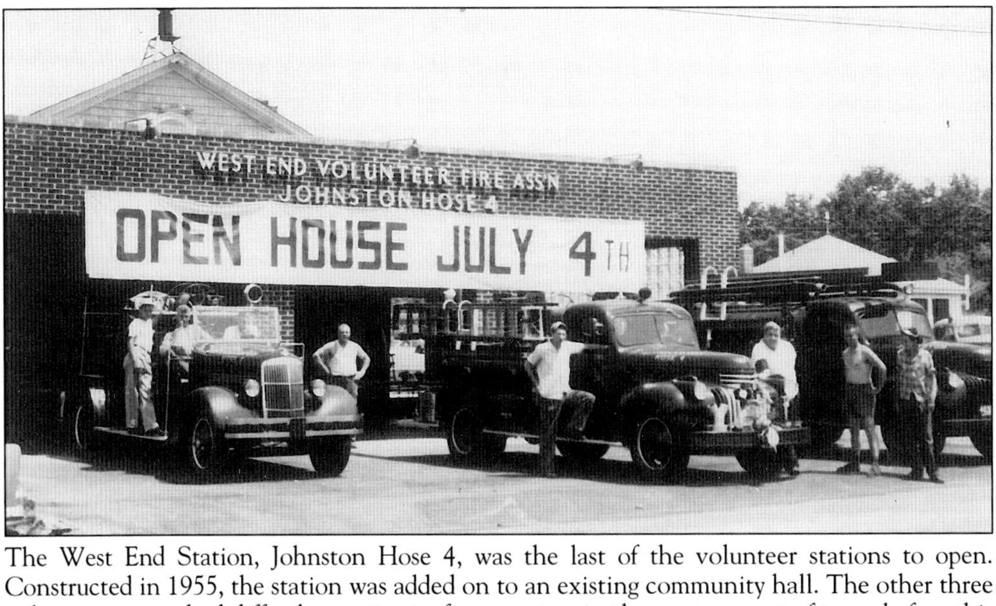

The West End Station, Johnston Hose 4, was the last of the volunteer stations to open. Constructed in 1955, the station was added on to an existing community hall. The other three volunteer groups had difficulty getting to fires on time in the western part of town before this station was built. As the population increased in the West End the people there needed their own station. (Photograph courtesy of Charles Redinger.)

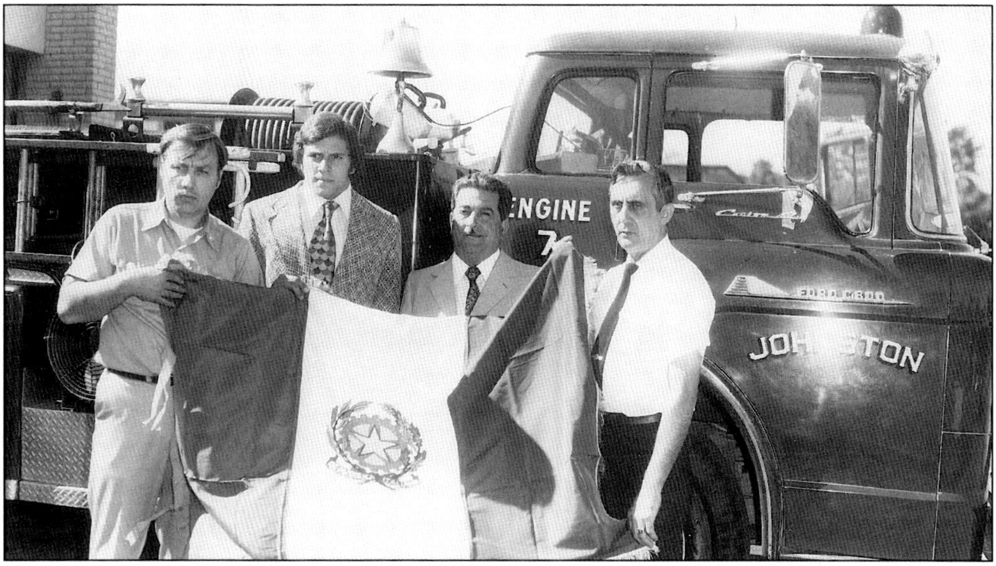

Mr. Pingerno Amato Sassari, second from the right, the local Italian Consul, presents an Italian flag to the fire department on Columbus Day, 1974. It was to be used during parades. Angelo "Ace" Cappelli (right) was fire chief of the town from 1972 until 1988. At the far left is Alan Zambarano, chief from 1991 until 1994. Tom DiLuglio, second from the left, was a state senator from Johnston at the time. (Photograph courtesy of Al Forte.)

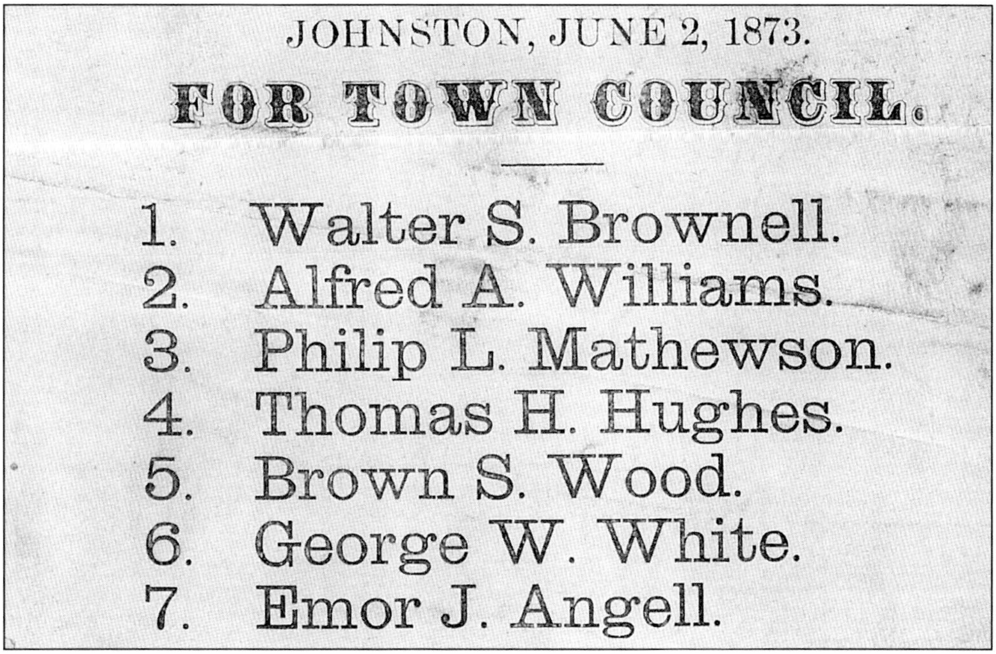

JOHNSTON, JUNE 2, 1873.

FOR TOWN COUNCIL.

1. Walter S. Brownell.
2. Alfred A. Williams.
3. Philip L. Mathewson.
4. Thomas H. Hughes.
5. Brown S. Wood.
6. George W. White.
7. Emor J. Angell.

This 1873 notice for a town council election shows no ethnic names. Only English names and an occasional Irish or German name were on ballots up to that time. In the early 20th century Italian names and an occasional French name could be found on the ballots. The Democratic Party was also weak at this time in town, as it was statewide. The Democrats did not control the town council from the Civil War until 1934. (Photograph courtesy of the Providence City Hall Archives.)

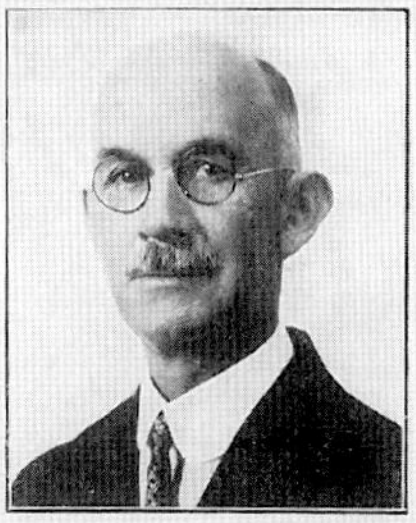

Its WILDER now in Johnston -
going wilder every day
WILDER, WILDER, WILDER -
in the good old-fashioned way
Even DOOLEY'S wilder -
He'll be wilder, so they say
When we vote for JACOB B.

VOTE, VOTE, VOTE -
and vote again for Jacob B,
We'll send him to the Senate
by a large majority.
He's *upright* and he's HONEST,
and he's strong for G. O. P.
So—we'll vote for JACOB B.

Jacob Butler White Wilder served in the Rhode Island House in the early teens and in the Rhode Island Senate in the late teens and early 1920s. This little poem harkens back to a simpler time. Today much more intense political tactics rule the game. Jacob married Gertrude Webb, and they had two children, Webb Westcott Wilder and Magel Wilder. (Photograph courtesy of Harold and Judy Beaudoin.)

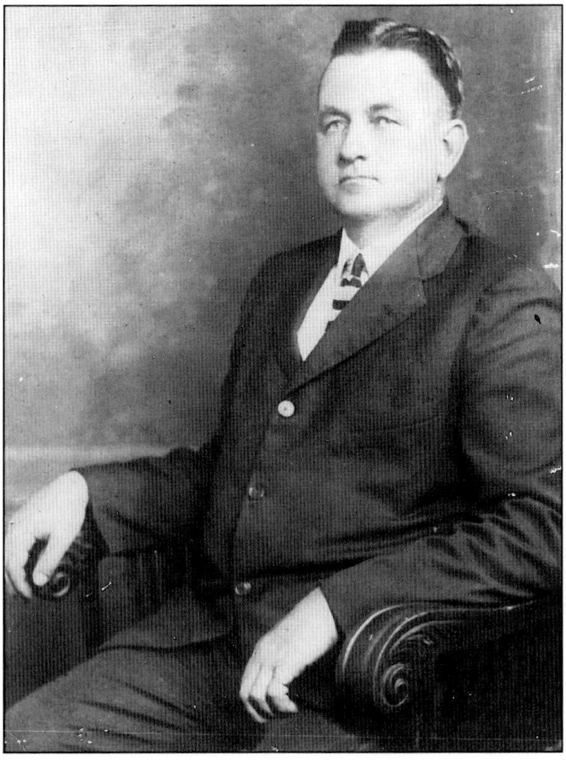

Willis Sweet held many positions in Johnston town government. At various times he served as building inspector, constable, and commissioner of weights and measures. He was also the first chief of the Graniteville Fire Station. Mr. Sweet lived at the old family homestead at 142 Putnam Pike, a house which still stands today. (Photograph courtesy of Arthur Harrington.)

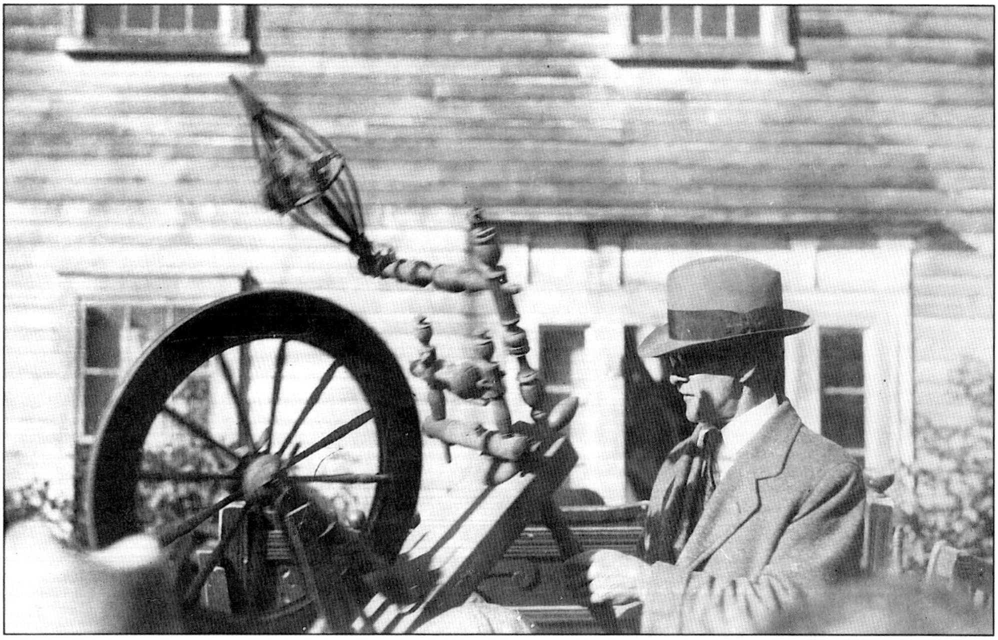

William H. Mathewson II was town tax collector and, hence, sometimes auctioneer. He lived on the family farm at the corner of Carpenter Drive and Greenville Avenue, where his daughter-in-law, Peg Mathewson, still lives. (Photograph courtesy of Elaine Mathewson Pereira.)

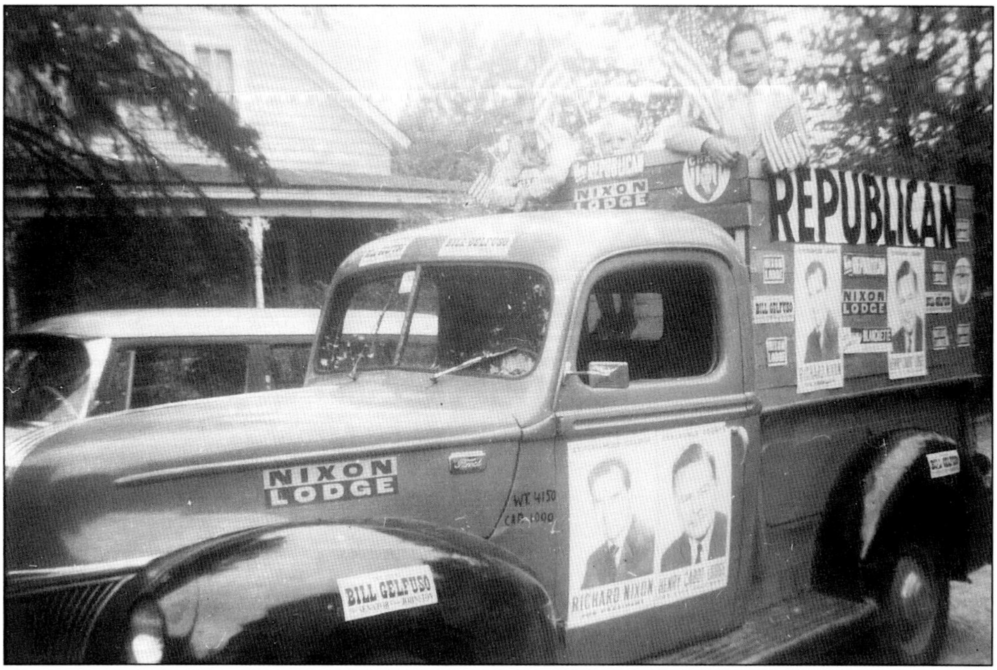

This 1960 image shows a 1939 Ford pick-up plastered with Richard M. Nixon and Henry Cabot Lodge campaign signs. It was a history-making campaign for many reasons—one being that live televised debates (between Nixon and John F. Kennedy) were used for the first time. (Photograph courtesy of Arthur Harrington.)

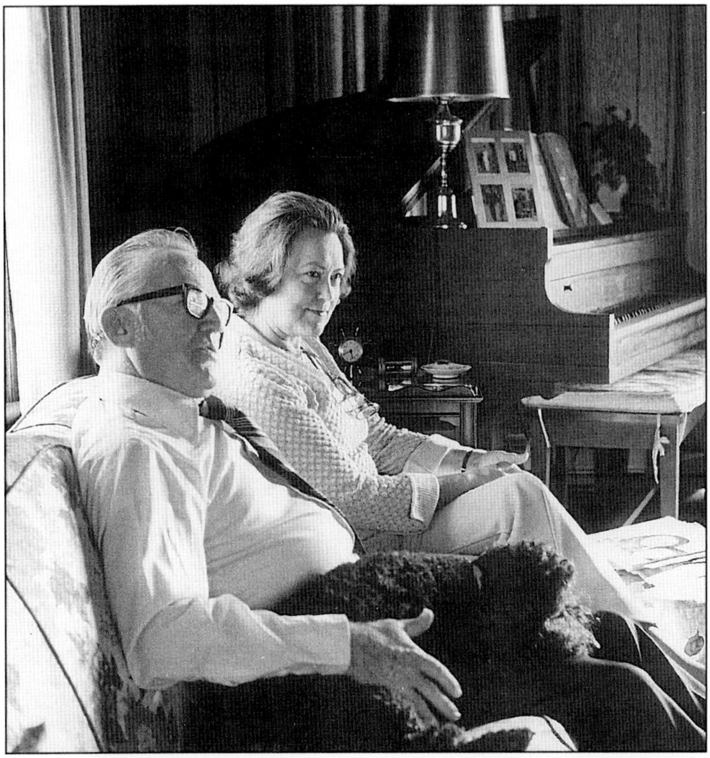

Charles Devaney represented Johnston in the state senate from 1960 to 1964. A lifelong Democrat, he retired from active politics to become a lobbyist for the New England Telephone Company. In his spare time, Mr. Devaney was master of ceremonies at the 1025 club from 1940 to the early 1950s. Leona Devaney, his wife, was a member of a jazz group that toured from Providence to New York City, including stints at the Copa Cabana. (Photograph courtesy of Donald Devaney.)

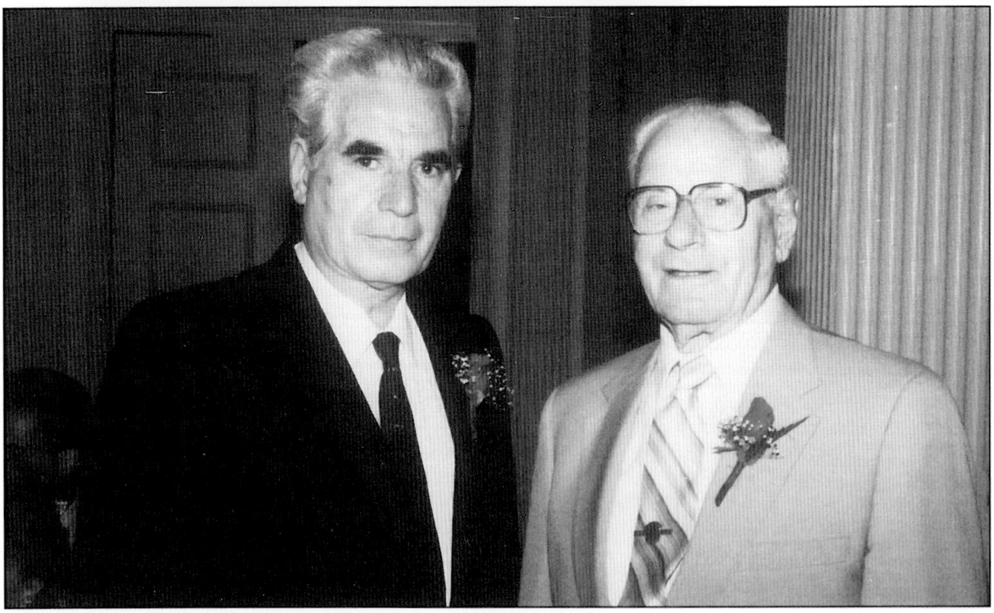

Johnston's first mayor, Ralph aRusso, is pictured on the left at a function with his uncle, Joseph Russo. Mr. aRusso became town administrator in 1971. His job title was changed to mayor in 1974 and he continued serving in that role until 1995, giving him a grand total of 24 years served as chief executive. That stint was said to be the longest reign in the state. He was born and grew up in Simmonsville, the son of Tom Russo. (Photograph courtesy of the late Joseph Russo.)

Five

Working

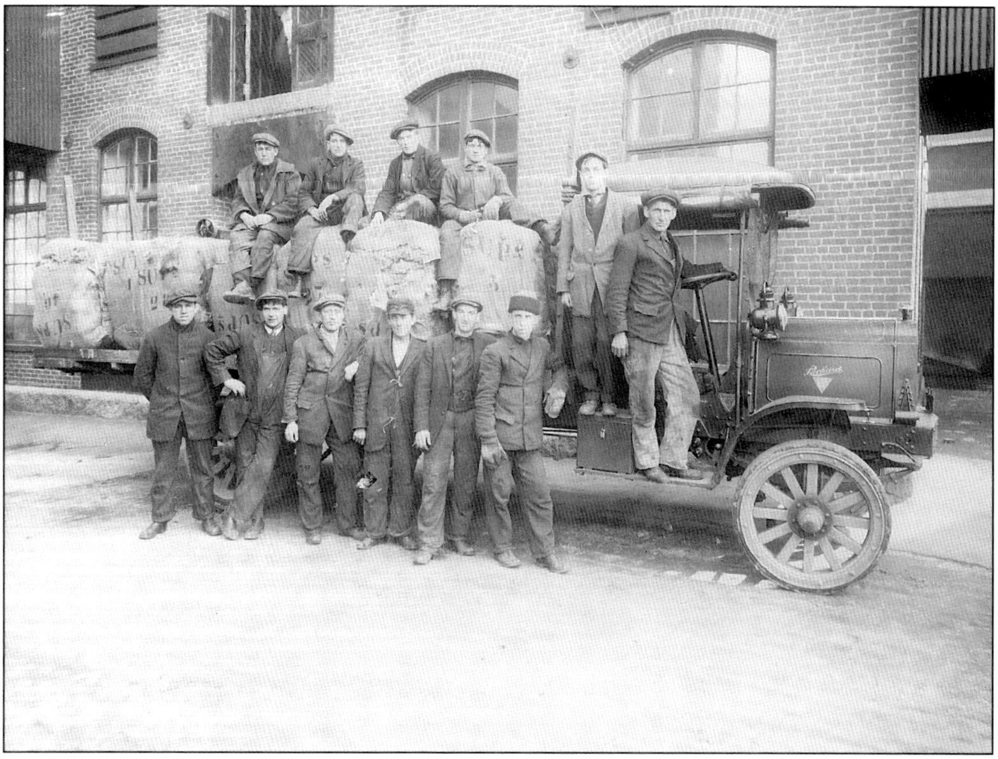

A Packard delivery truck is seen in the early teens outside the British Hosiery Mill on Mill Street in Thornton. On the truck are bales of raw wool. At the cab is Harry Tingle, the boss driver. Standing third from the left is Louis Leo. On the truck, second from the right, is Wilfred Coupe, Sam Coupe's uncle. (Photograph courtesy of Sam Coupe.)

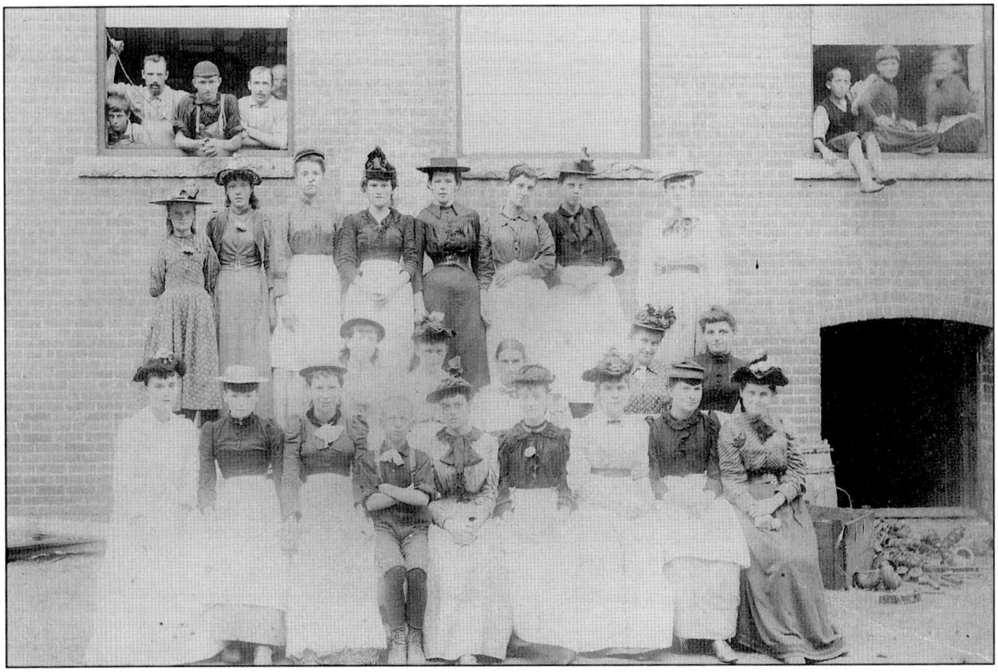

Female workers are shown here at the British Hosiery Mill probably in the 1890s. Unlike the accompanying shot of the male workers, this photo includes some very young children, a reminder that no matter how peaceful the images may seem, conditions in the mills were often brutal. (Photograph courtesy of Sam Coupe.)

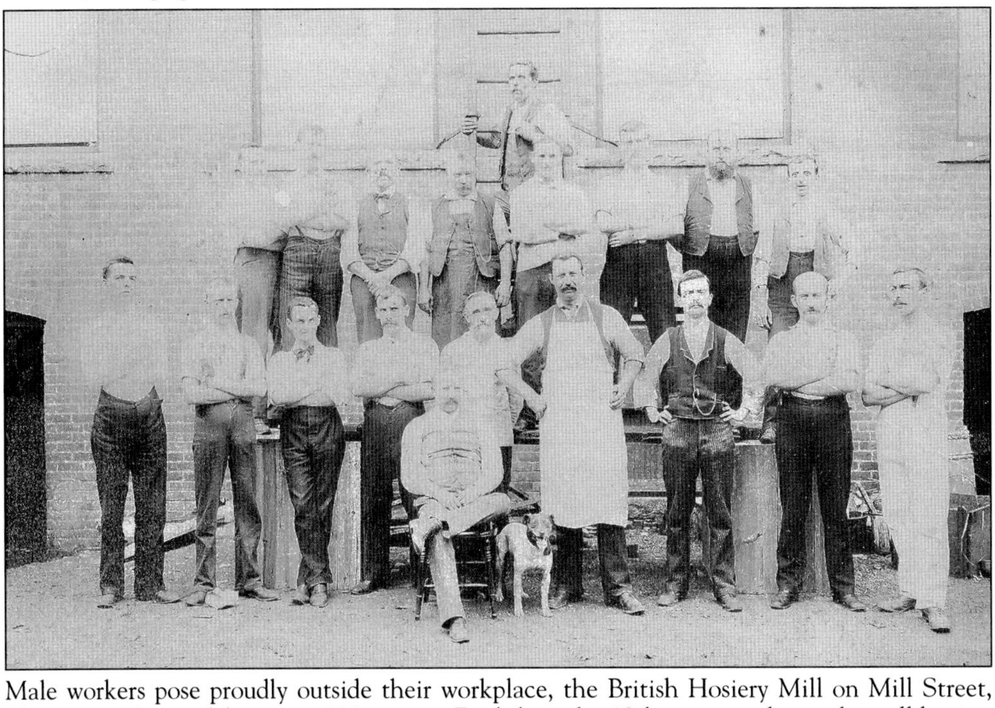

Male workers pose proudly outside their workplace, the British Hosiery Mill on Mill Street, Thornton. The workforce was 100 percent English in the 19th century, the workers all having emigrated from the old country. (Photograph courtesy of Sam Coupe.)

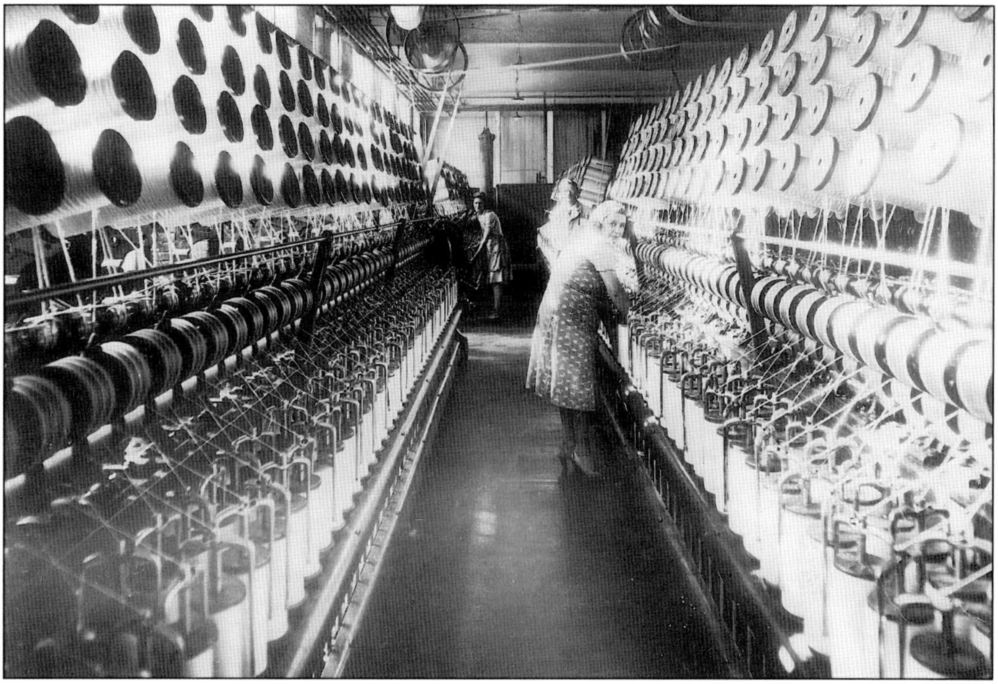

The woman in the foreground of this late 1940s photo is Bertha (Bodenrader) Youde, mother of Millie Youde. She is working on a heavy drawing machine in the Pocasset Mill on Pocasset Street, when the mill was owned by the Walter Marshall Spinning Company. The two people behind her are thought to be foreman Sam Harper and Sue Saccoccio. (Photograph courtesy of Millie Youde.)

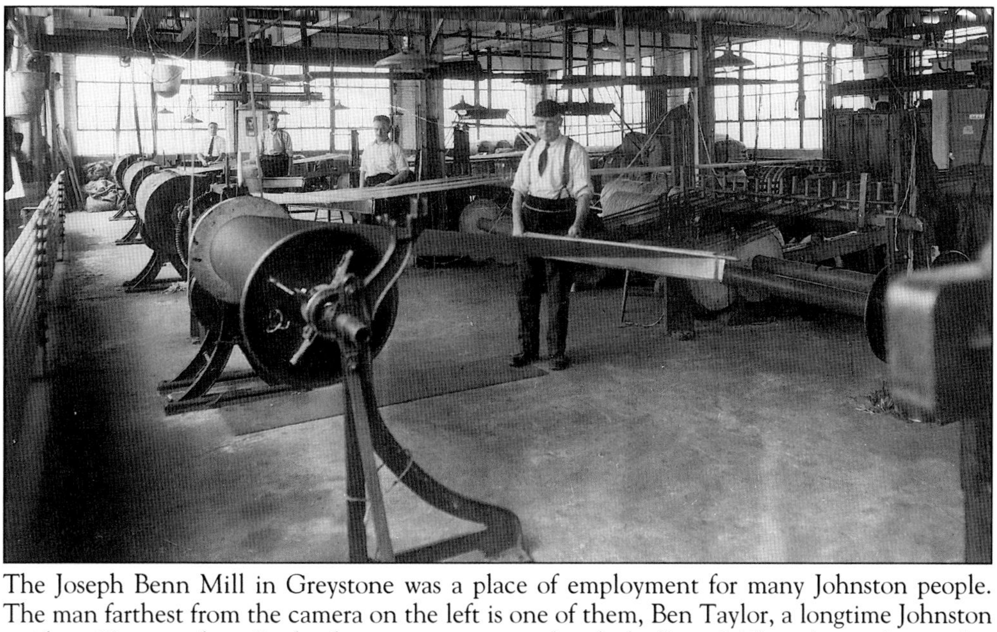

The Joseph Benn Mill in Greystone was a place of employment for many Johnston people. The man farthest from the camera on the left is one of them, Ben Taylor, a longtime Johnston resident. He came from England on a contract signed with the Benn Mill, and agreed to work a 52-hour week for $6.50 a week. Like other Graniteville people, he would walk across the river to work at Greystone. (Photograph courtesy of Gary Lynn.)

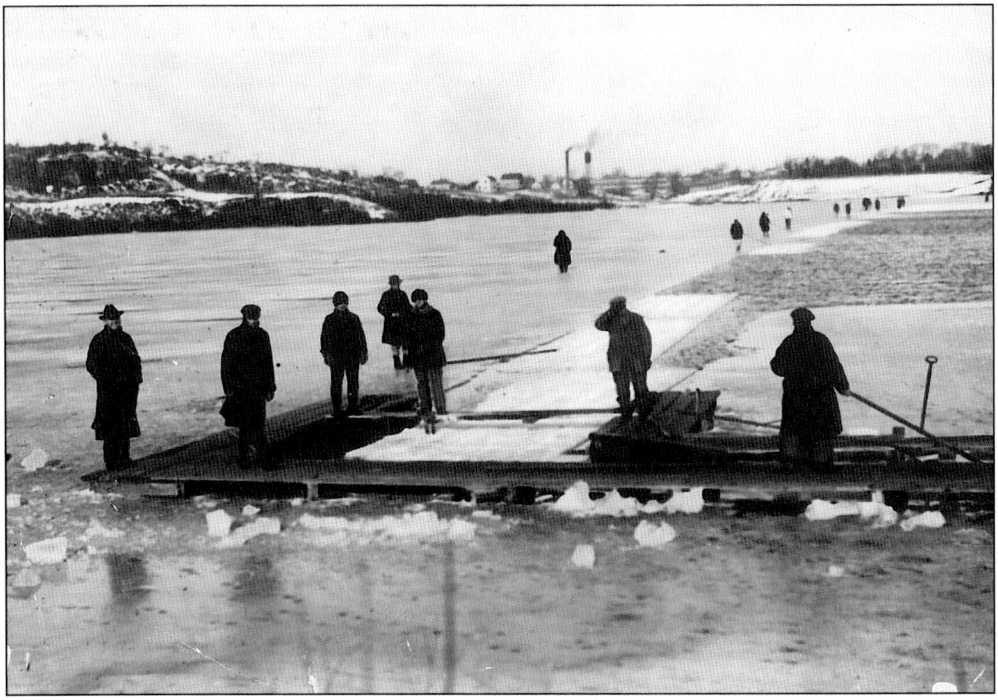

The back of this photograph reads: "The trench and breaking pen." The men are cutting ice at Randall's Pond in Cranston in the early 20th century. The Pocasset Mill village can be seen in the distance. Ice was cut on ponds all over Johnston to supply local household and business needs. (Photograph courtesy of Evelyn Stone Beaumier.)

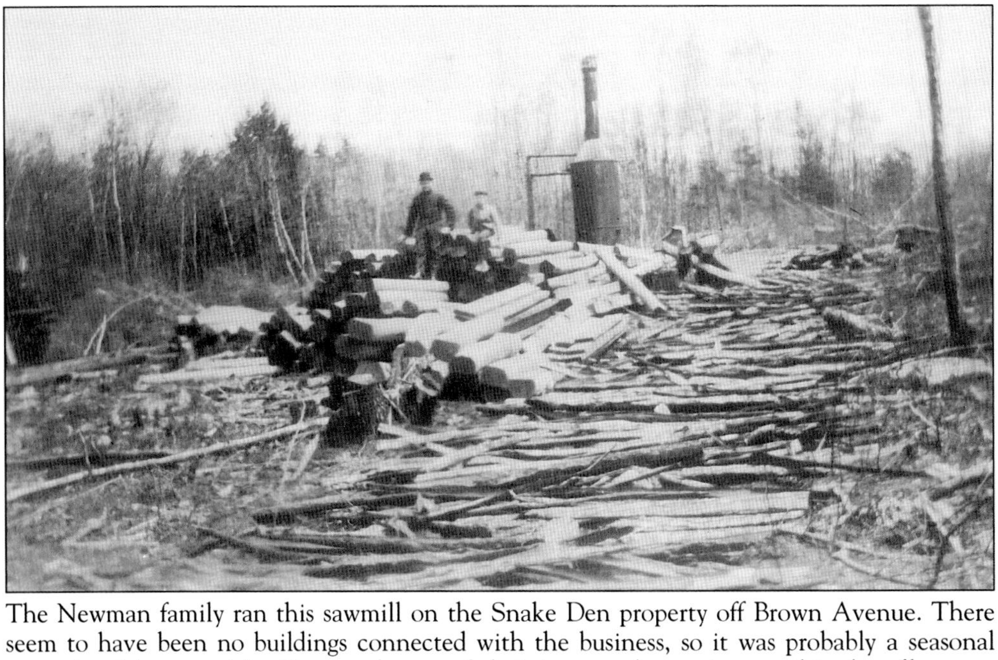

The Newman family ran this sawmill on the Snake Den property off Brown Avenue. There seem to have been no buildings connected with the business, so it was probably a seasonal operation. Many rural families supplemented their incomes by cutting wood in the off-season. (Photograph courtesy of the Newman family.)

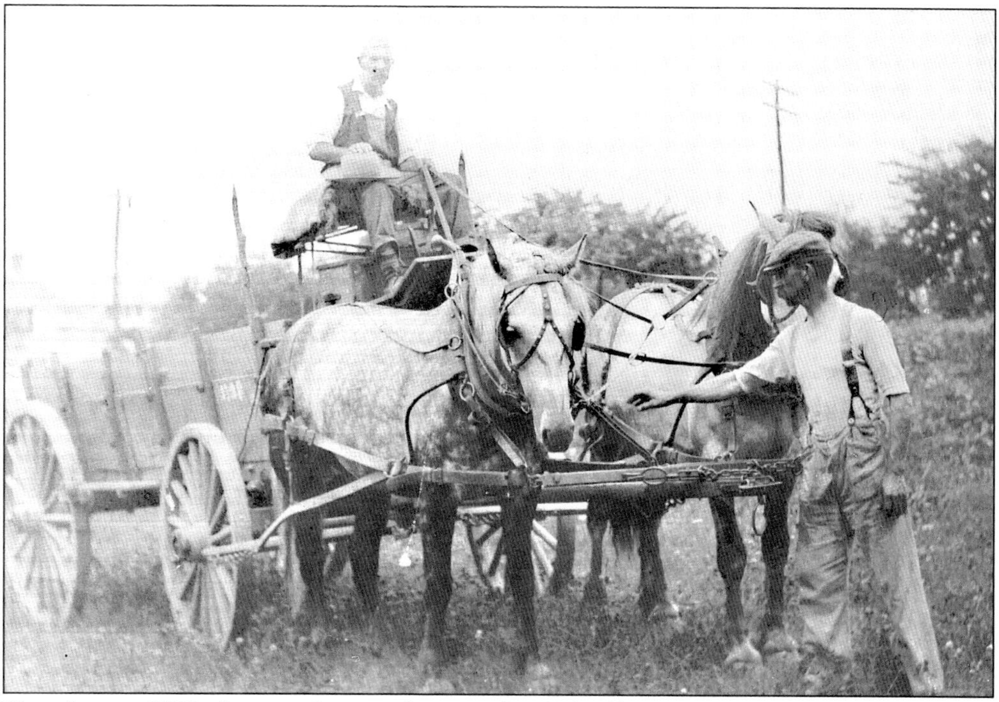

This August 1912 photograph was taken on the Colwell Farm, Greenville Avenue. Morris Brown is the teamster at the reins while Leon S. Colwell, the father of deceased Police Chief Chester B. Colwell, is standing in front of the wagon. (Photograph courtesy of Elizabeth Colwell Mowry.)

Labra Russo, the father of the five Russo boys (Joe, Jack, Mike, Andy, and Ligian), can be seen on the extreme left in this view at Budlong Fields on the site of the present Garden City. His sons are with him as well as a couple of hired workers. They cut hay, hauled it by wagon to Morgan Avenue, and used it on their farm. They also sold some of the hay to other local farms. (Photograph courtesy of Bob Russo.)

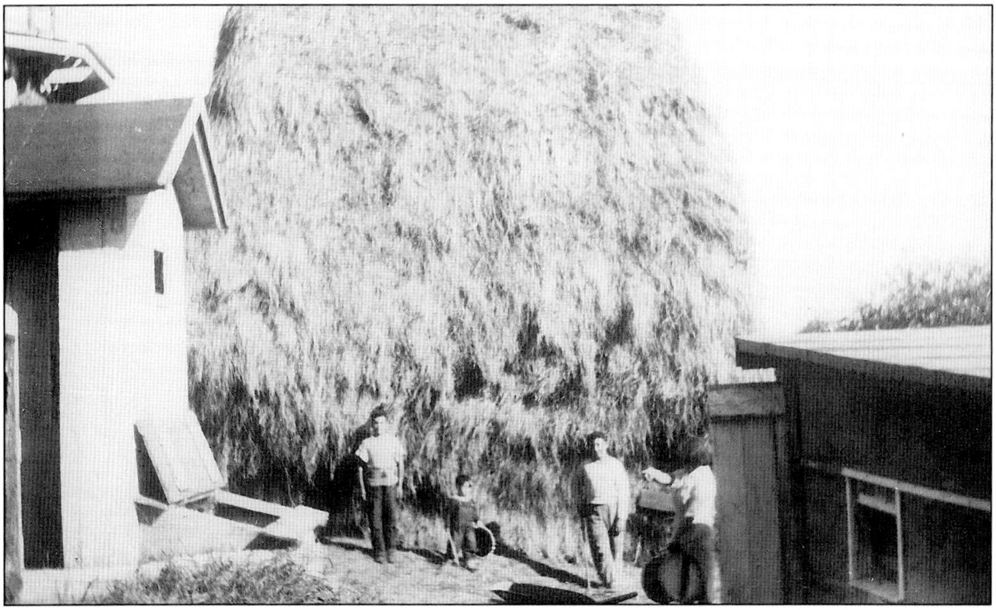

That is a lot of hay! This stack, seen here in 1937 on the Russo Farm, 315 Morgan Avenue, weighed about 100 tons. It was hauled in from Budlong Fields in Cranston to feed the Russo family's herd of cows. Paul Russo is to the far left, and his brother Bob is on his left. The stack burned in 1938. (Photograph courtesy of Paul Russo.)

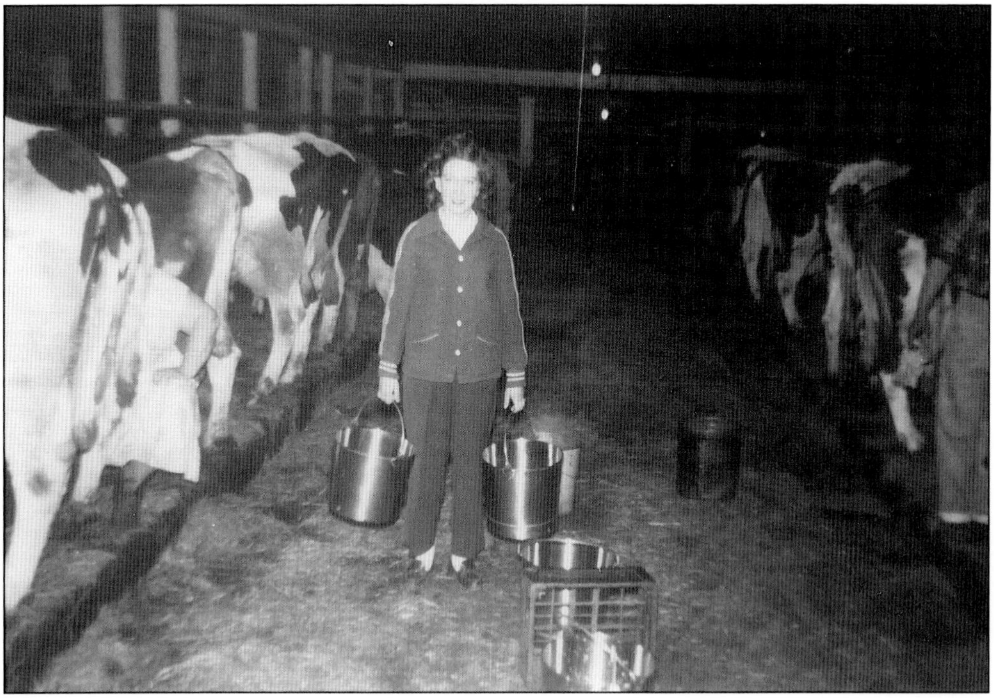

Betty (Colwell) Russo is seen working inside the cow barn at the Russo farm in the 1940s. Milking was done by hand, but the buckets were metal by this time. Betty, the daughter of deceased Police Chief Chester Colwell, later married Paul Russo. (Photograph courtesy of Betty Colwell Russo.)

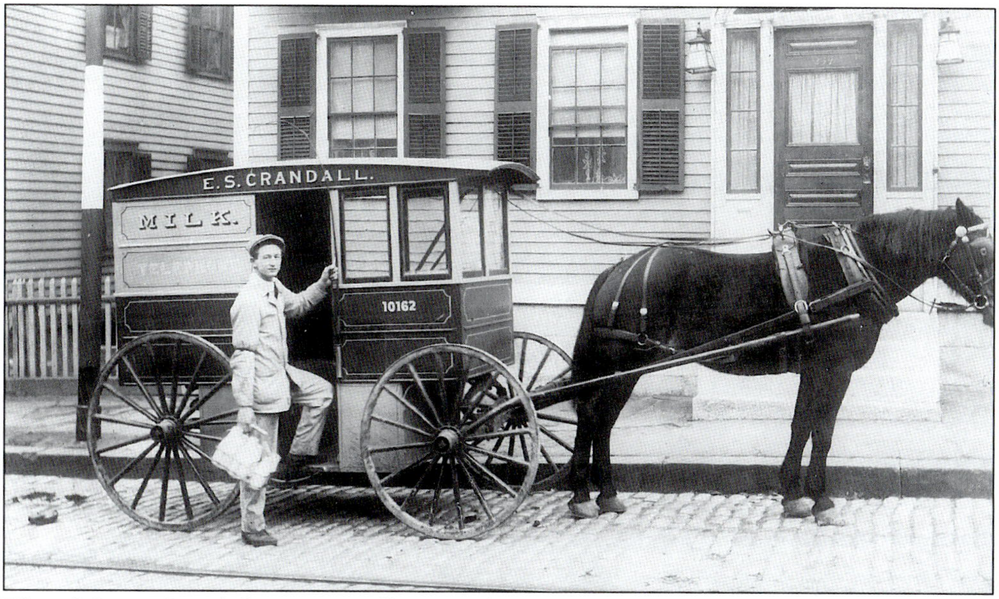

Edward Sweet Crandall was originally a grinder at Brown & Sharpe. After retiring from that company, he went into the milk business, starting a dairy on Alverson Avenue in Providence. He later moved to Lowell Avenue. Area farmers brought their milk to him, and he delivered it to customers on wagons such as the one shown here on Point Street in Providence. In 1938 he built a huge barn on Morgan Avenue in Johnston so he would have his own cows to supply his milk. (Photograph courtesy of Keith Crandall.)

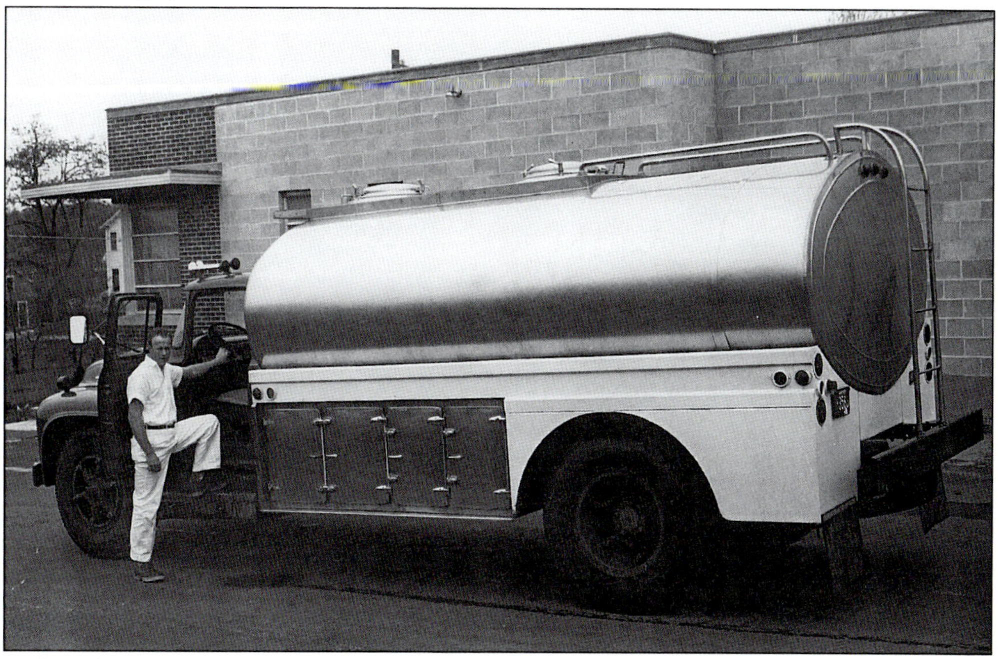

Arthur Shortman, a cousin of the Crandalls, prepares to drive the Crandall family's bulk pickup tank truck. Their dairy building, built in 1955, allowed the milk-processing operation to move from Lowell Avenue in Providence to Johnston. Edward Sweet Crandall had previously opened his dairy barn on the Morgan Avenue site in 1938. (Photograph courtesy of Keith Crandall.)

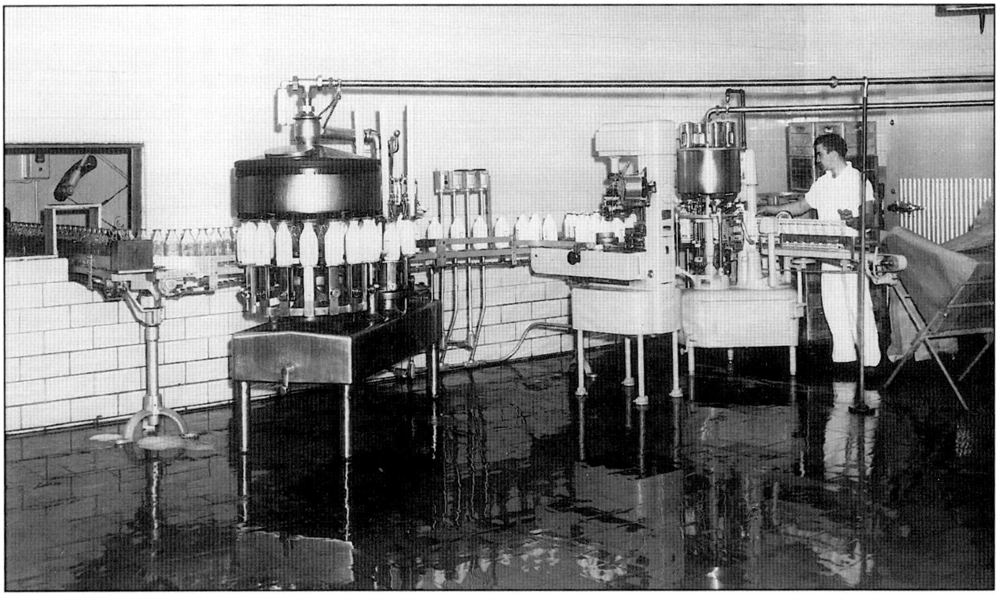

Here we see the inside of the E.S. Crandall Dairy on Morgan Avenue. The bottles coming down the belt through the window on the left have just left the washer. They would then go through the bottle filler, have their caps inserted, and have cellophane placed over the caps. The man on the right is operating a paper bottle filler. (Photograph courtesy of Keith Crandall.)

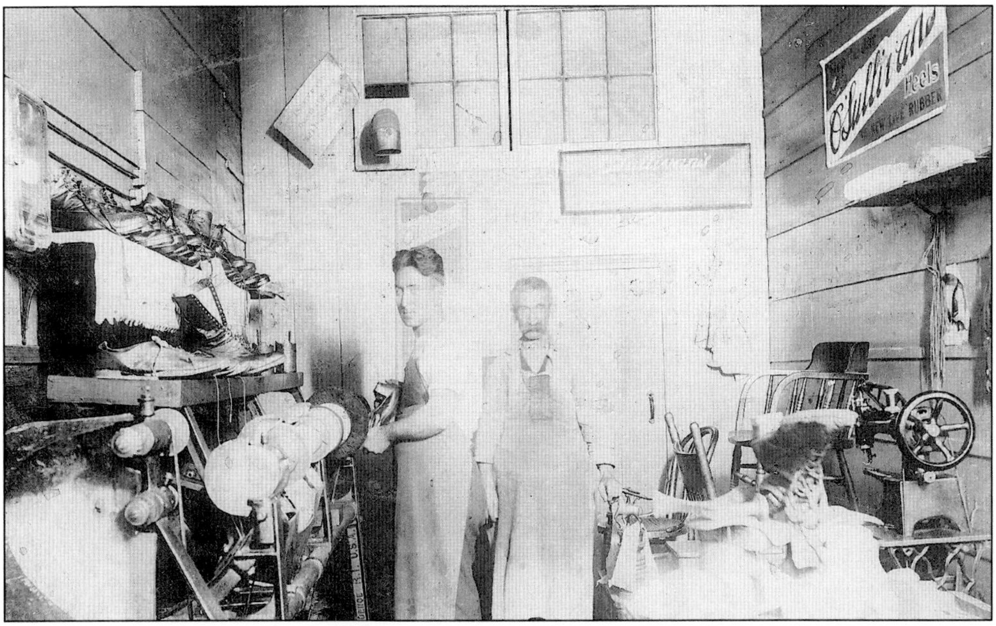

This view from the late teens shows Pasquale Rinaldi with his father, Michael, in Pasquale's cobbler shop at 440 Plainfield Street. Michael was a barber, but on occasion he would help his son. Pasquale married in Italy. He arrived in Johnston with his family and parents in 1913, settling in the village of Thornton. One aspect of Pasquale's business would be hard for us to imagine today—he offered pick-up and delivery service. (Photograph courtesy of Janice Rinaldi.)

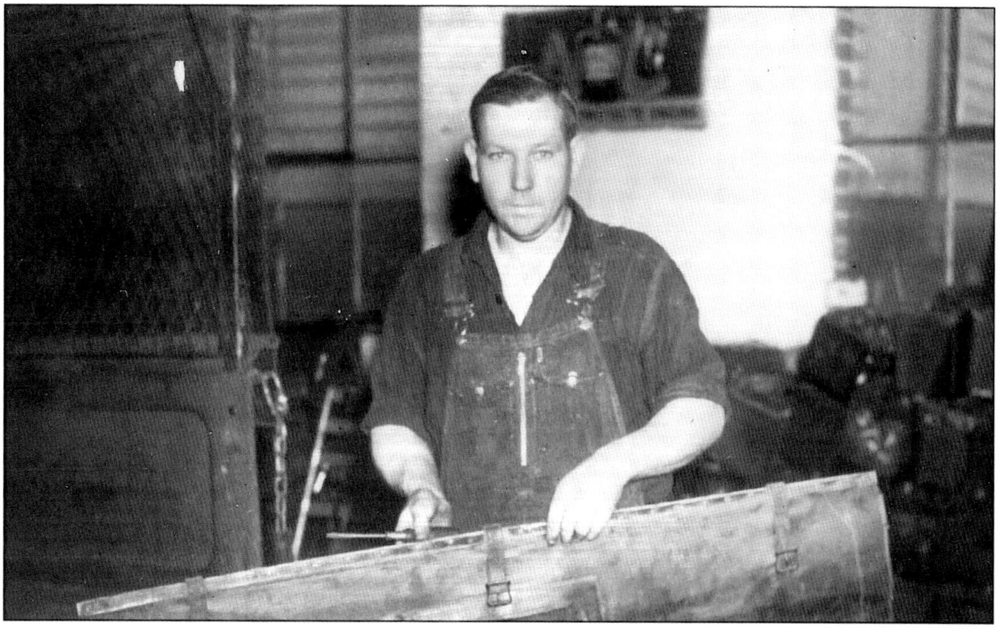

Jimmy Shaw is seen working on upholstery from a car about 1943 at his garage on Greenville Avenue. Jimmy, who still works every day, turned 90 in November 1998. His sister Elizabeth, a couple of years younger than he is, handles the books on a daily basis. (Photograph courtesy of Jimmy Shaw.)

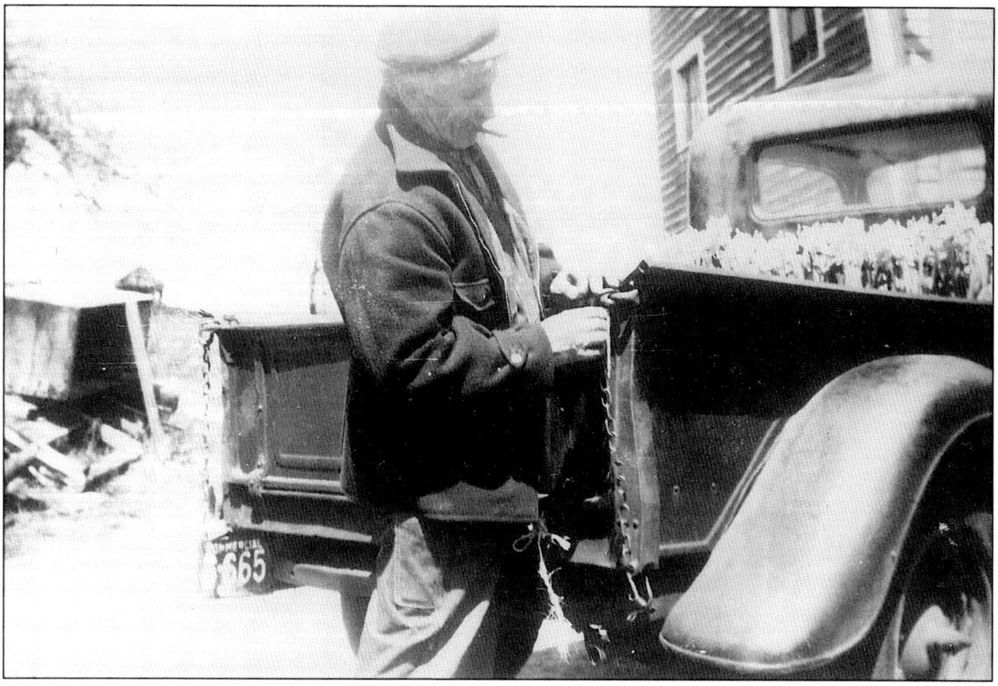

John Altrui loads flowers onto his truck at the Altrui farm, Simmonsville. Italian farmers in Hughesdale, Thornton, and Simmonsville grew flowers, apples, vegetables, and kept bees for honey for the truck market trade at the Farmers' Market in Providence. (Photograph courtesy of William Macera.)

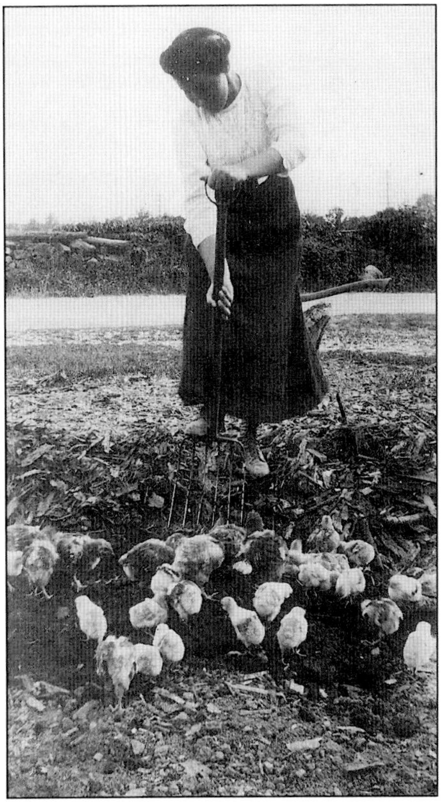

Eliza (Whipple) Langford is seen digging earth worms to feed the chicks in front of her. The Langford home was on the south side of Shun Pike, their farm adjoining the Upper Simmonsville Reservoir. Locals know the reservoir as Langford's. Eliza was a daughter of Zack Whipple from Brown Avenue. (Photograph courtesy of Susie Brown.)

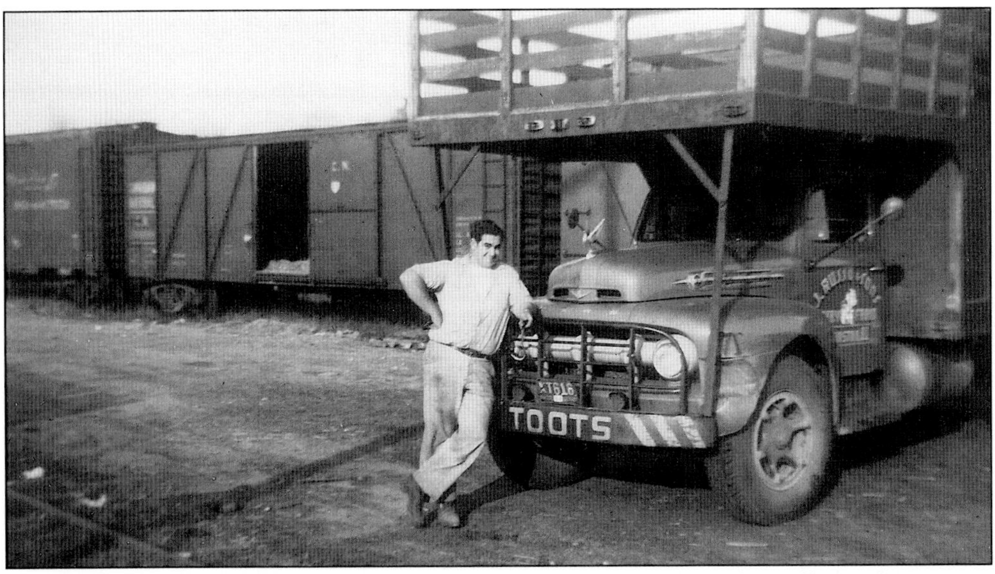

Paul Russo awaits a delivery of hay from a freight car in the Olneyville yard. Previous generations in his family had done their own haying in the Budlong Fields in Cranston, but times had changed by 1952, when this shot was taken. The family farm had over 100 cows in the 1940s. Paul and his brother Bob ran Russo's Dairy. (Photograph courtesy of Paul and Betty Russo.)

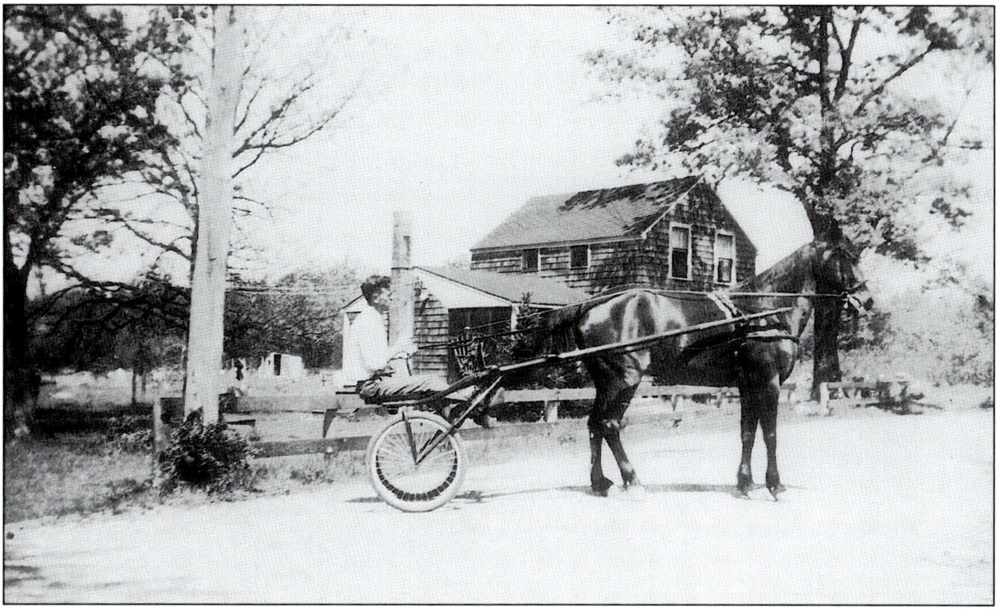

James Mitchell is seen here in 1943 training a racehorse called "The Titan" so it would become accustomed to joycarts. Frank Mitchell Sr., his father, owned and raced harness horses during this time. James and his brother, Frank Jr., were both blacksmiths, shoeing horses all over the area. The house in back of James was the Mitchell's home at 28 Milton Street, off George Waterman Road. (Photograph courtesy of James E. Mitchell.)

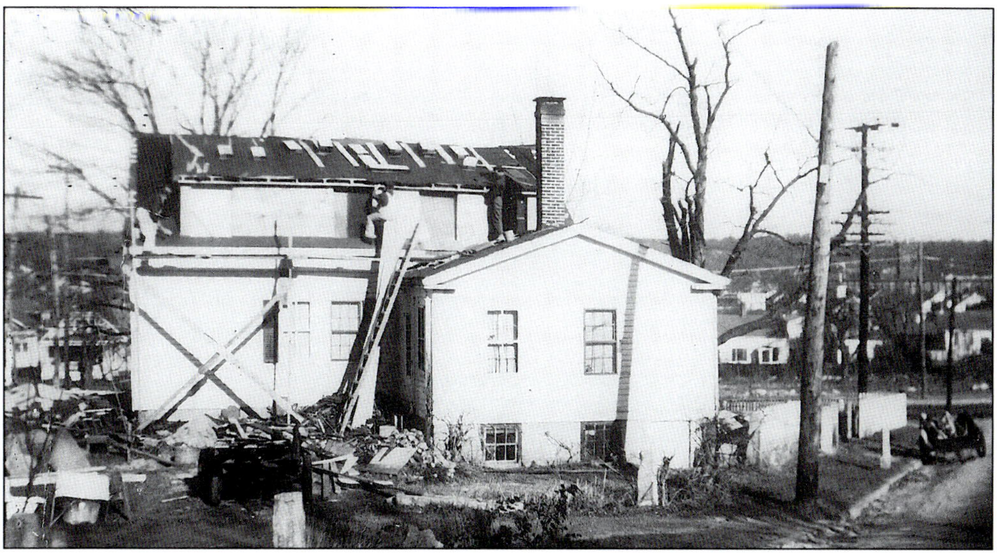

This photograph from 1937 shows a dormer being constructed on the roof of the Emor Angell House at 138 Putnam Pike at the corner of Pine Hill Avenue. On the far left is Walter Pearson and to the right is George Harrington. These two workmen were employed by Albert Thornton, a local contractor who at one time was superintendent of schools in Johnston. (Photograph courtesy of Steve Toro.)

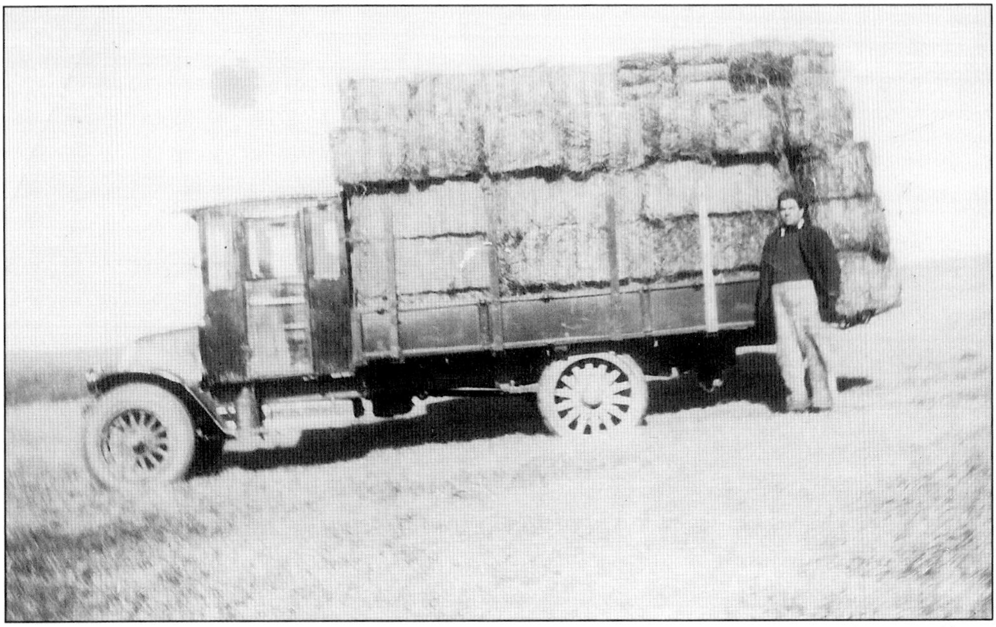

Jack Russo, the father of Bob and Paul Russo, is shown here with his hay truck at Budlong Fields in Garden City about 1920. The truck had solid rubber tires and needed to be cranked to start. It must have been a bumpy ride back to Morgan Avenue. (Photograph courtesy of Paul & Bob Russo.)

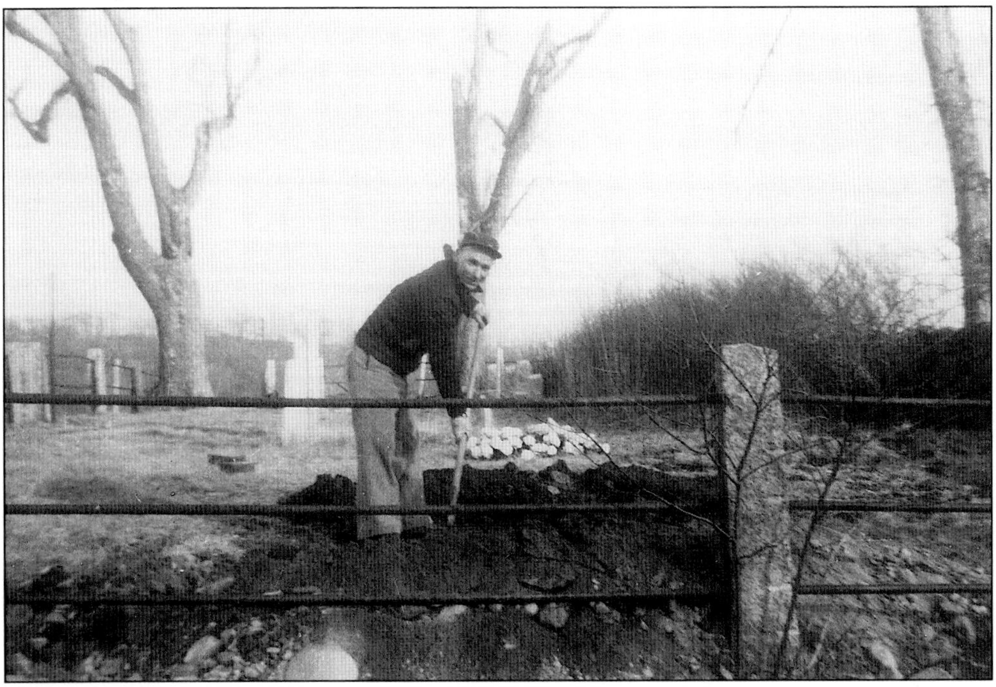

George Kinsley digs a grave at the Atwood family cemetery on Morgan Avenue. The 1955 burial of Minerva Taft was the last to date in this lot, although the cemetery can still be used. Small family lots like this one can be found all over Johnston and all over the state. (Photograph courtesy of Mabel Sprague.)

Six

FAMILY AND FRIENDS

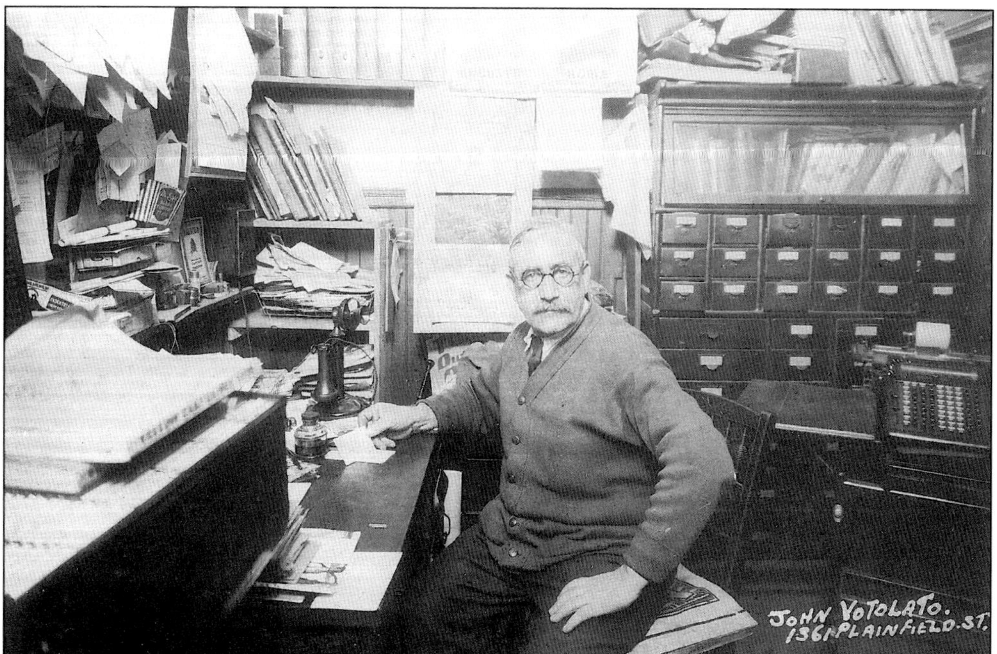

John Votolato originally ran a hardware store next to the Collins Drugstore but moved the business to the Myrtle Hall building after he purchased the latter. He was the first Italian town councilman in Johnston, and he helped many Italian immigrants adjust to life in the new country. This photograph shows him at his desk in his office at 1361 Plainfield Street in the Myrtle Hall building. (Photograph courtesy of Barbra Votolato McGuirl.)

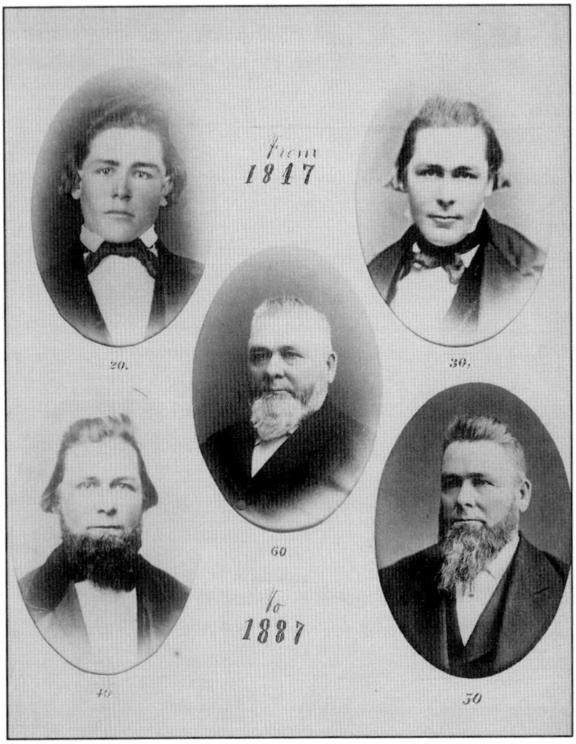

George White lived on Cherry Hill Road and later at the corner of Cherry Hill Road and Greenville Avenue. He is shown here every ten years starting from the time he was 20 years old in 1847 to when he was 60 in 1887. His son Leroy and his grandson Leroy Jr. lived at the Greenville Avenue farm until about 1990. It is now the site of Whytebrook Terrace. (From the collection of the Johnston Historical Society.)

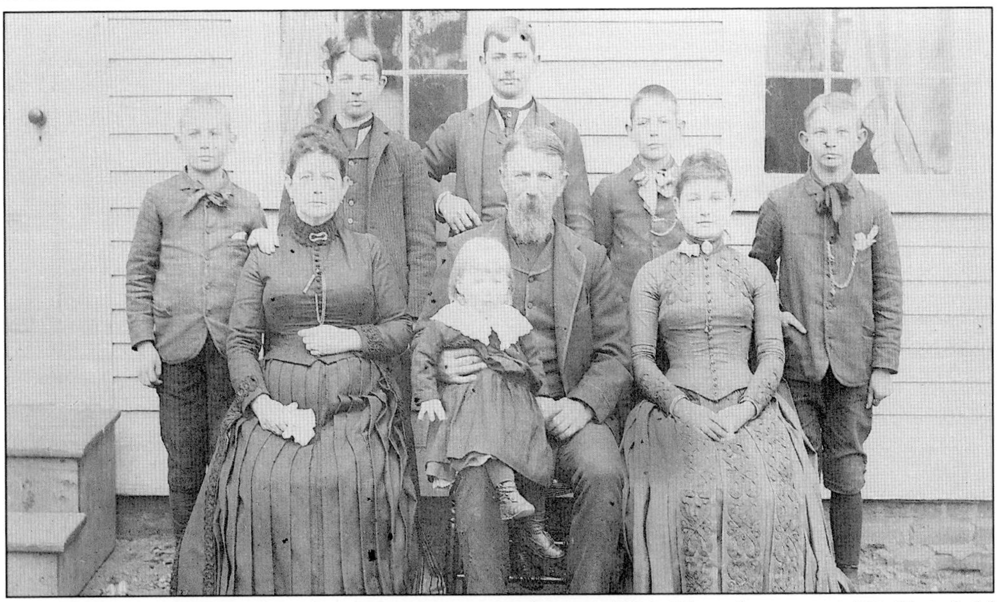

This William Albert Luther family portrait was taken in 1890. Their home at 1421 Plainfield Street is still intact. They are, from left to right, as follows: (seated) Ada C. (Rogers) Luther, William Albert Luther, Annie Luther, and Caroline P. Luther (on Dad's lap); (standing) Frank R. Luther, Byron S. Luther, George O. Luther, Edgar H. Luther, and William Albert Luther. Sterry K. Luther's father, Addison Luther, a brother of William Sr. Sterry, was town clerk in Johnston for many years during the early 20th century. (Photo courtesy of Fred and Martha Mikkelsen.)

George C. Calef was born in Vermont in 1837 and came to Providence in 1858 to seek his fortune. He and two of his brothers opened a very successful family market there, and George also owned a large livery stable in the city. He took great interest in the school system in Johnston, serving as a trustee of the Manton School District for many years. Largely through his efforts Johnston's first high school was established in the Annex area. He also served on the town council. (Photograph courtesy of Alan Iemma.)

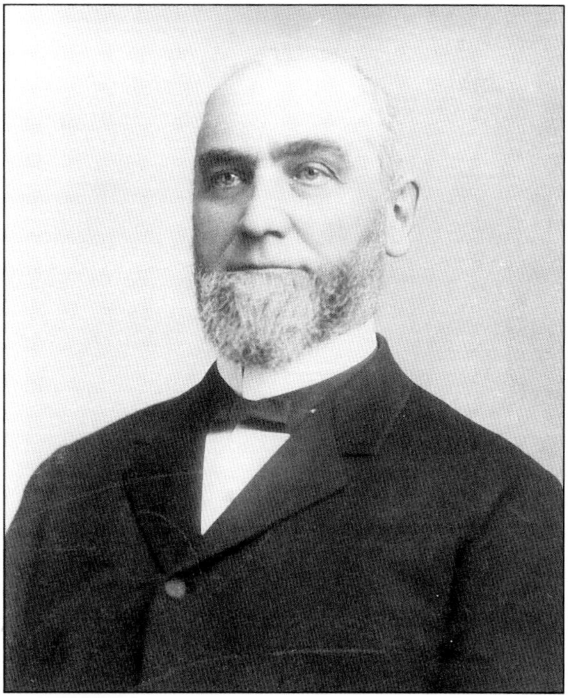

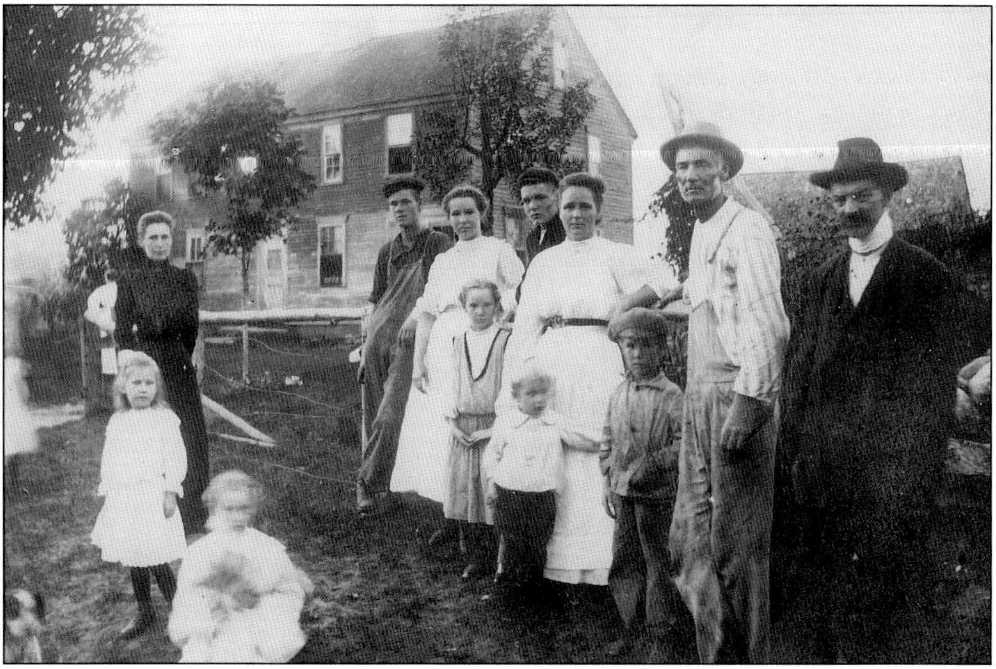

The Steere House on Snake Den Road (now Belfield Drive) is shown here about 1909. The house, which burned in the 1920s, was situated on the north side of the road, about halfway in from Hartford Avenue. George Washington Brown is second from the right, and the other people are his family from two marriages. His first wife was Julia (Randall) Brown and his second wife was Martha (Cady) Brown. George was Susie Brown's grandfather. (Photograph courtesy of Susie Brown.)

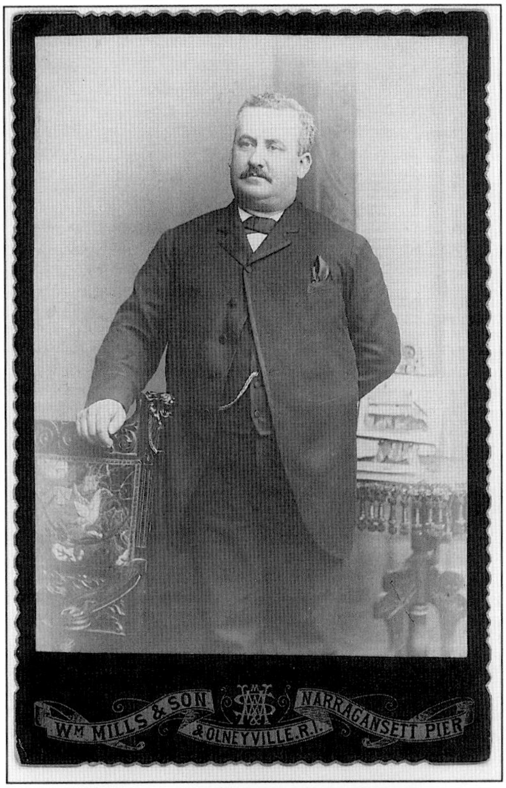

Senator George Frederick Aldrich Beane was very prominent in business and political affairs in Johnston during the last decades of the 19th century. He ran a very prosperous coal, hay, grain, teaming, and livery business on Plainfield Street. In the public arena he was president of the town council for a number of years, highway commissioner of District 1, a founder and active member of the Rough and Ready Fire Engine Company, and a state senator in the 1890s.

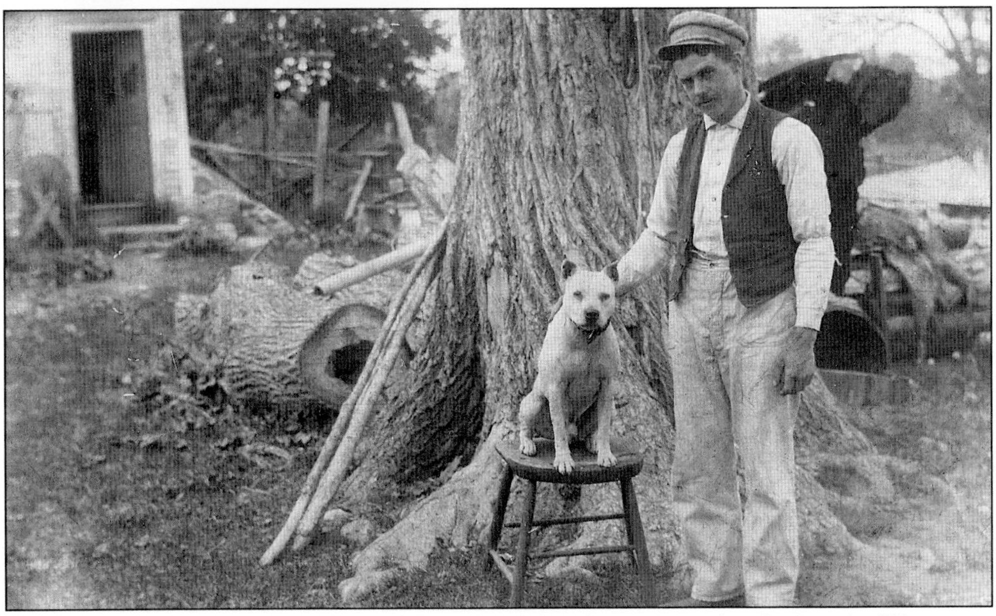

James Edward Waterman (1871–1916) poses with his dog next to the shed at the Waterman farm on Cherry Hill Road. The scene is probably from the 1890s. Mr. Waterman was one in a long line of his family to farm this land. The well-kept family cemetery sits at the corner of Cherry Hill Road and Atwood Avenue. He was the son of James N. Waterman and Susan D. Evans. (Photograph courtesy of James Waterman Jr.)

Aunt Dolly Onsley lived on Morgan Avenue and was Ben Onsley's grandmother. They were Native Americans from the Wampanoag Tribe. Mabel Sprague remembers her parents telling her about Aunt Dolly coming to do laundry at their house around the turn of the century and having dinner with them. The photo was taken in Mabel's house. (Photograph courtesy of Mabel Sprague.)

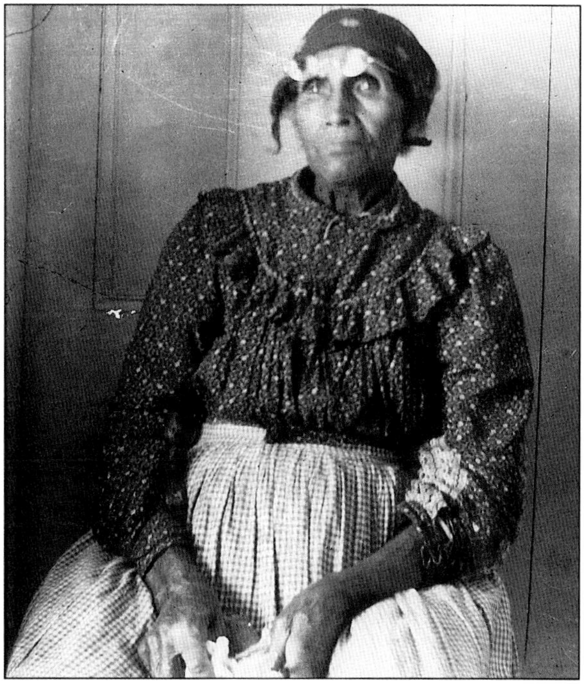

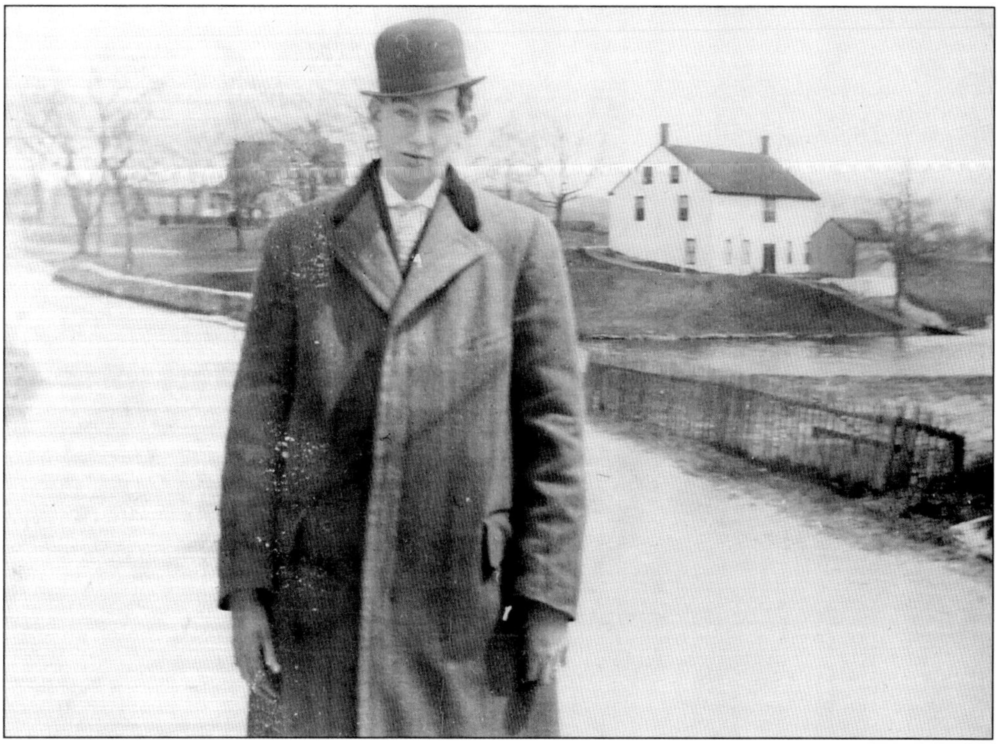

"Long Slim Nick" Vanner is seen here in front of the bridge on Morgan Avenue over the Pocasset River. A textile mill house made of stone is on the right and the Peckham House is on the left. The stone house was torn down many years ago. (Photograph courtesy of Mabel Sprague.)

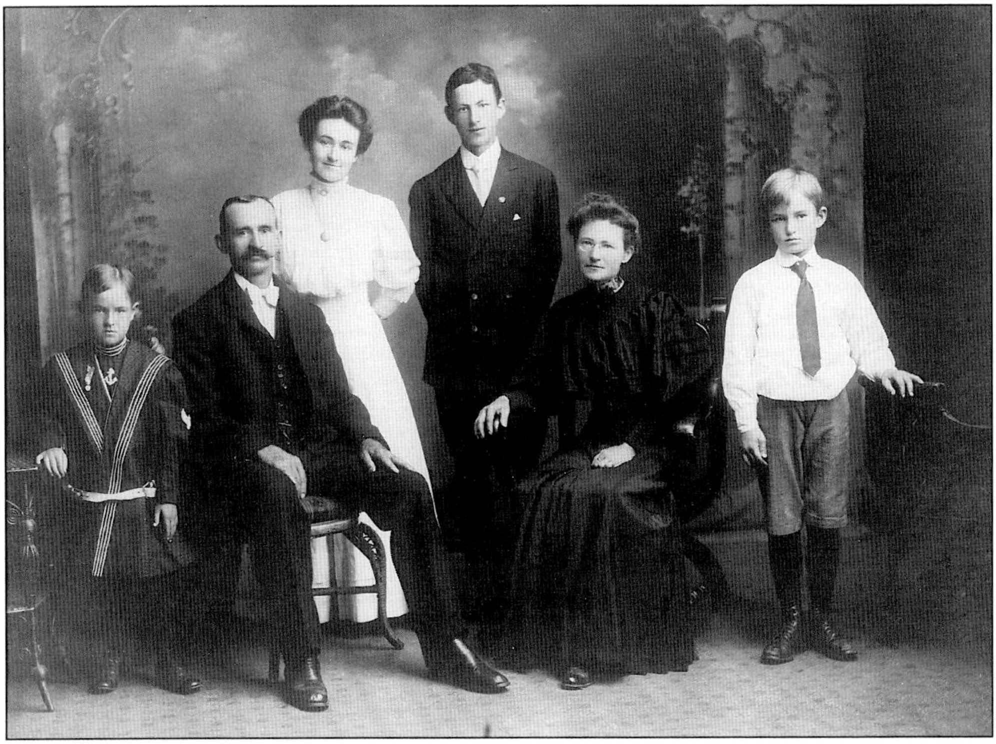

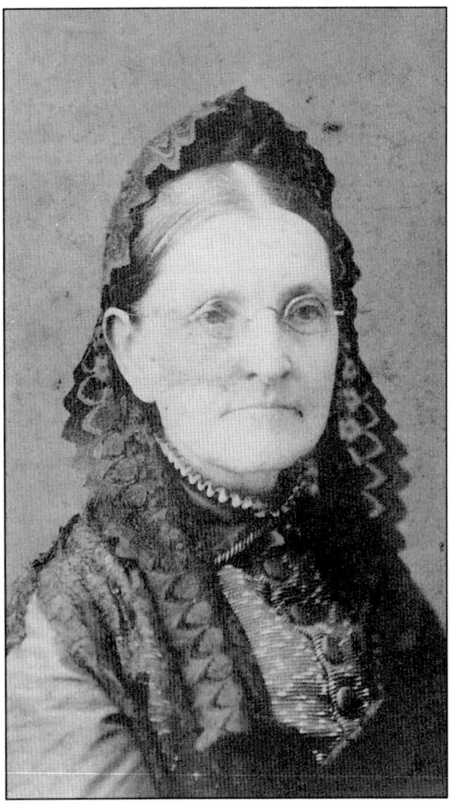

John and Katherine Newman (seated) and their family are pictured here *c.* 1906. Their children are, standing from left to right, Alfred (born 1901), Katherine, Henry, and George W. They later had another child, Evelyn. Alfred was the father of Herb Newman, who still lives on Pine Hill Avenue. John bought a milk business on Greenville Avenue from his nephew Arthur Newman in 1916, and ran the business under the name of J.F. Newman Dairy. In the 1920s it was sold to the Hood Company. (Photograph courtesy of Herb Newman.)

This photograph from the late 19th century is of Phebe Fenner, the wife of Welcome Fenner. Mrs. Fenner lived in the house now standing at 222 Morgan Avenue, which was supposedly built in the 1830s by Mr. Fenner as a wedding gift for his new bride. Welcome Fenner was a millwright. (Photograph courtesy of Harold and Judy Beaudoin.)

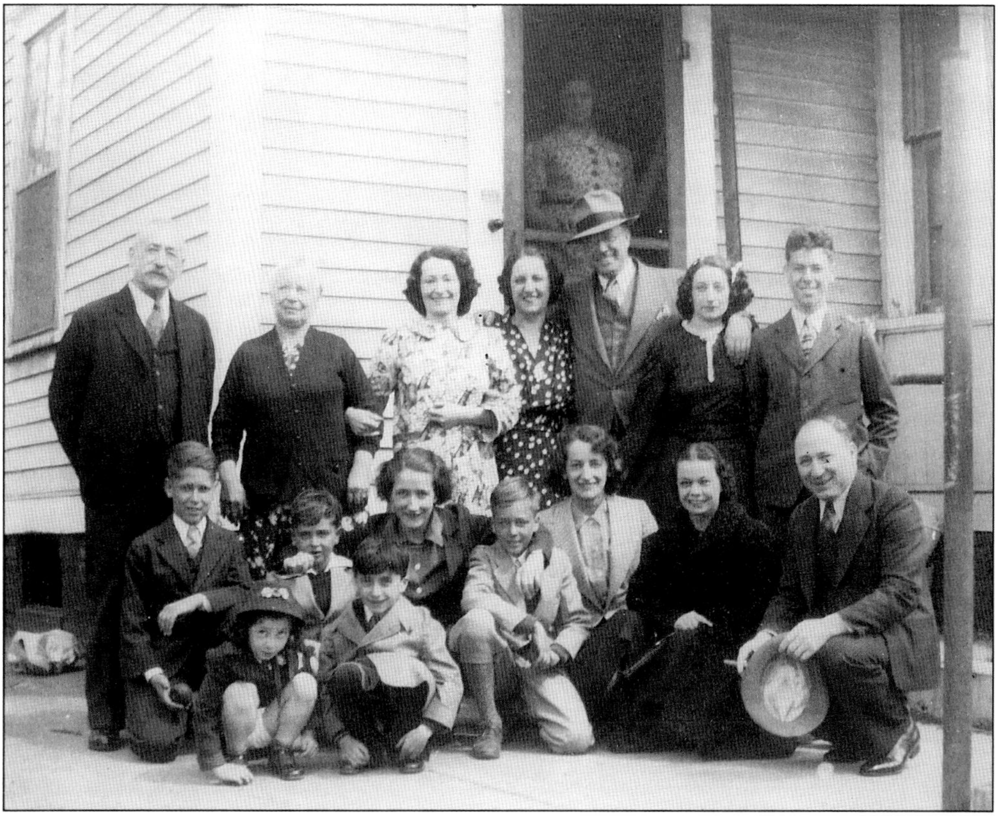

The Votolato family of Thornton is pictured in the 1930s. They are, from left to right, as follows: (front row) two unidentified children; (middle row) unknown, unknown, Mary Votolato, unknown, Nancy Votolato, Mary Votolato, and Judge Arthur Votolato; (back row) John Votolato, Pasqualena Votolato (John's wife), Mary Sullivan, unknown, Vin Votolato, Virginia Votolato, and unknown. (Photograph courtesy of Barbra Votolato McGuirl.)

William Aitchson was a well-known figure in Thornton in the early 20th century. He ran the Aitchison Hotel at 1381 Plainfield Street (a popular eating and drinking establishment next to Ferri's Tavern), owned much of the land in the area of the present St. Rocco's Church, had a square and its fountain named after him, and sponsored St. Ronan's soccer team before WW I. He died in 1927. St. Rocco's bought the property for the present church from his family in the 1940s.

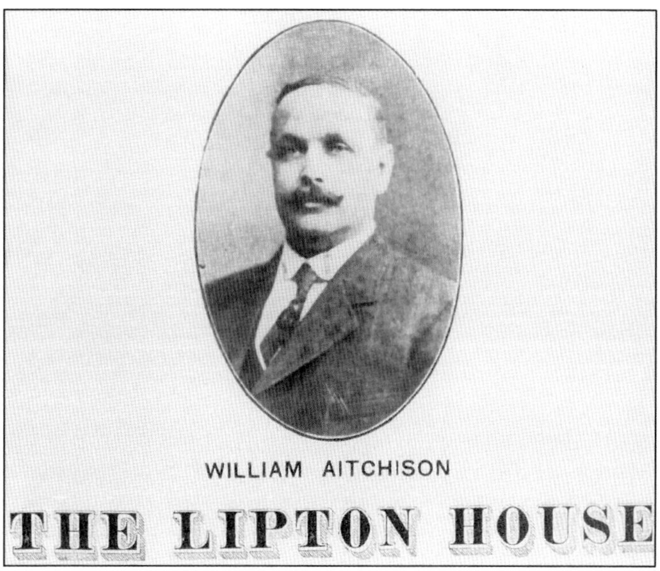

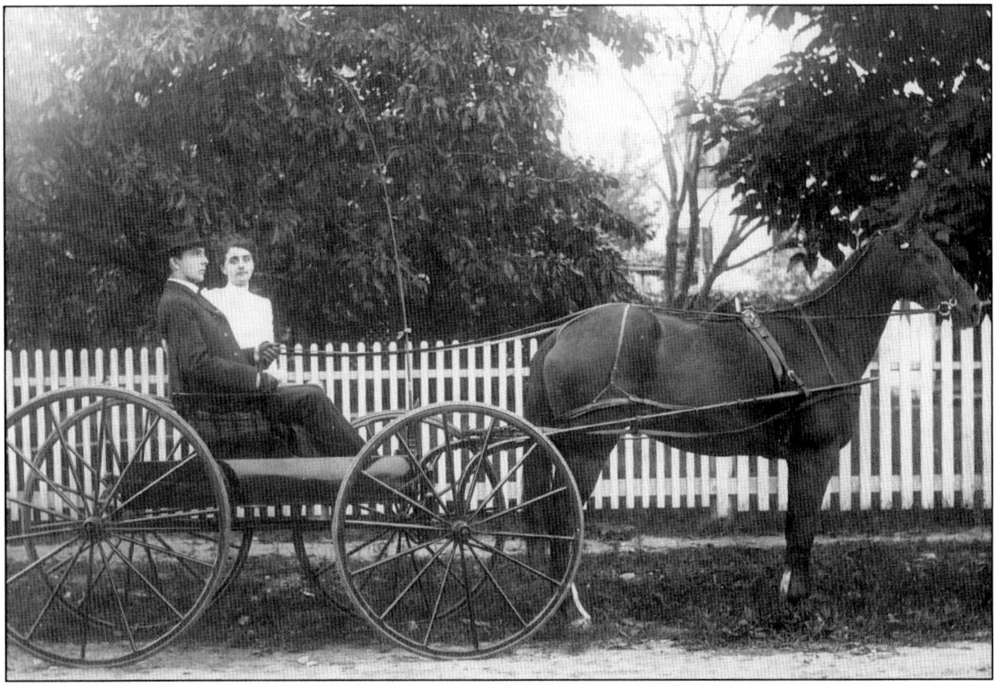

The two people in the fine-looking buggy are Laban F. Cram and Irene Bertha Cram, being pulled by Bessie the mare. The photo was probably taken around the turn of the century on present-day Cherry Hill Road. The Peter Randall House is in the background. Mr. Cram was related to the Waterman family through his mother; he died in 1904 at the age of 23. (Photograph courtesy of James Waterman Jr.)

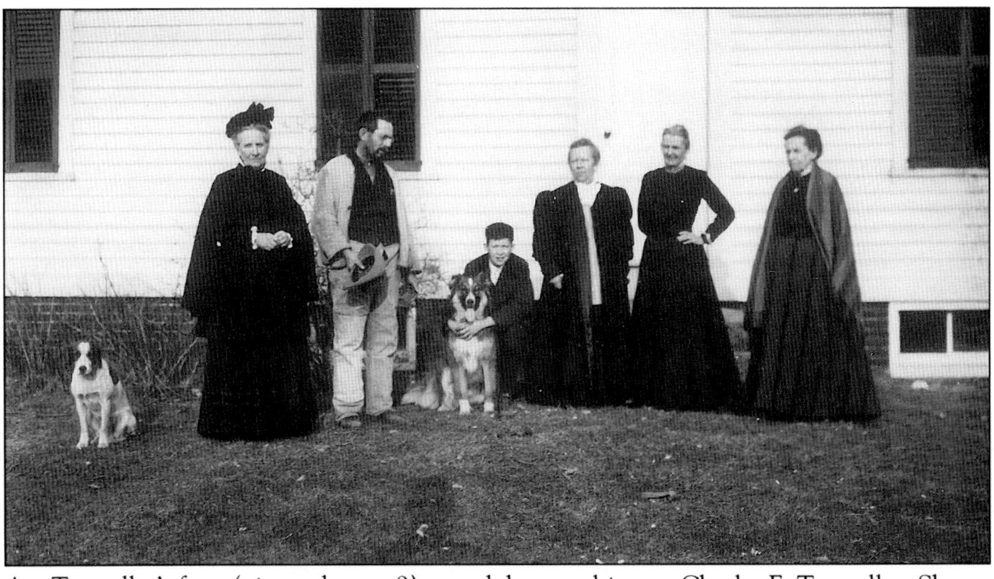

Asa Tourtellot's farm (pictured on p. 9) passed down to his son, Charles E. Tourtellot. Shown in front of his farmhouse c. 1910 are, from left to right, Sanondess Jenks, Charles E. Tourtellot, Webb Wilder and "Laddie," Elizabeth Wilder, "Tillie" Tourtellot (wife of Charles), and Mary Tourtellot. Three of the women were Charles's sisters. Young Webb Wilder was the grandson of Elizabeth Wilder. (Photograph courtesy of Harold and Judy Beaudoin.)

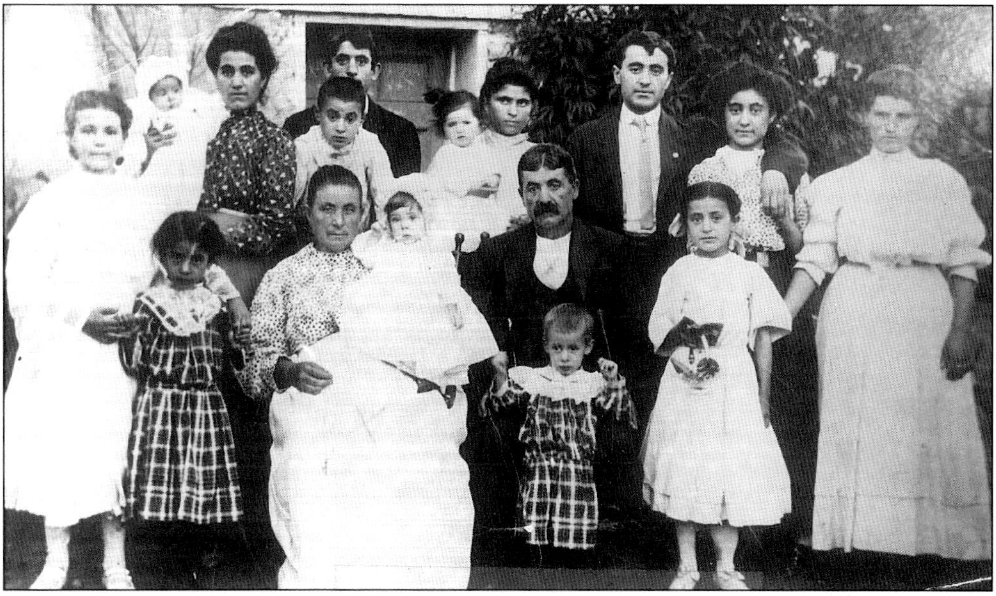

This LaFazia family photograph was taken in the teens next to their house, still standing on Zanfagna Street in Thornton. In the center is Pasquale LaFazia with his wife, Caterina (Confredi) LaFazia. Behind Pasquale is Josephine (Nardillo) LaFazia holding her first child with husband Alfonso on the right. Other family members are Joseph, Angelina, Clara, and Theresa. Pasquale and Caterina were married in Italy and arrived in Thornton in the early 1900s. (Photograph courtesy of Alfonso J. LaFazia.)

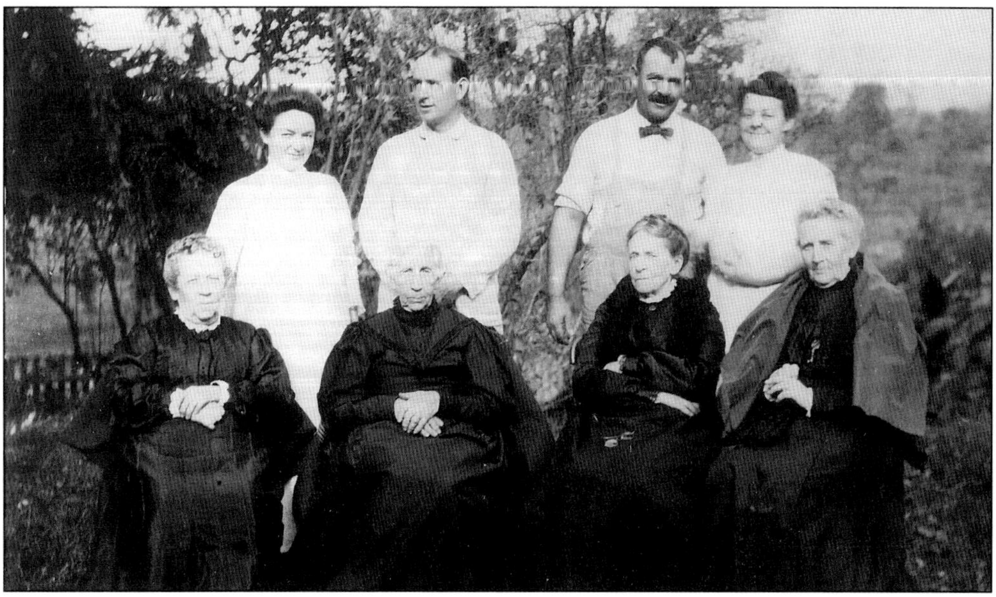

Taken around 1917, this picture shows a grouping of the Tourtellot and Wilder families, who lived on adjoining farms. In the front row are the four daughters of Asa and Eliza Tourtellot, while in the back row are two of Elizabeth Wilder's sons and their wives. From left to right they are as follows: (front row) Elizabeth Weaver Wilder, Phebe R. Angell, Mary Mahala Tourtellot, and Sanondess Austress Jenks; (back row) Ida Kimball Wilder, Raymond Wilder, Frank Wilder, and Lillian Gardner Wilder. (Photograph courtesy of Mabel Hopkins.)

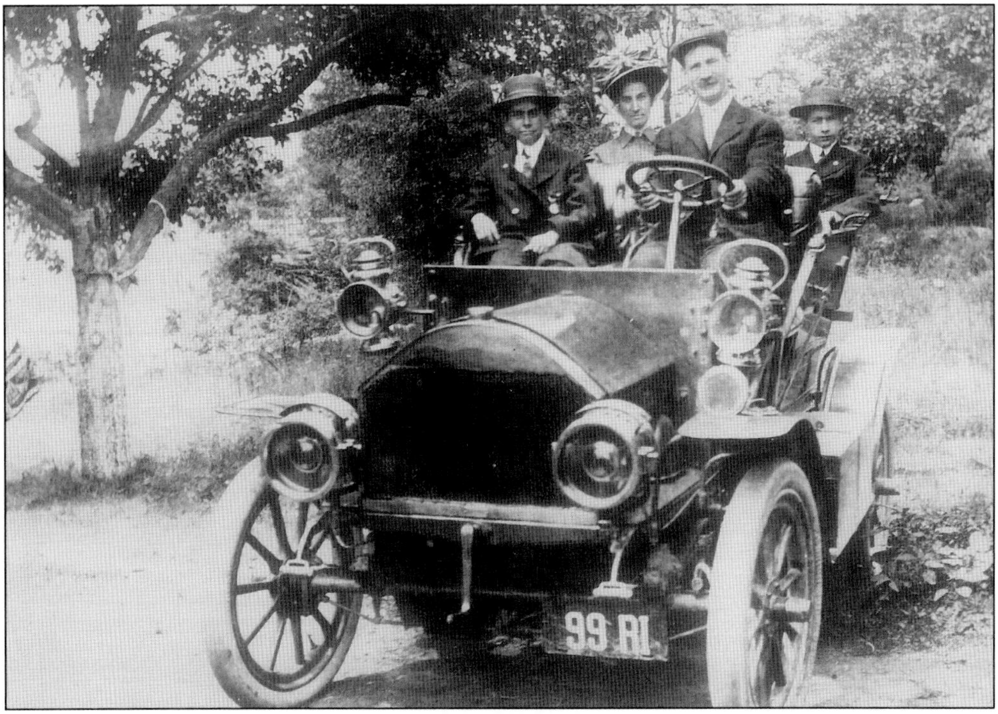

What a license plate!! Any true Rhode Islander would fight for this one. James Charnley, owner of the Greystone Market on Angell Avenue, is at the wheel of his 1909 Columbia. Annie, his wife, is in back with their son Frank, and Clarence is in front with his Dad. (Photograph courtesy of Laura Charnley Panicucci.)

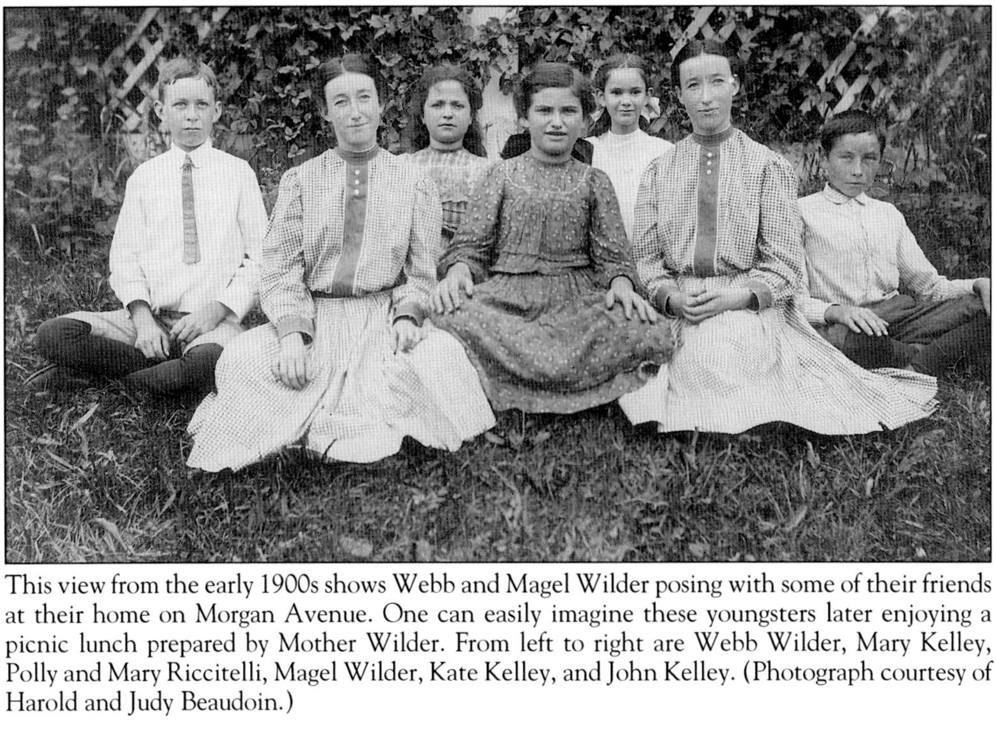

This view from the early 1900s shows Webb and Magel Wilder posing with some of their friends at their home on Morgan Avenue. One can easily imagine these youngsters later enjoying a picnic lunch prepared by Mother Wilder. From left to right are Webb Wilder, Mary Kelley, Polly and Mary Riccitelli, Magel Wilder, Kate Kelley, and John Kelley. (Photograph courtesy of Harold and Judy Beaudoin.)

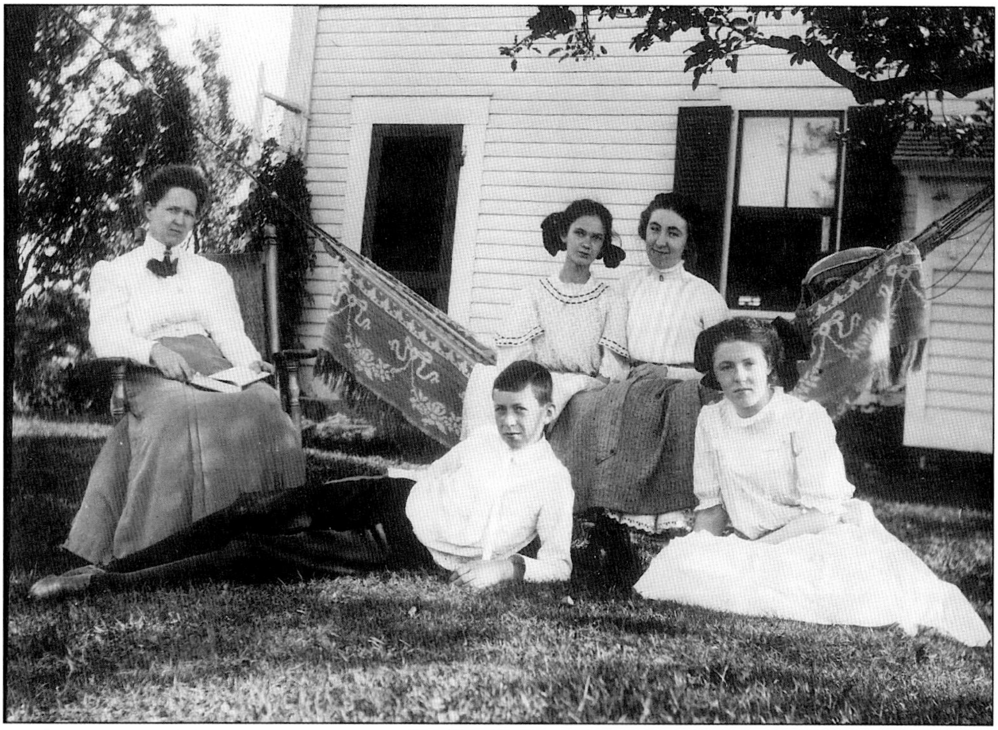

This is an early-20th-century view of the Wilder family in back of their home at 281 Morgan Avenue. Gertrude Wilder is on the left, Magel Wilder and Ethel Collingwood are in the hammock, and Webb Wilder and Mary Collingwood are on the ground in this nostalgic view of a simpler time. (Photograph courtesy of Harold and Judy Beaudoin.)

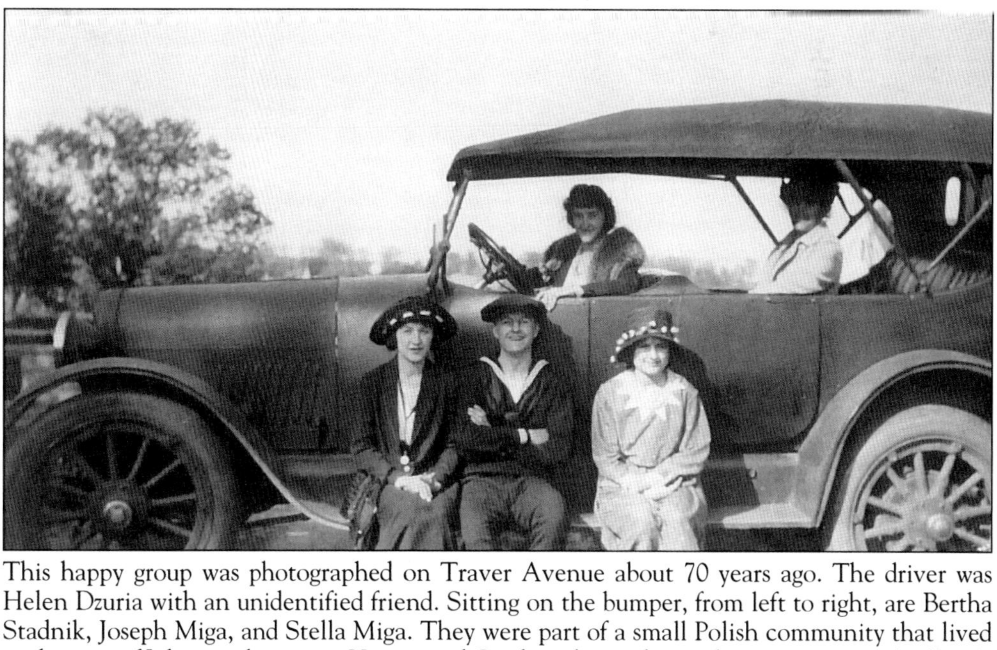

This happy group was photographed on Traver Avenue about 70 years ago. The driver was Helen Dzuria with an unidentified friend. Sitting on the bumper, from left to right, are Bertha Stadnik, Joseph Miga, and Stella Miga. They were part of a small Polish community that lived in the area of Johnston known as Homestead Gardens, located near the intersection of Killingly Street and Greenville Avenue. (Photograph courtesy of Dorothy Innocenti.)

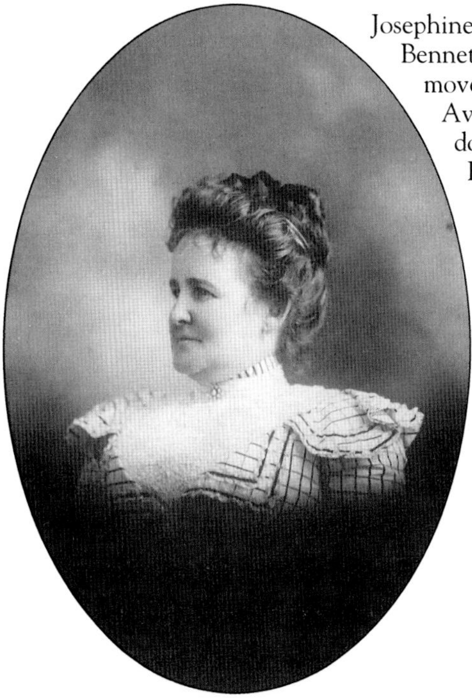

Josephine Peckham, the wife of Leander Peckham, was a Bennett by birth. In 1897 she and her husband, Leander, moved into a fancy Victorian house at 278 Morgan Avenue that they had built. They are said to have done much entertaining. (Photograph courtesy of Harold and Judy Beaudoin.)

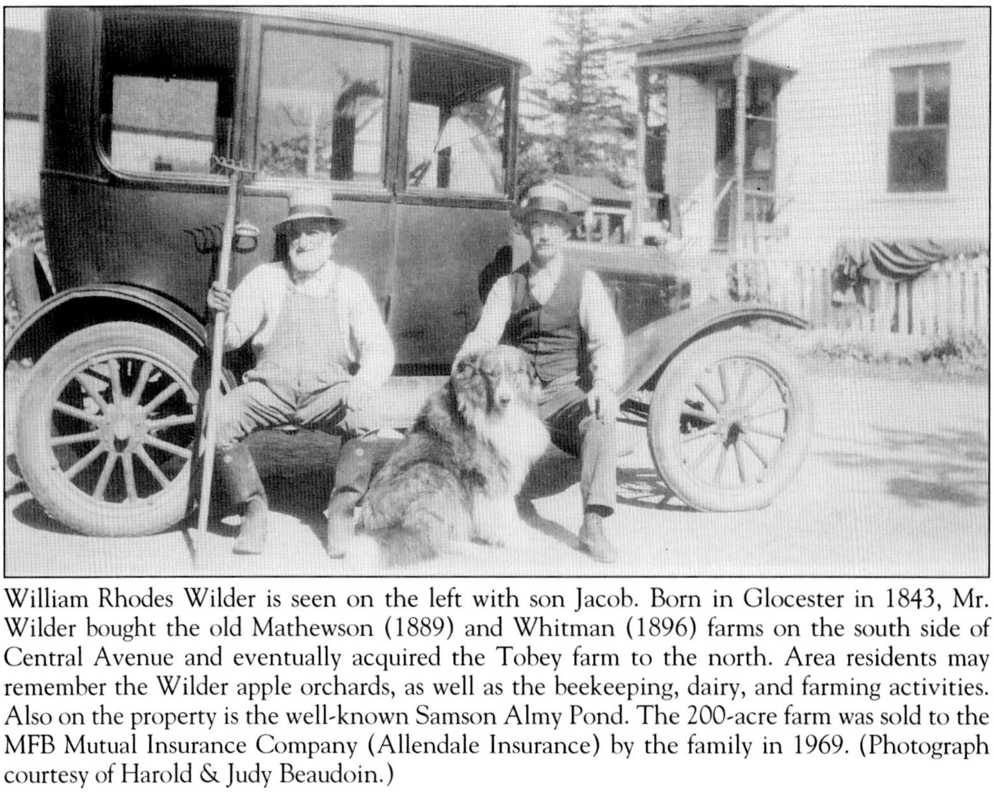

William Rhodes Wilder is seen on the left with son Jacob. Born in Glocester in 1843, Mr. Wilder bought the old Mathewson (1889) and Whitman (1896) farms on the south side of Central Avenue and eventually acquired the Tobey farm to the north. Area residents may remember the Wilder apple orchards, as well as the beekeeping, dairy, and farming activities. Also on the property is the well-known Samson Almy Pond. The 200-acre farm was sold to the MFB Mutual Insurance Company (Allendale Insurance) by the family in 1969. (Photograph courtesy of Harold & Judy Beaudoin.)

Stanley and Catherine Miga were both born in Poland and immigrated to the United States, settling in Johnston on Traver Avenue. Mr. Miga, a milkman, was killed on December 17, 1923, when his horse-drawn milk wagon was involved in an accident with an electric trolley car. (Photograph courtesy of Dorothy Innocenti.)

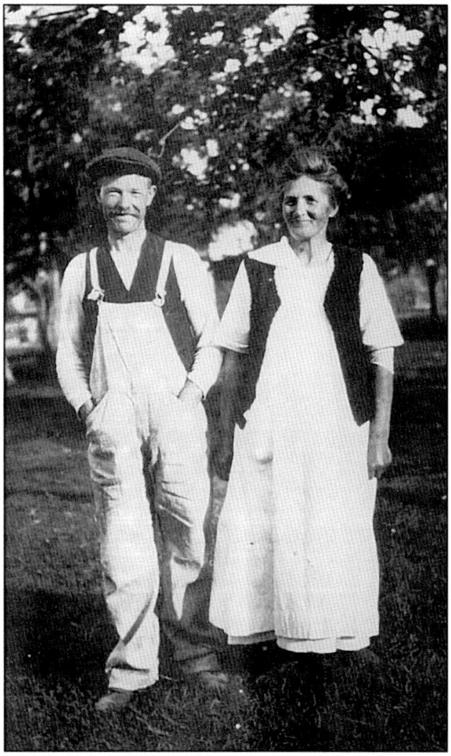

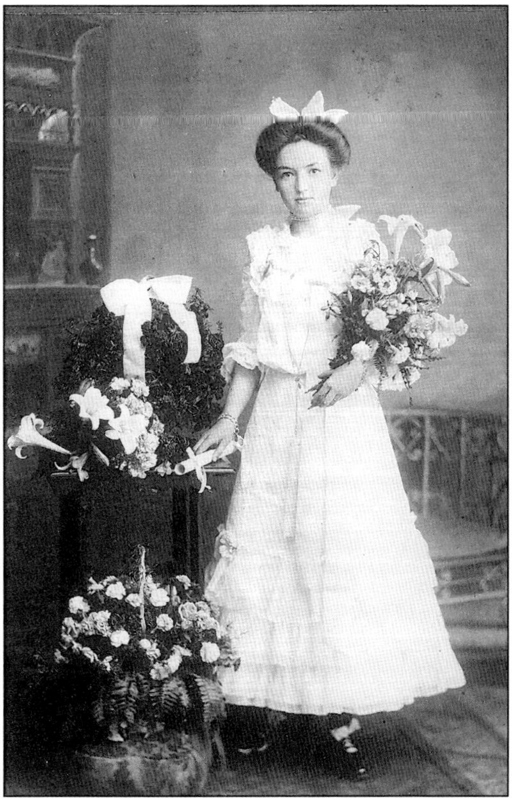

This picture, dating from 1902, is of Miss Ida Kimball at her school graduation. Born in Johnston in 1887, she married Raymond M. Wilder, a son of William and Elizabeth Wilder, in 1911. Ida and Raymond Wilder farmed and raised dairy cows on what was the eastern end of the Wilder's farm on Central Avenue. (Photograph courtesy of Harold and Judy Beaudoin.)

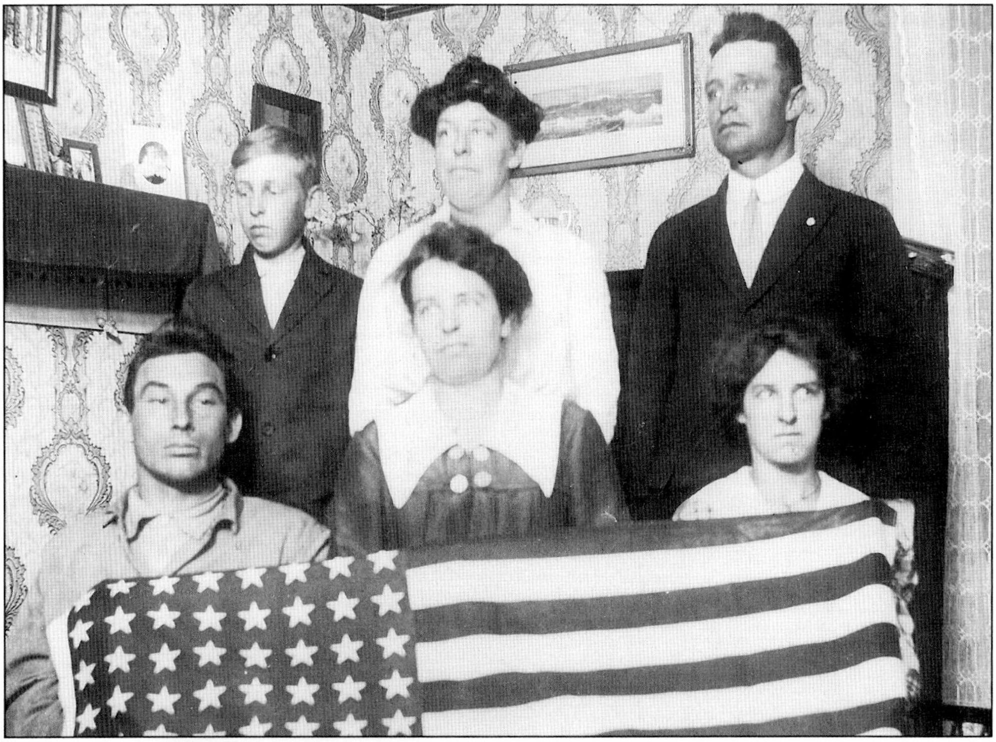

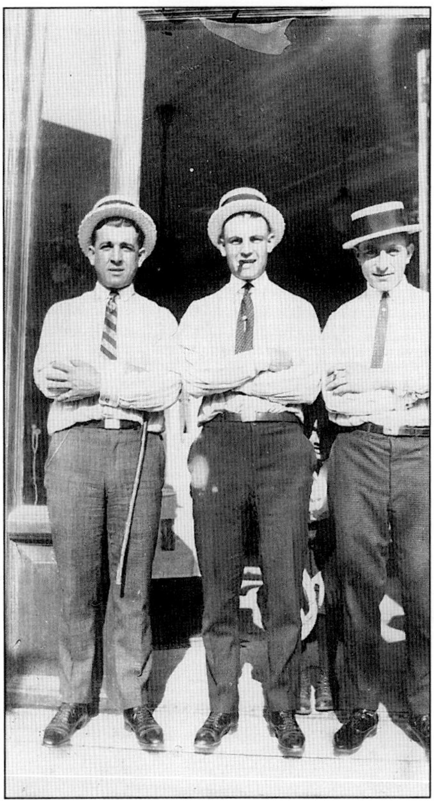

We are not sure why no one is looking at the camera, but we guess they had their reasons. Pictured are, from left to right, as follows: (front row) Edward Newman and Cora and Gladys Coughlin; (back row) Everett, May, and Frank Coughlin. The Coughlin and Newman families were both from the area of Manton near the fire station. (Photograph courtesy of Gert Newman Rice.)

Looking dapper in their straw hats in the 1930s are, from left to right, Anthony "Handsome" Ferri, Ercole "Bob" Barone, and Carl "Nation" Simone. Ferri ran a barbershop in the Ferri Block while Barone ran the bowling alleys in Thornton from the late 1920s into the 1940s. "Nation" was an excellent soccer player who earned his nickname, it is said, from his ability at knocking home combinations on the pool table. (Photograph courtesy of Carl Rainone.)

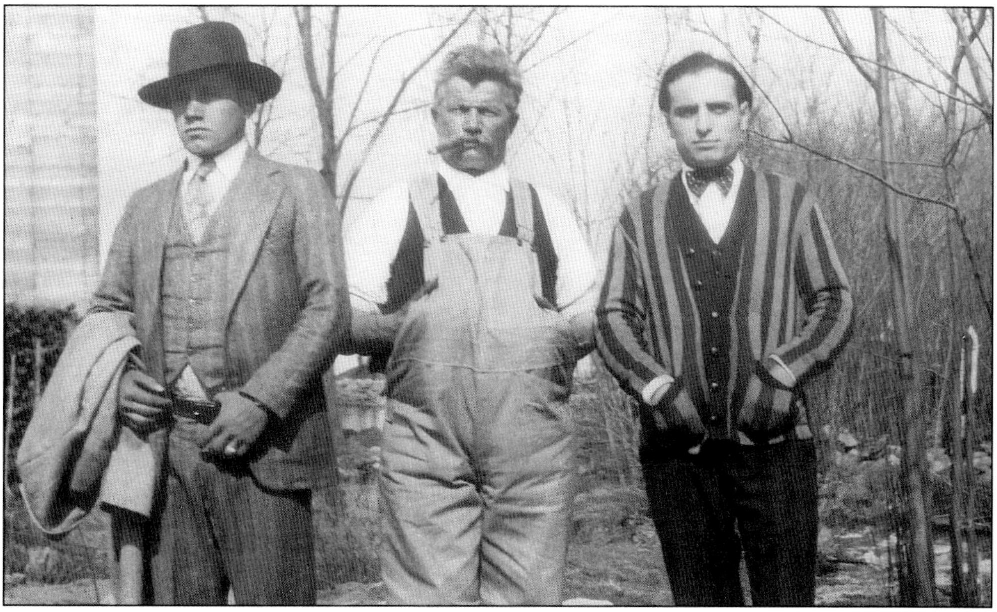

This early 1930s photograph was taken on the Ruotolo property on Simmonsville Avenue. From left to right are Tom Ruotolo, owner of the Old Village Farm and Dairy and Old Village Oil; his father, Nick Ruotolo, who was a farmer; and John Cerra, who married Mary Ruotolo, Nick's daughter. (Photograph courtesy of Linda Ruotolo.)

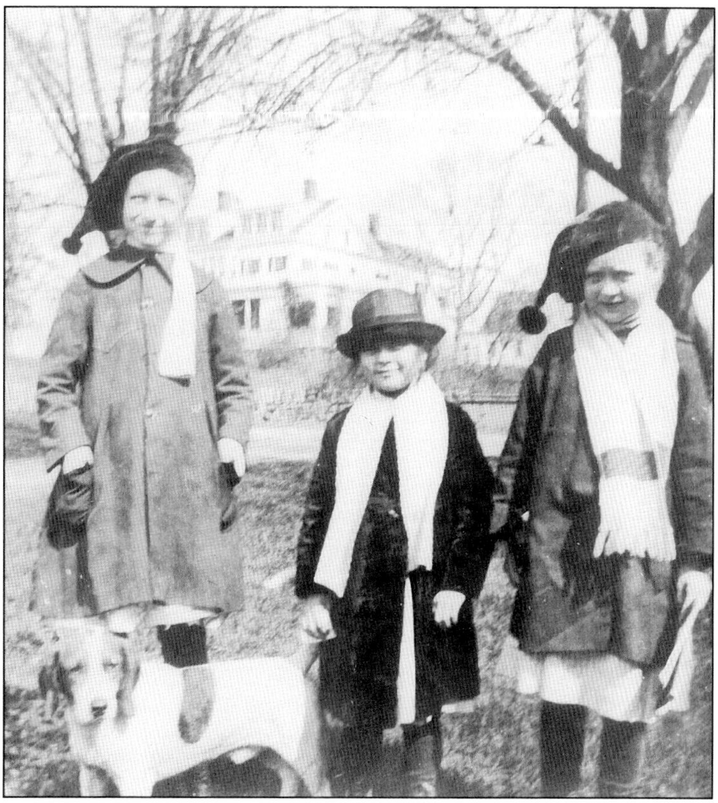

Mabel (Atwood) Sprague (center) is flanked by her two sisters, Blanche (left) and Alice (right), both longtime teachers in town. They are standing in the yard of their home at 216 Morgan Avenue about 1920. The Alverson/Tillinghast/Crandall house is behind them. Mabel still lives in the family home. (Photograph courtesy of Mabel Atwood Sprague.)

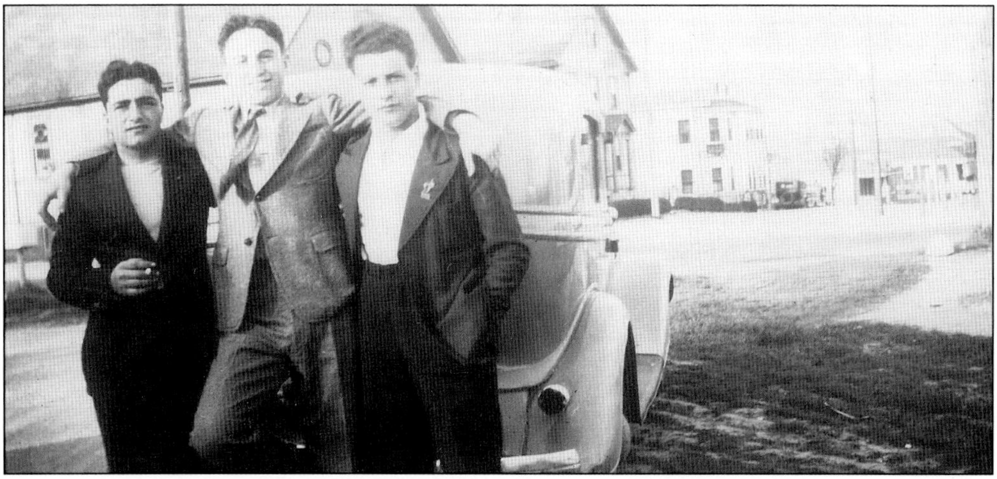

Pete Bucco, Angelo "Stump" Pezzullo, and Louis "Smokey" Ullucci pose in front of a 1932 Ford about 1940 on Greenville Avenue. The original Our Lady of Grace Church is on the left with the vestry on the right. (Photograph courtesy of Louis "Smokey" Ullucci.)

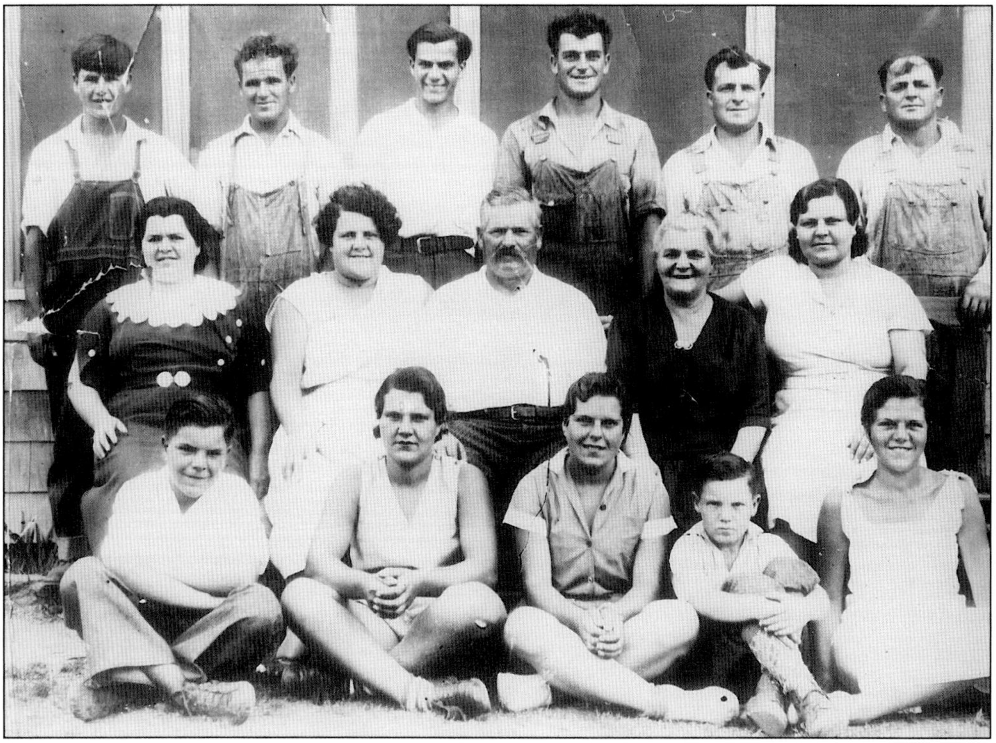

Part of the Caparrelli family from Plainfield Pike poses here for a photograph. Mr. Caparrelli owned an 80-acre farm that stretched from the present-day Dunkin Donuts, where the main house stood, to Taylor Road. Shown here are, from left to right, as follows: (front row) Raymond, Edith, Christina, Rudolph, and Elizabeth; (middle row) Lillian, Mary, Costanzo (the father), Antonia (the mother), and Rose; (back row) Luigi, Costanzo Jr., Joseph, Peter, Anthony, and Benny. The family photo was taken for a contest to send the largest family in the Providence area to the Chicago World Fair in the 1930s. Missing from the photo are Jasmine and Laura. (Photograph courtesy of Christine Caparrelli Smith.)

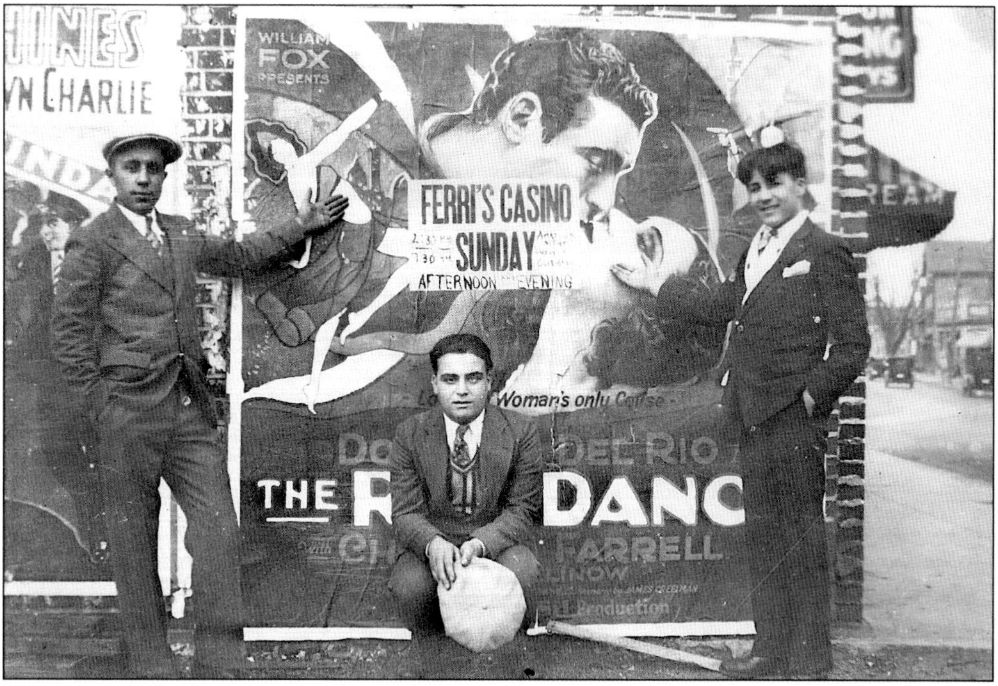

E. Iannuccilli (left), A. Cambia (center), and Nick Ferri stand in front of an advertisement for a Delores Del Rio movie in 1929. Ads such as these were the main means of getting information out to the population about movies. The boys are standing at the back of the Ferri Block, where the movie was shown. (Photograph courtesy of Carl Rainone.)

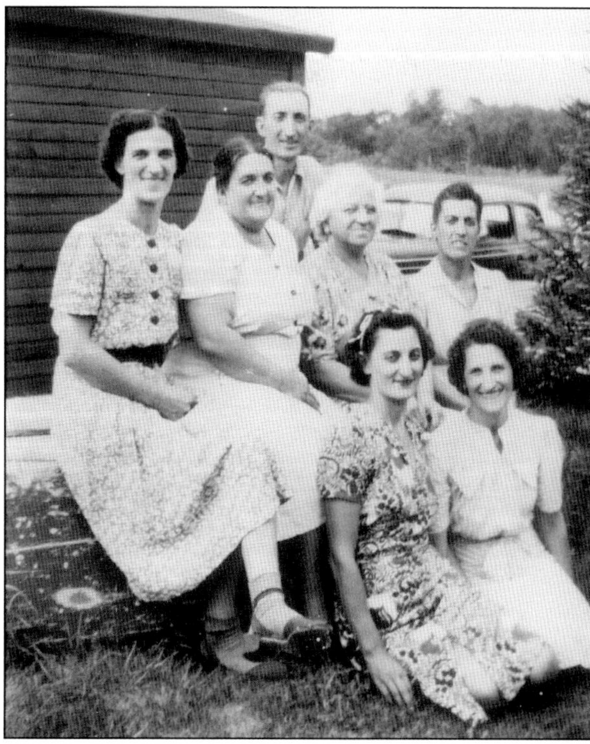

The seven people pictured here are the children of Anthony and Marie Travelyn (changed from Travalini). They are, from left to right, as follows: (front row) Susan and Marie; (back row) Carrie, Antonette, Pasco, Jenny, and Rose. The family lived on Atwood Avenue, just east of Central Avenue. (See the bottom of p. 52 in *Johnston, Volume I*, for a view of their house.) (Photograph courtesy of Marie Travelyn Florie.)

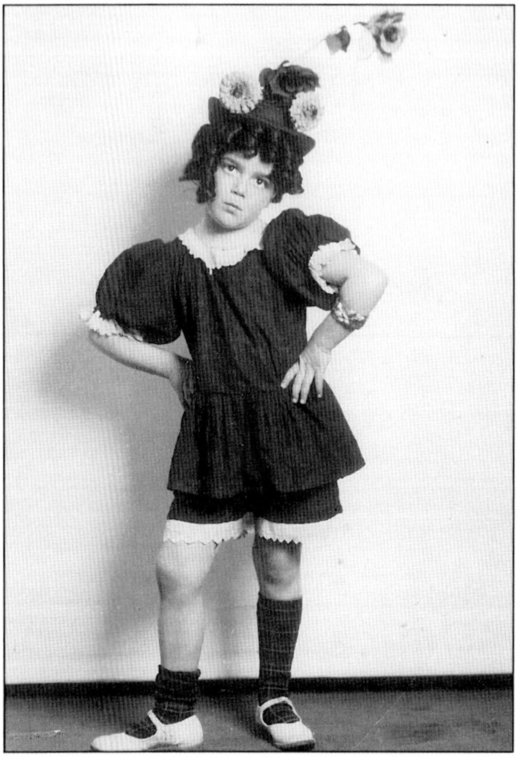

Joan (Caparrelli) Ventetuolo poses in the early 1940s in her minstrel outfit, which she wore while singing and dancing in the various minstrel shows held in town. Joan was also involved with Celia Moreau and her Kiddie Revue, a Saturday morning radio show on WJAR. Also participating were Buddy Cianci, Art Lake (announcer), and Johnstonians Vin Manfredi, Eleanor Ross, and the Capobianco boys, Ernie and Angelo. (Photograph courtesy of Joan Caparrelli Ventetuolo.)

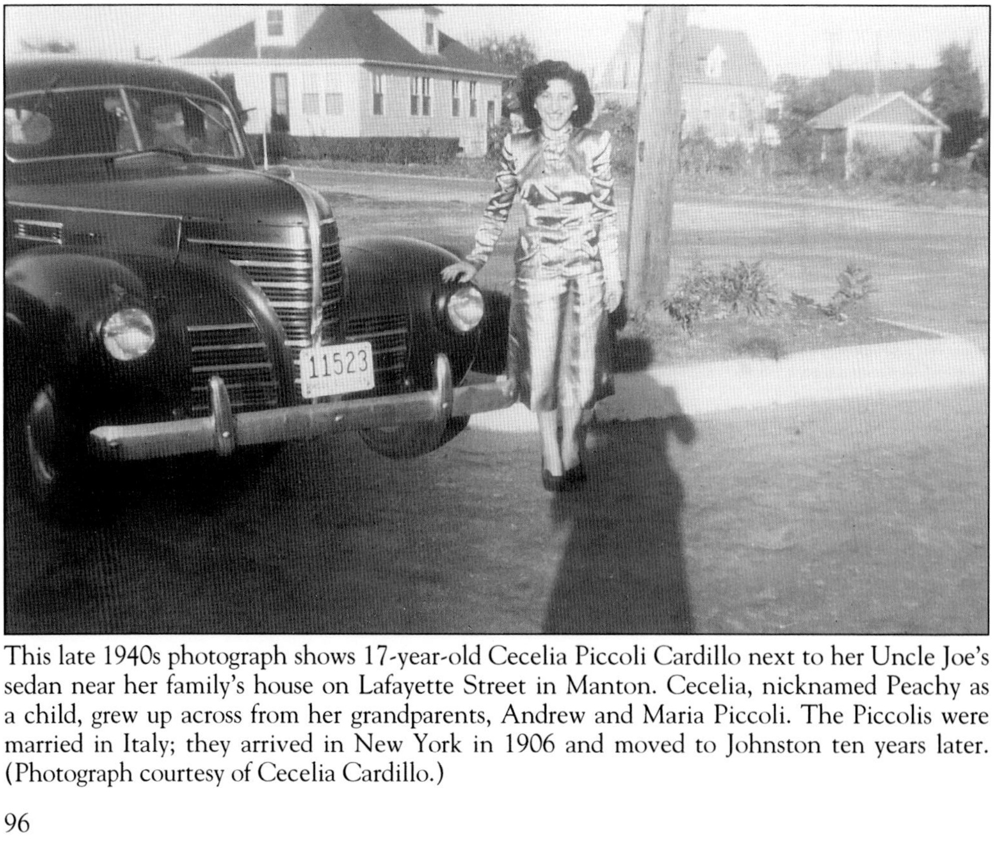

This late 1940s photograph shows 17-year-old Cecelia Piccoli Cardillo next to her Uncle Joe's sedan near her family's house on Lafayette Street in Manton. Cecelia, nicknamed Peachy as a child, grew up across from her grandparents, Andrew and Maria Piccoli. The Piccolis were married in Italy; they arrived in New York in 1906 and moved to Johnston ten years later. (Photograph courtesy of Cecelia Cardillo.)

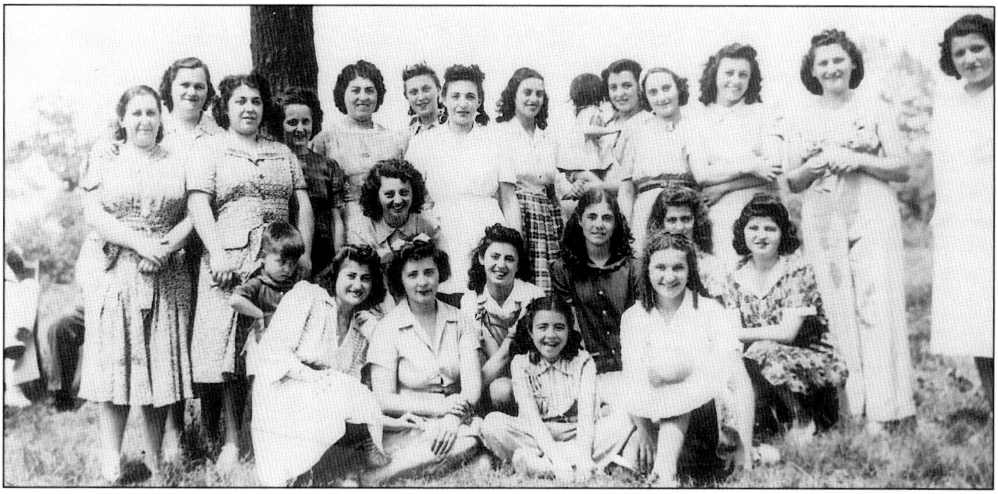

In this 1940 photograph, the LaFazia women, siblings, in-laws, cousins, and children are seen gathering at the new Club 400, located in West Warwick, for the first LaFazia family outing. The family was so large that separate photographs were taken of the men and the older women. Although not held annually, the outings continued until the late 1970s. (Photograph courtesy of Alfonso J. LaFazia.)

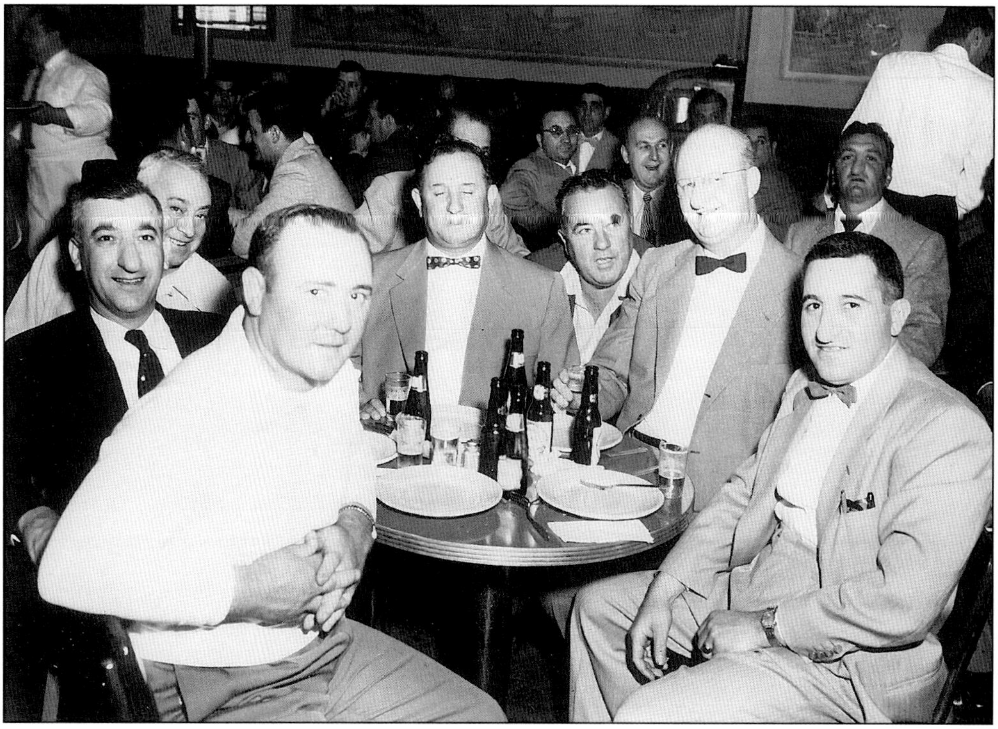

This gathering of the "Big Nose Club" took place at the Iafrate Brothers Restaurant (later Sonny Russo's) in Thornton. It was not a real club, but a once-a-year get-together at which micrometers were used to measure the biggest "honker." Pictured from left to right, starting from the third on the left, are Al Vacca, Louis Vacca, "Sweetheart" Vitullo, Al Salzillo, Carl Cinami, unknown, Gil Hartley, Angelo Lanni, and Carlo Tundis. (Photograph courtesy of Sam Coupe.)

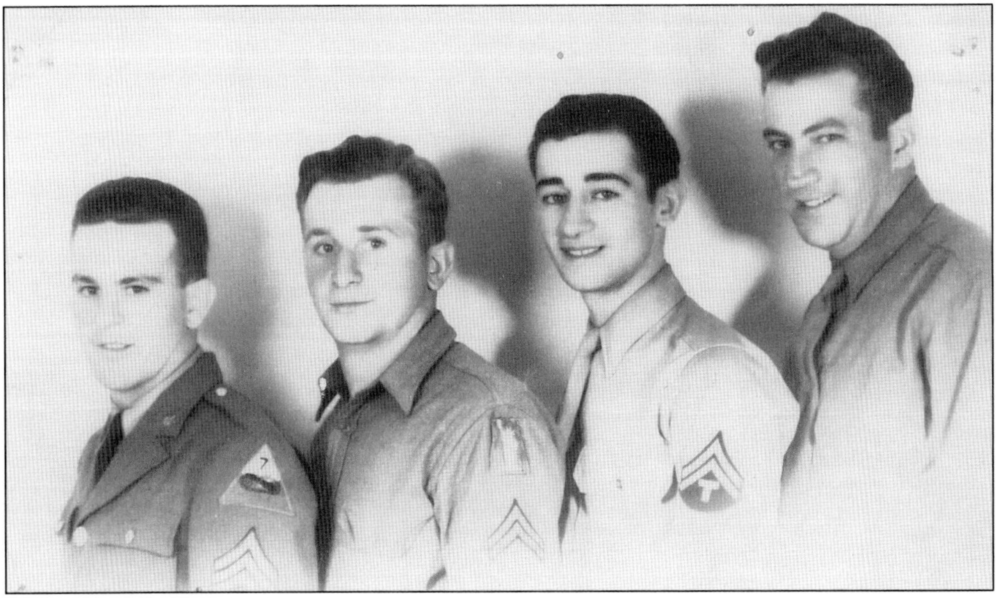

These four friends answered their nation's call during WW II, as did Johnston residents from all over the town. Pictured are, from left to right, Americo "Mutt" Martinelli, Ray Mendozzi, Lennie "Seaweed" Macari, and Anthony "Canopener" Cinami. (Photograph courtesy of Barbra Votolato McGuirl.)

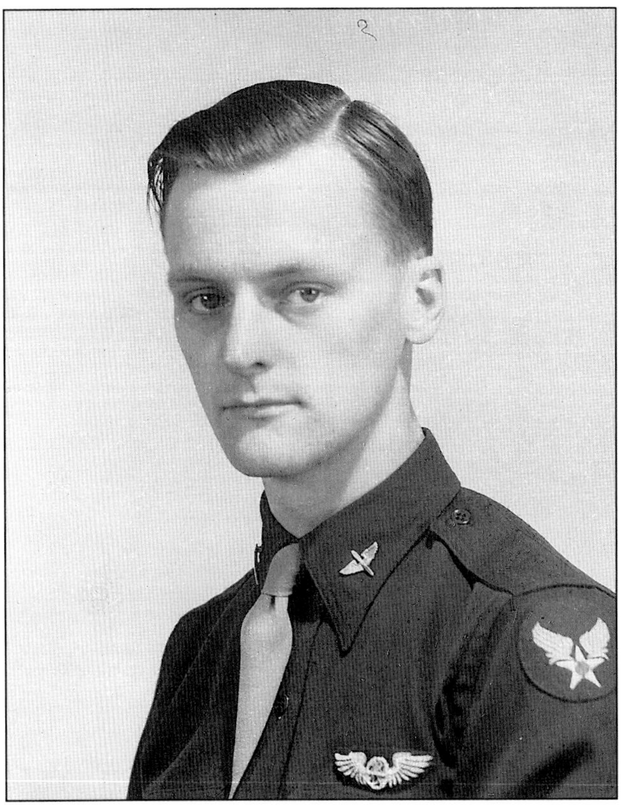

William R. Thorpe was born in Johnston in 1921 at 94 Putnam Avenue. He was a navigator on a B-17 bomber of the 100th Bomber Group during WW II. On a daytime bombing run over Berlin his plane was shot down and he was killed. His father received his last letter on the day he died, March 6, 1944. William was buried in Belgium. His name is on the Graniteville Memorial on Putnam Pike. (Photograph courtesy of Margaret Thorpe Pearson.)

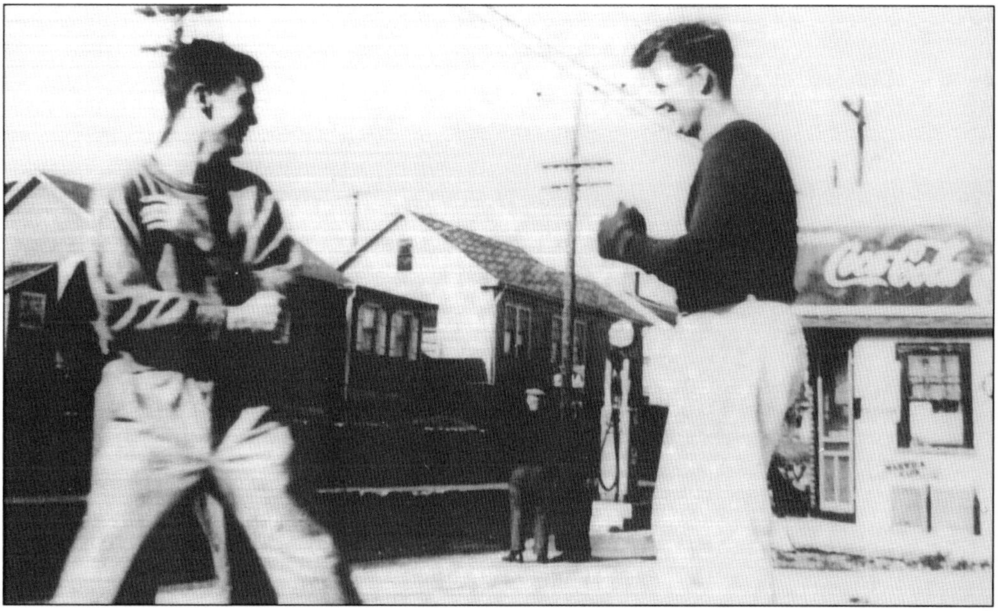

Two young men, known only as Henry and Woodie, are shadow boxing while on break from a WW II salvage drive. They are at the top of Cottage Street in Graniteville. In back of them is Hesketh's Variety Store and Gas Station, which sat next to the old Graniteville Fire Station. (Photograph courtesy of Laura Charnley Panicucci.)

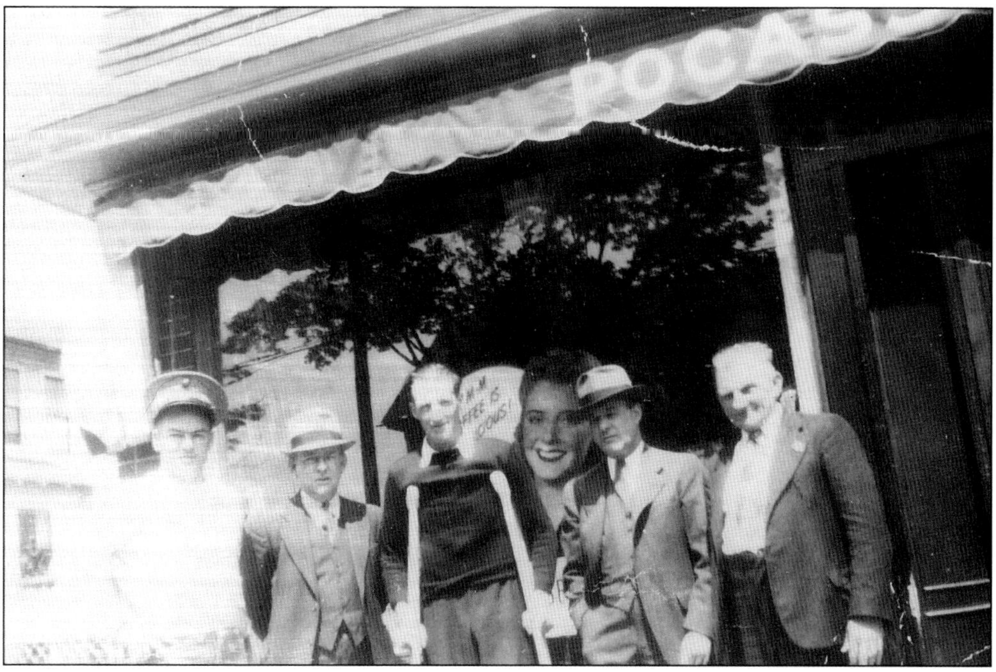

These men gathered in front of the Pocasset Market every Sunday after 10 o'clock Mass at St. Brigid's Church to solve the world's problems. Pictured during WW II are, from left to right, Jim Geary, Irving Zander, George Carrington, Stubby Leonard, and Herman Fleury. The Pocasset Market was started by Ernest and Julia Capobianco and was run by the family into the 1990s. (Photograph courtesy of Jim Geary.)

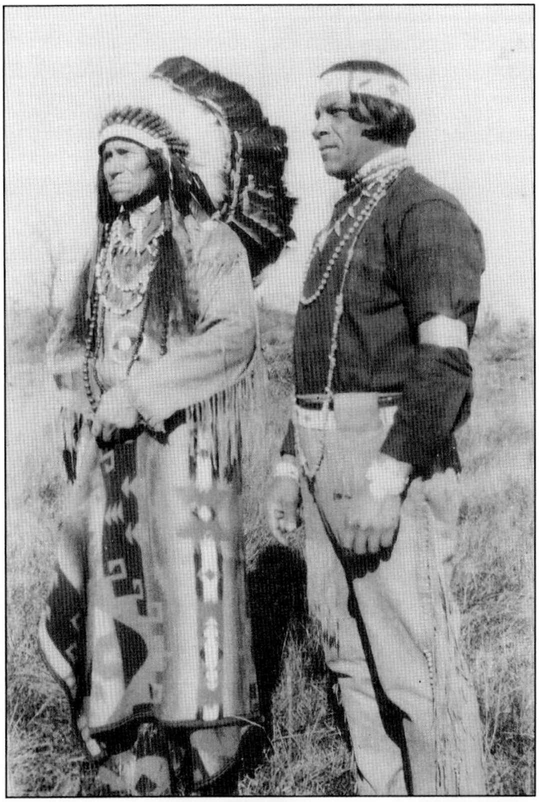

Chief Great Owl (Ben Onsley) and his son, Chief Rainbow (Ernie Onsley), are pictured in the 1930s in Johnston. They lived at the corner of Morgan and Borden Avenues. Members of the Wampanoag Tribe, they were active in Native American events around the state. Their last name was changed from Walmsley. Ben's descendants, the Steppos, still live in the family house that Ben built on Morgan Avenue. (Photography courtesy of Sandra Steppo Decesaris.)

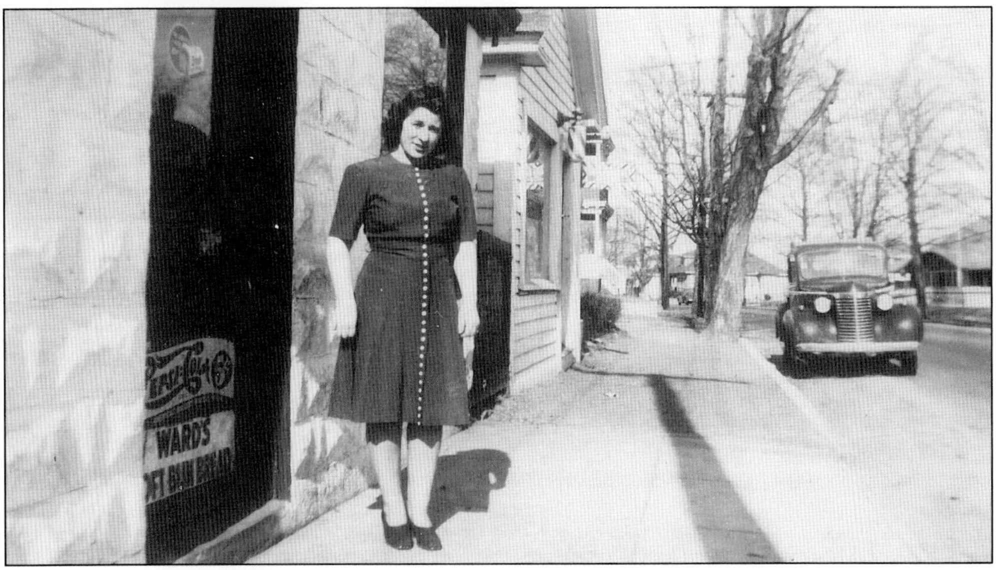

Mary (Pezza) Rinaldi is seen standing in front of Pezza's Market (her father's shop) and next to Fico's Barbershop on Plainfield Street. Fico later moved his shop a few doors west. In the distance is the Pocasset Casino several months before it burned to the ground. During the war years, Mary helped her father run the market in place of her brother Lawrence, who was away in the service. Mary's family arrived in Pocasset in 1919 when she was three years old. (Photograph courtesy of Janice Rinaldi.)

At the Brown farm on Belfield Drive is William M.S. Brown (on guitar) and Edwin E. Essex (on the violin). Essex, a salesman from Providence, was a family friend and played with William to entertain family and friends. William's daughter Susie accompanied them on piano when they played inside. (Photograph courtesy of Susie Brown.)

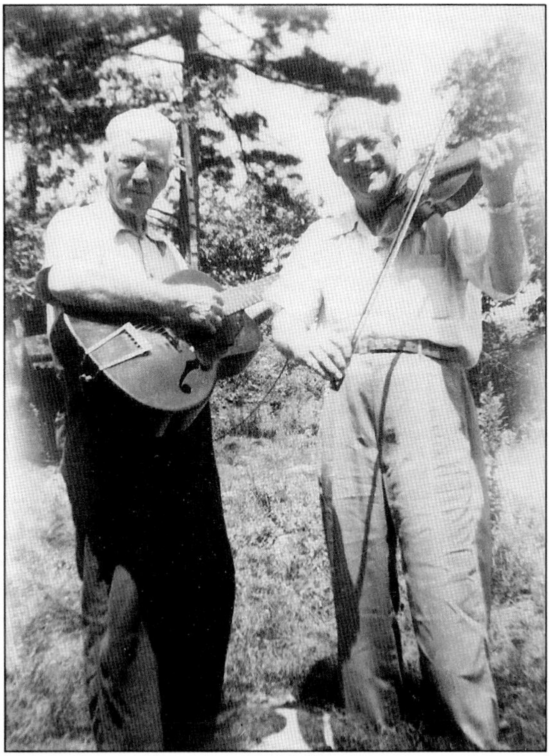

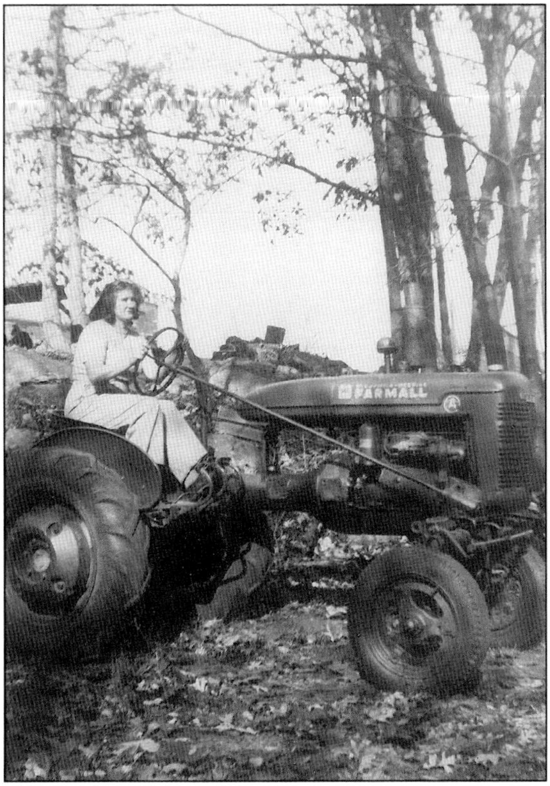

Susie Brown is on the tractor on her family farm on Belfield Drive. On a small farm, such as theirs, everyone pitched in to help things run smoothly. Her dad, William, was a carpenter and painter by trade and also ran the farm. Her mother was Mary Katherine (Belfield) Brown, for whom Belfield Drive was named. (Photograph courtesy of Susie Brown.)

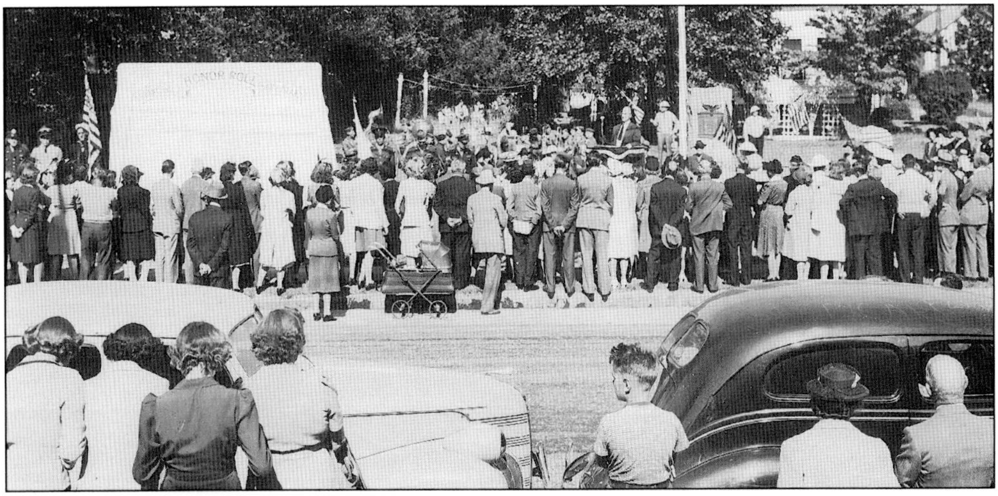

In September 1943 a large crowd turned up for a WW II memorial dedication in Graniteville. The memorial was newly completed. A service each Memorial Day, run by the Graniteville Baptist Church, still draws large crowds. (Photograph courtesy of Arthur Harrington.)

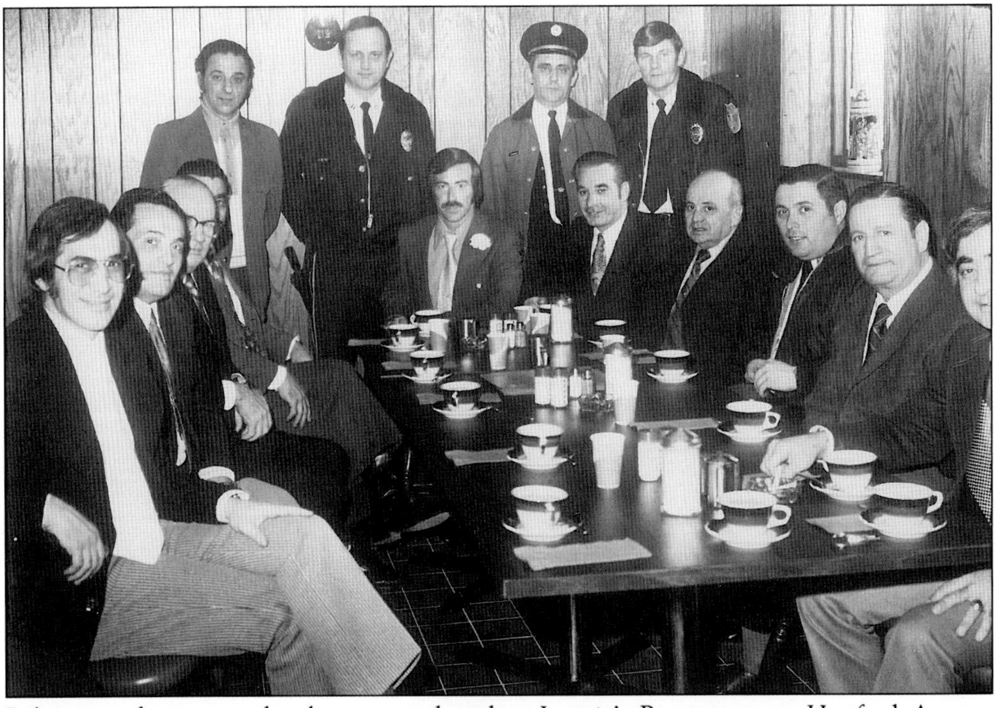

Politicians, firemen, and policemen gathered at Lennie's Restaurant on Hartford Avenue for the grand opening in the 1970s. Pictured are, from left to right, Vito Petrone (federal co-ordinator under CETA), Robert Butmarc (electrical inspector), Edward Heelon (plumbing inspector), unknown, "Chief" Generali, Deputy Chief Louis Zambarano, Leonard Macari (seated, the owner), Fire Chief Ace Cappelli, Mayor Ralph Russo (seated), Deputy Chief of Police Joe Devine, Horace Corrente (finance director), John Shaw (town fire prevention officer), Albert Ferruolo (building inspector), and Ernest Acciardo. (Photograph courtesy of Angelo "Ace" Cappelli.)

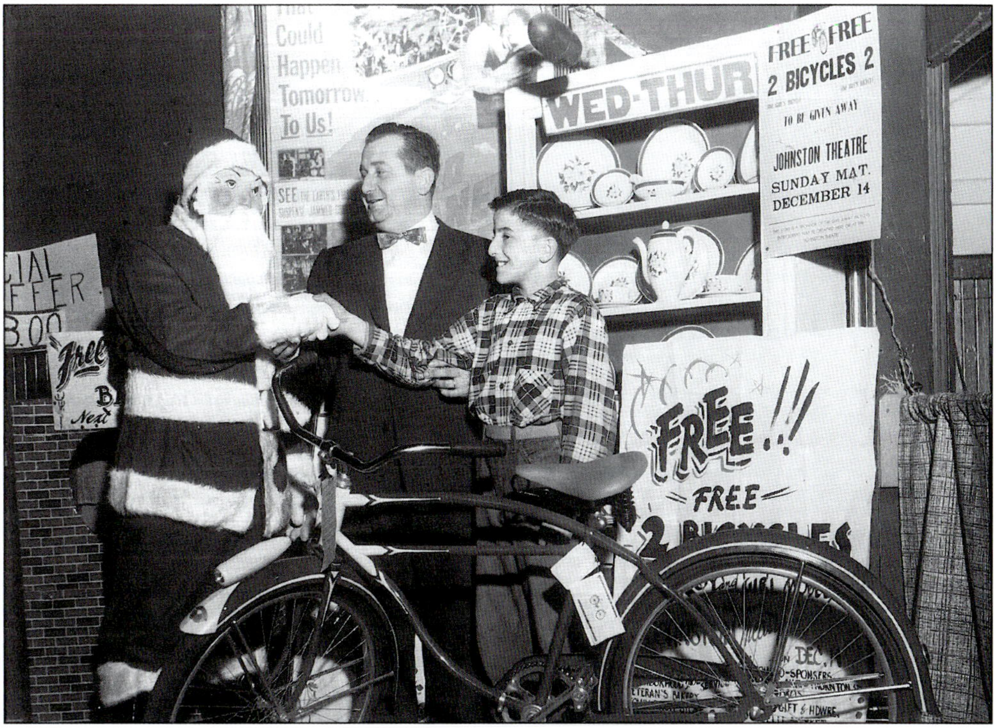

An excited 11-year-old Rocco Macari accepts a new bike *c.* 1950 from Santa Claus (John Ferri) and Mr. Mendozzi, who donated the bike. The Mendozzi family ran Little Rhody Gift and Hardware Store on Plainfield Street. The photograph was taken in the Johnston Theater in the Ferri Block. Note the advertisement for china place settings on the back wall, which were given as prizes to lucky movie-goers. (Photograph courtesy of Barbra Votolato McGuirl.)

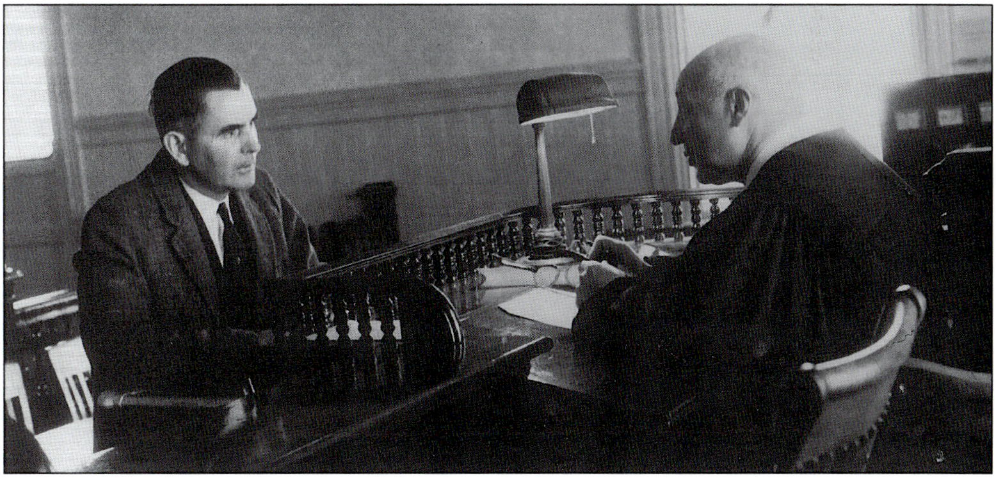

Arthur N. Votolato Sr. of Thornton, the son of John and Pasqualina (Viti) Votolato, was a judge at the Cranston District Court. He was born in Johnston and lived there until 1953. After graduating from North Eastern Law School, he was admitted to the bar in 1926 and is thought to be the first Johnston-born Italian American to be so admitted. He kept his law offices in Myrtle Hall on Plainfield Street until his death in 1988. (Photograph courtesy of Barbra Votolato McGuirl.)

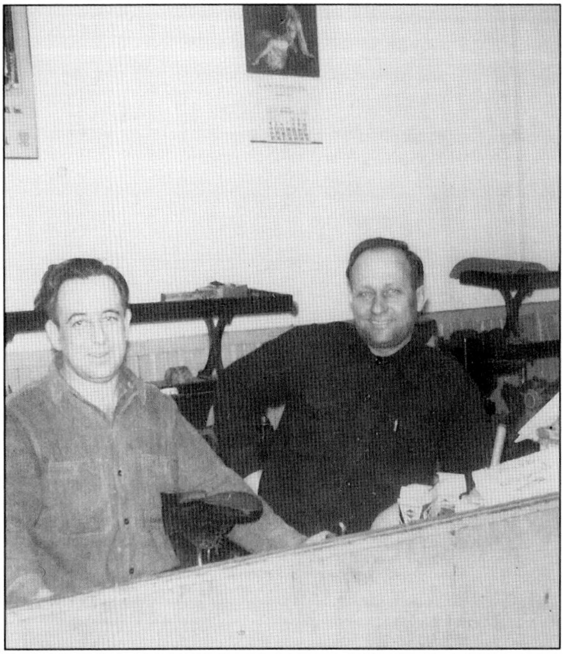

Arthur Rinaldi is seated on the left in his cobbler shop in Myrtle Hall, 1363 Plainfield Street. With him is Ralph Mariano. Arthur learned his trade as a young man from his father, Pasquale, and was a cobbler all his life. Arthur was raised in "Frog City," married Mary Pezza in 1941, and with his family moved to Pocasset in the early 1960s. (Photograph courtesy of Janice Rinaldi.)

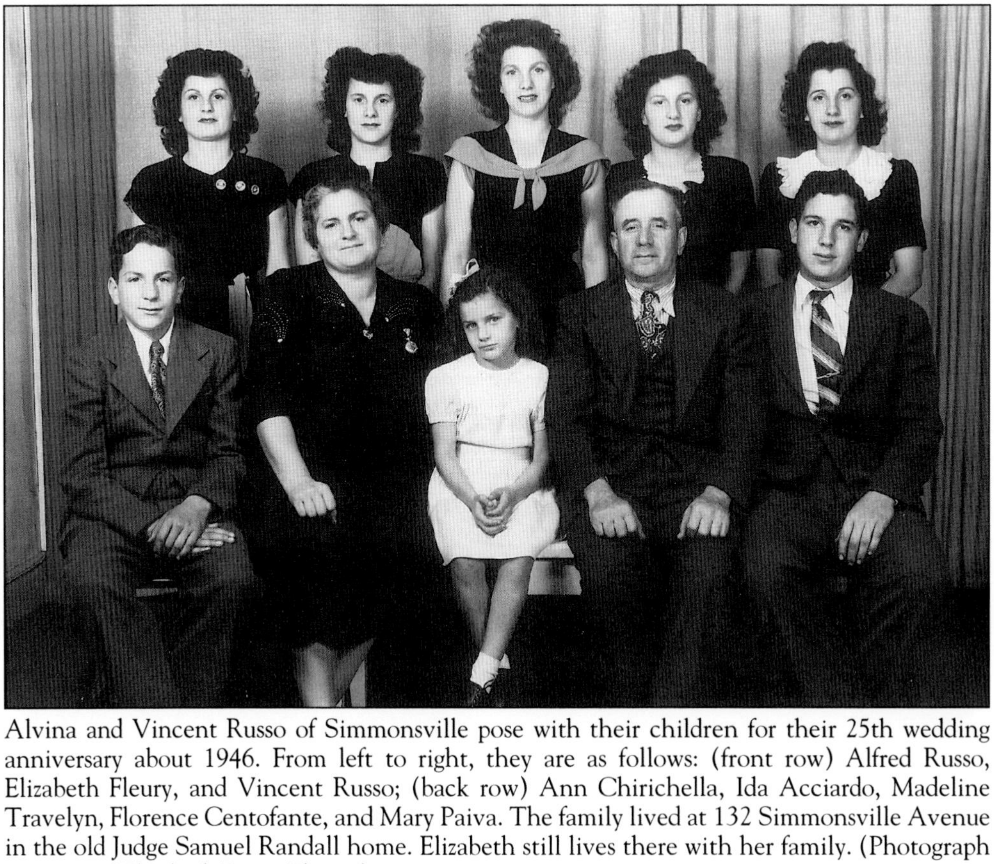

Alvina and Vincent Russo of Simmonsville pose with their children for their 25th wedding anniversary about 1946. From left to right, they are as follows: (front row) Alfred Russo, Elizabeth Fleury, and Vincent Russo; (back row) Ann Chirichella, Ida Acciardo, Madeline Travelyn, Florence Centofante, and Mary Paiva. The family lived at 132 Simmonsville Avenue in the old Judge Samuel Randall home. Elizabeth still lives there with her family. (Photograph courtesy of Elizabeth Russo Fleury.)

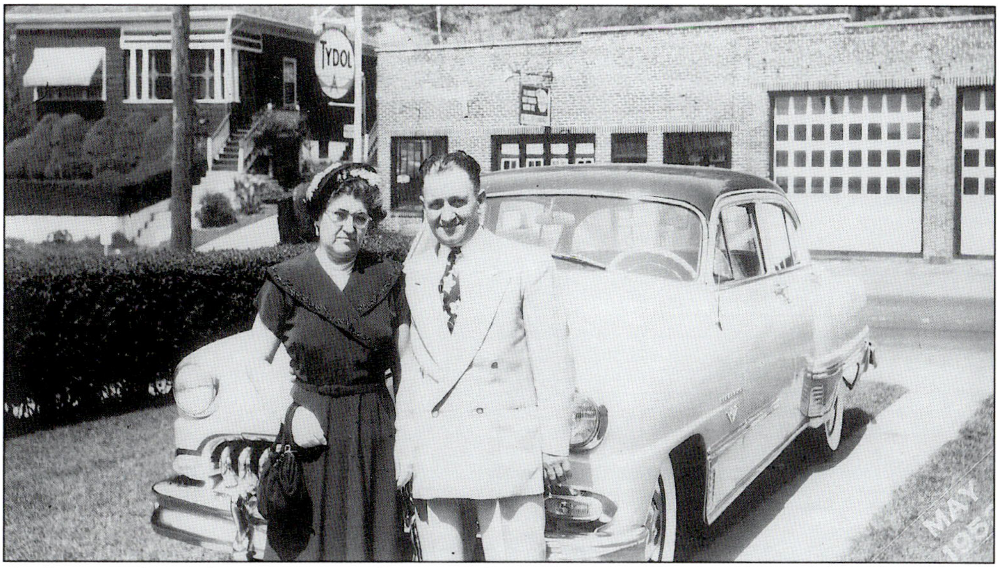

Anthony and Josephine Ricci raised sons Anthony and John at 986 Plainfield Street. The two structures in the background still stand. The brick building is a Tydol service station run at various times by George Cunningford and Fred Miller. Their shiny new automobile is a DeSoto, a make that has long been out of production. (Photograph courtesy of John Ricci.)

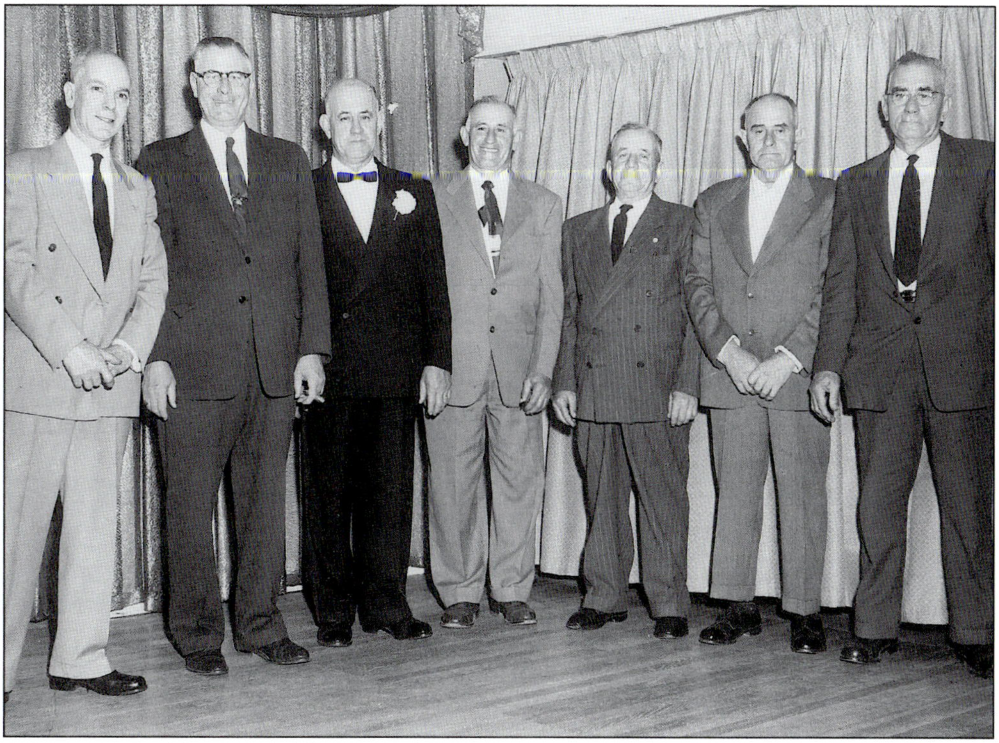

At Connie Deihlman's wedding in February 1955, seven children of Pasquale Russo (1862–1942) and Concetta Ricci (1859–1932) got together for this photograph. They are, from left to right, Pat Gatta (standing in for his wife, Mary), Joe Russo, Tony Russo, Giuseppi Russo, Vincent Russo, Jack Russo, and Tom Russo. (Photograph courtesy of Elizabeth Russo Fleury.)

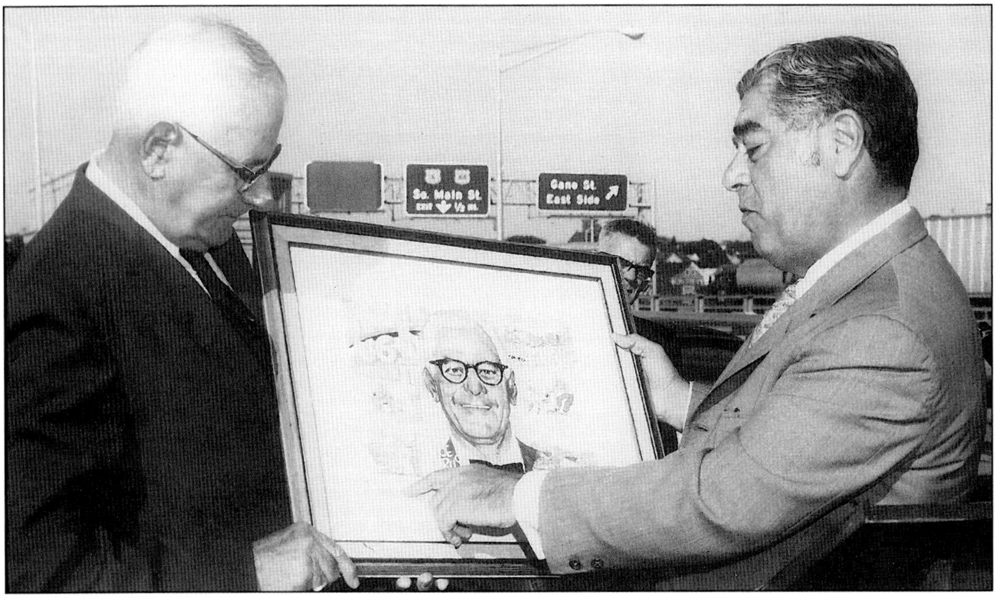

Joseph Russo of Simmonsville (left) poses with Governor Frank Licht in the early 1970s at the Washington Bridge in Providence. Joe retired as supervising civil engineer for RIDOT after 46 years with the state. In 1941 he was put in charge of all bridge construction in Rhode Island. He oversaw construction of the new Red Bridge and the new Washington Bridge in Providence. (Photograph courtesy of Elizabeth Russo Fleury.)

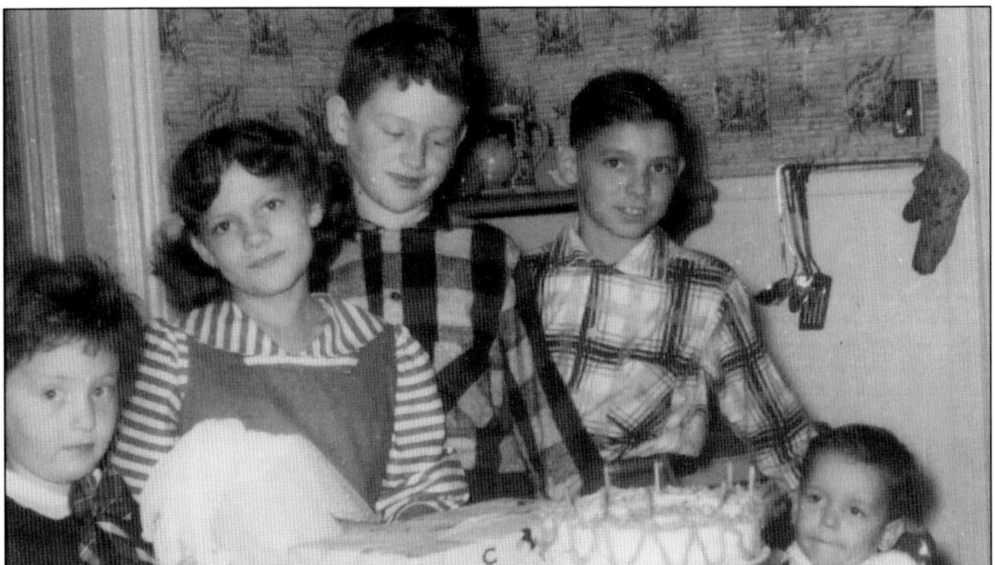

It's birthday time at the Steppo house in 1957. Sister and brother Adrienne and Louis McGowan are first and third from the left. Sister and brothers Sandra, Melvin, and David are second, fourth, and fifth from the left. The McGowans and the Steppos were next-door neighbors living in mill houses that formerly belonged to the Pocasset Mill. The houses were roomy and sturdy. There were also a lot of "baby boomer" children to play with. The baseball field (the old Pocasset Oval) and the river just down the street provided plenty of opportunities for fun. (Photograph courtesy of Sandra Steppo DeCesaris.)

Millicent Newsham is at the wheel of her family's electric-powered toy Thunderbird while a friend, Christine Frappier, stands by. Millicent's grandparents, John and Lillian Brown, ran the J.O. Brown Dairy on Walnut Street in Thornton. Her grandfather kept the little car for his grandchildren, Millicent, Steven, and David Brown, to use around the neighborhood. (Photograph courtesy of Millicent Brown Newsham.)

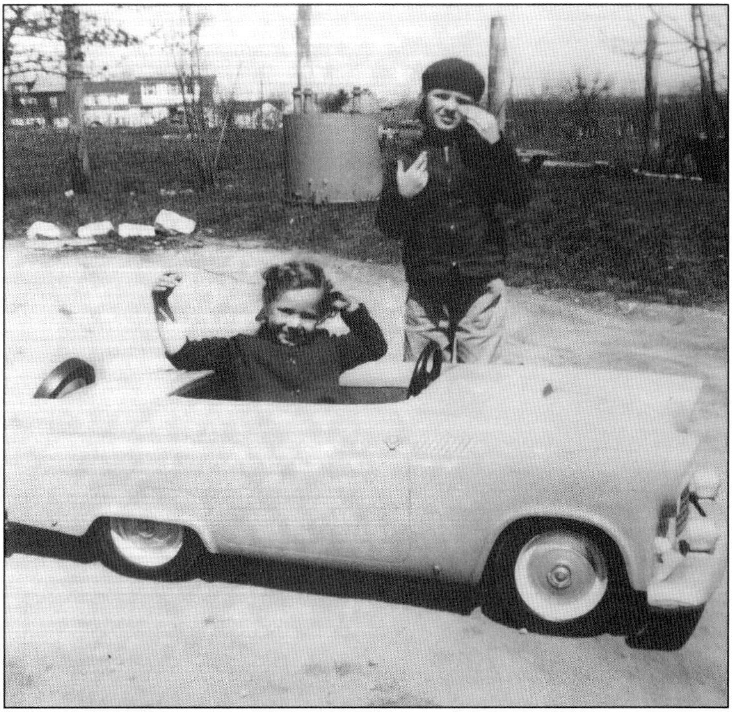

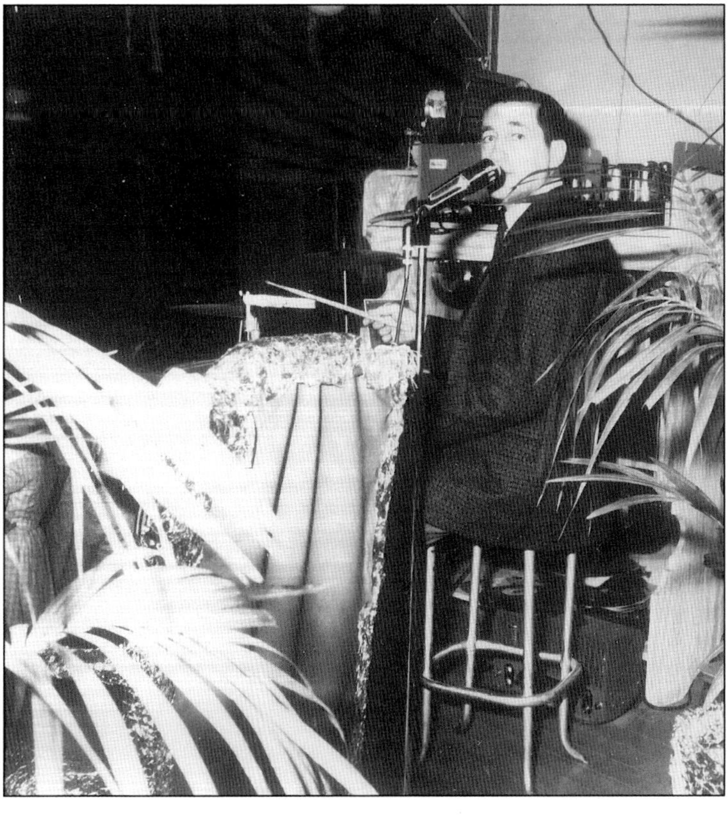

The late Mario Votolato sits at his drums at the Swinghaven Canteen in Myrtle Hall, Plainfield Street. Mario and his wife, Ann, ran the canteen from about 1946 until the 1960s. He also ran ABC Flag for many years, the Johnston Theater in the Ferri Block, and Myrtle Theater. He gave us a lot of help with our historical work in the village and is greatly missed. His daughter, Barbra, continues to run the flag shop. (Photograph courtesy of Barbra Votolato McGuirl.)

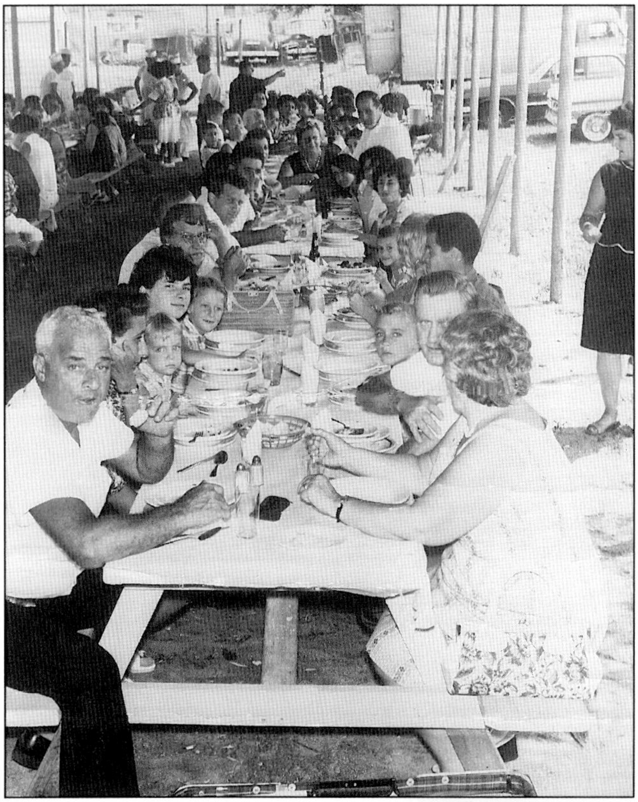

This Ricci-Marro family reunion was held *c*. 1965 at the Plainfield Manor on Plainfield Pike. The manor, on the site of DiRaimo's Auto sales, is now gone but was used in the past for reunions, fund-raisers, and the like. John Clark and his son John Jr. are second and third on the right. On the far left is Pete Marro, and across from him is his wife, Beatrice. Next to him is Ethel Clark (John's wife) and their daughter, Maryann Brenda. (Photo courtesy of John Clark.)

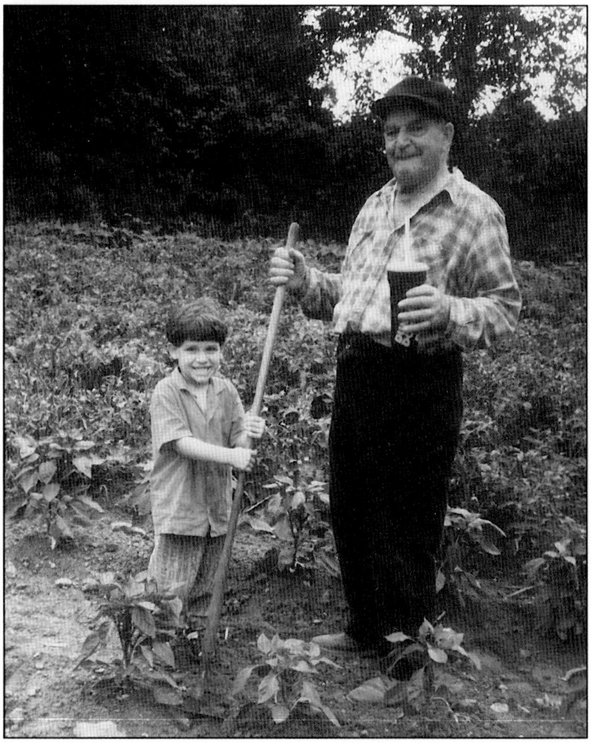

Pete Caparrelli of Taylor Road is seen with his grandson, Alex Pappas, about five years ago. Pete, still going strong at age 93, was one of the 22 children of Costanzo and Antonia Caparrelli, who lived along Plainfield Pike. He drove a bus for the Johnston School System for many years in addition to farming. (Photograph courtesy of Mr. & Mrs. Thomas Hartshorn.)

Seven

Entertainment and Recreation

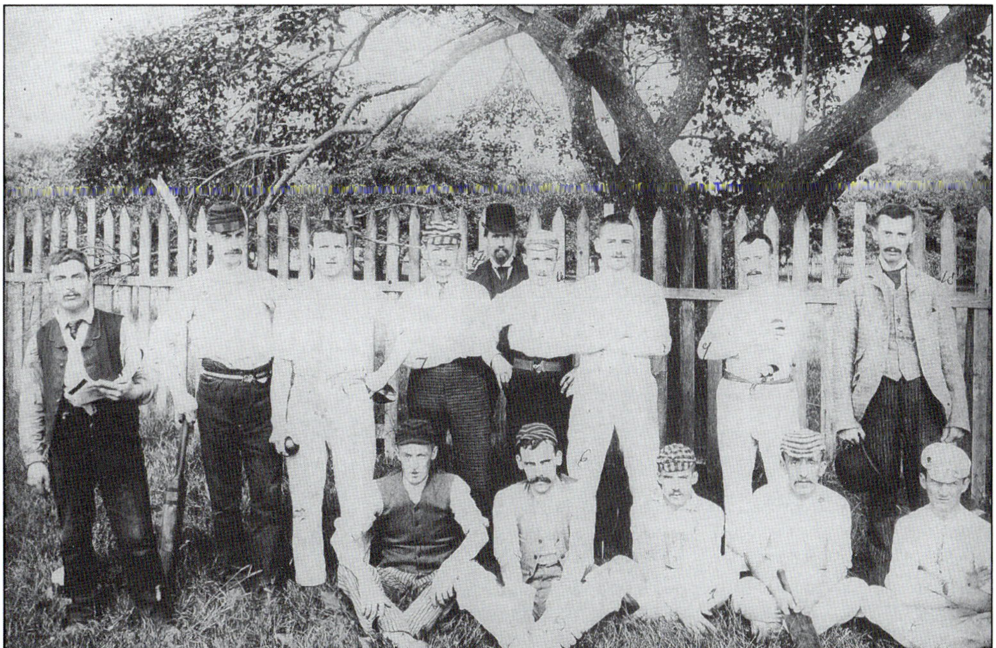

This *c*. 1890 image of a cricket team was taken when Thornton was an all-English village. The players are, from left to right, as follows: (front row) George Ledence?, unknown, John Tomlinson, unknown, and Tom Youde; (back row) George Heteren?, unknown, unknown, ? Burton, Tom Kaunley?, ? Hayes, Albert Weston?, Herbert Hickly?, and ? Cawthern?. This was probably the Thornton Cricket Club, which became the British Hosiery Co. Cricket Club. (Photograph courtesy of Sam Coupe.)

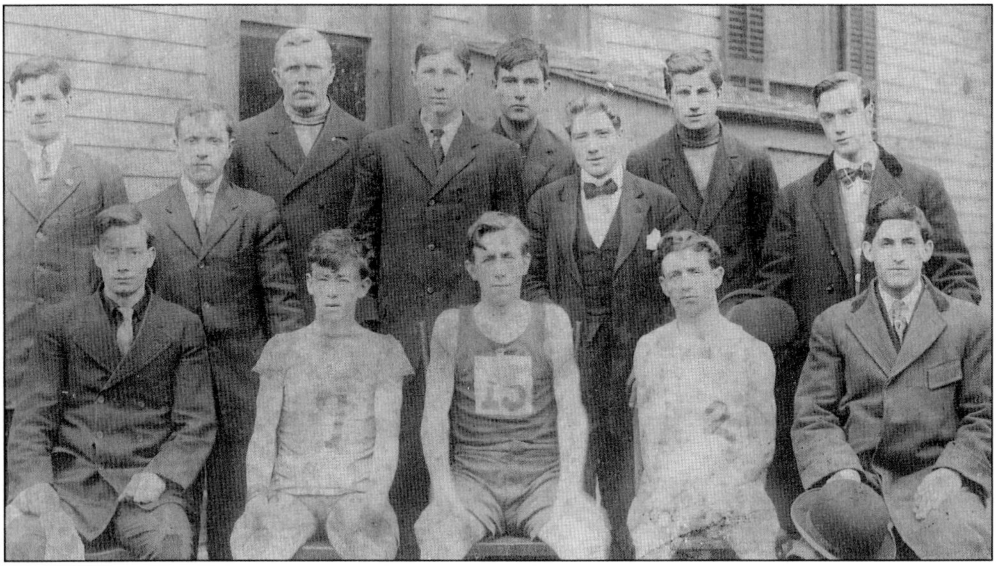

The Primrose Athletic Club sponsored the soccer team shown in this 1908 image. The man to the far right in the first row is Pasco Iafrate, who ran a barbershop in Thornton. He tore down the old Congregational church in Thornton and built the present Mainelli's Spa. The man third from the left in the middle row is John "Pete" Shaw. To his right is Mike Leo, who ran the pool room in the Ferri's Block. Second from the left in the front row is Frank "Doc" Trainor, a worker at Victoria Mills. (Photograph courtesy of Fred Iafrate.)

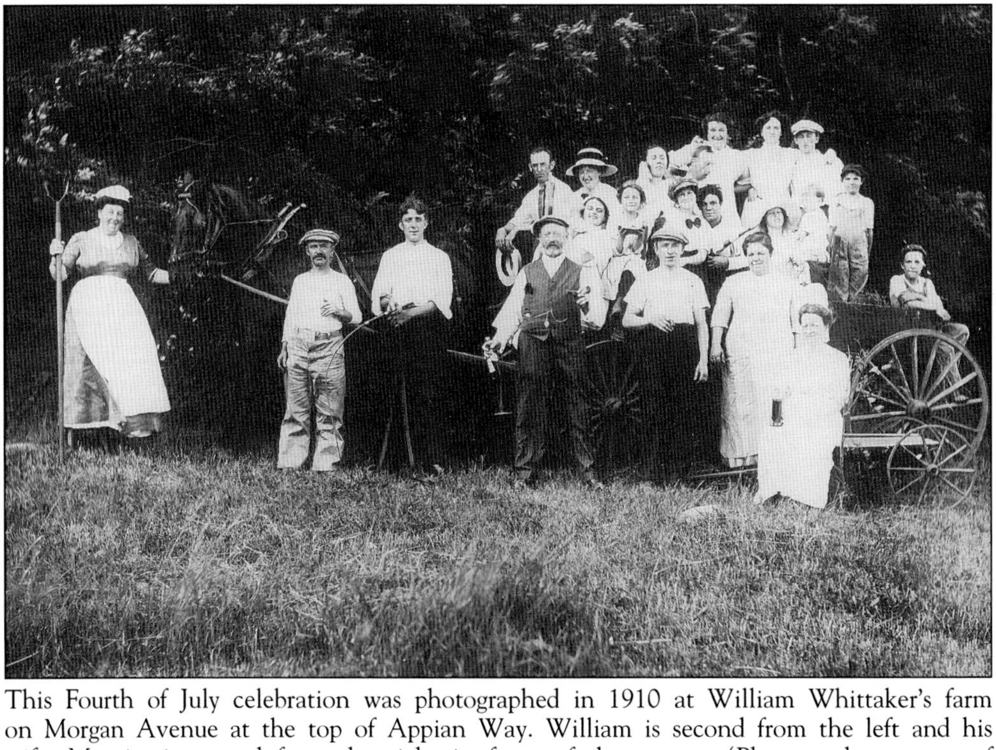

This Fourth of July celebration was photographed in 1910 at William Whittaker's farm on Morgan Avenue at the top of Appian Way. William is second from the left and his wife, Maggie, is second from the right in front of the wagon. (Photograph courtesy of Bob Whittaker.)

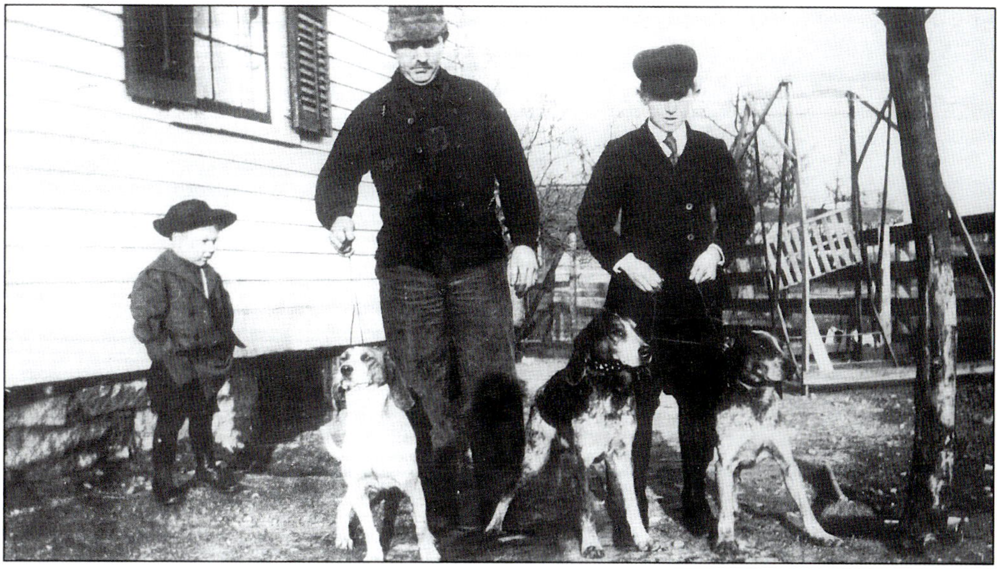

Jim Shaw Sr. and his son George prepare for the hunt about 1914 while Jim's youngest son, Jim Jr., looks on longingly. Jim Jr. says he caught up later and became a lifelong hunter for food. The Shaws hunted rabbits for supper at various sites in Foster and North Kingstown. (Photograph courtesy of Jim Shaw.)

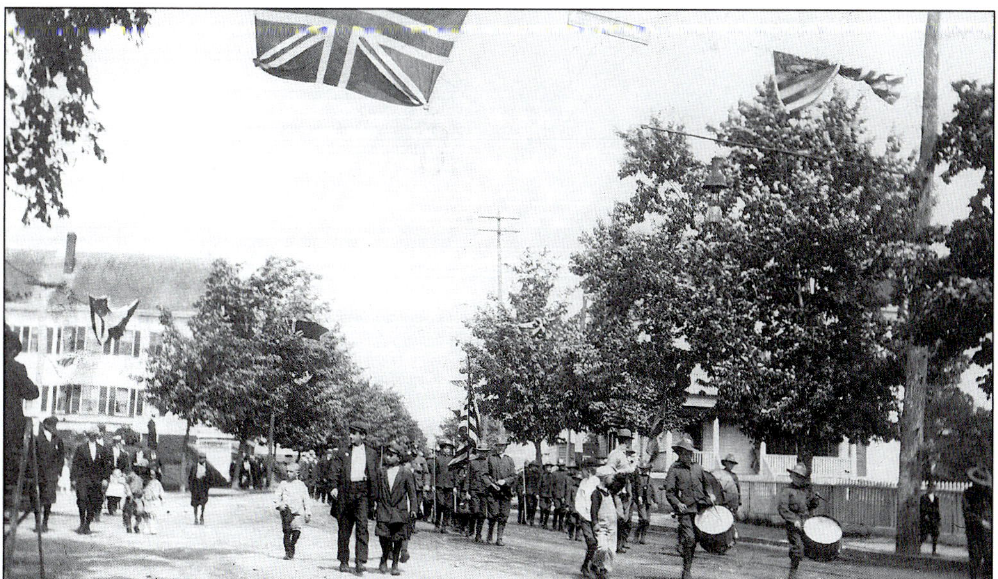

Boy Scouts are shown here marching down Plainfield Street at Aitchison Square, probably in the late teens. The tenement on the left is still in place. Over the street flies the American flag and the Union Jack, showing the village's ethnic make-up at that time. (Photograph courtesy of Sam Coupe.)

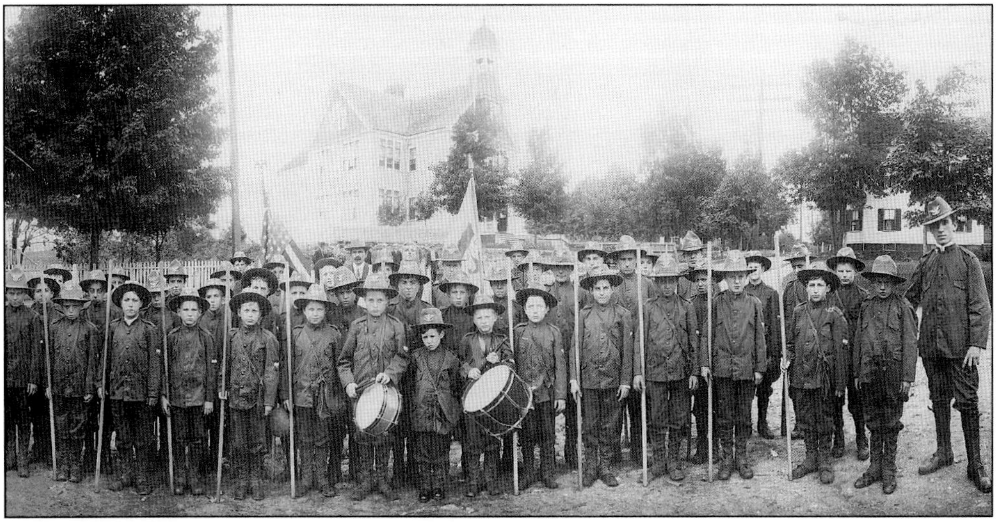

This very early view of a Boy Scout troop was taken in the middle or late 1910s. The old Thornton School in back of them burned in 1919. The scout master was Mr. Aurecchia. Irving Youde is between the drums in the front row. Five places to the left of him is Joe Perry. (Photograph courtesy of Tom Hartshorn.)

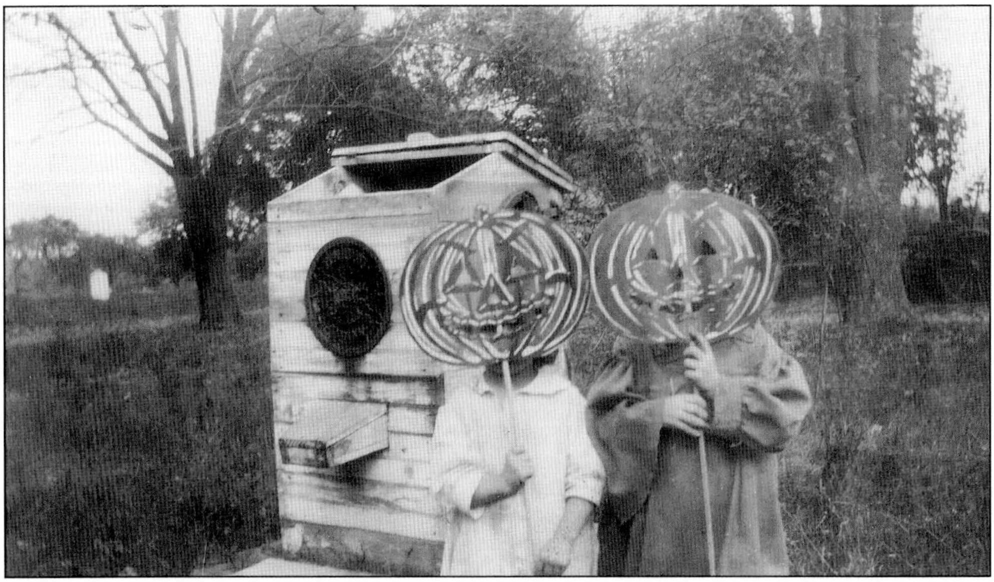

These two Halloween trick or treaters are anxious for the night to begin. Mildred and Laban Waterman, children of James Edward Waterman, pose on their farm at 330 Cherry Hill Road. As a note of interest, the well house in the picture now stands at 6 Blueberry Lane. (Photograph courtesy of James Waterman Jr.)

The Pocasset Rovers played at the Pocasset Oval in back of the Pocasset Social Club (Pocasset Casino), but their main field was Ferri's Field in back of St. Rocco's Church. They are pictured here in 1921 in front of the Pocasset Social Club on Plainfield Street. In the first row, second from the left, is Irving Youde. To the far right in the back row is Sam Youde, Irving's father. Sam was the superintendent at British Hosiery when it was owned by George Boyden. (Photograph courtesy of Millie Youde.)

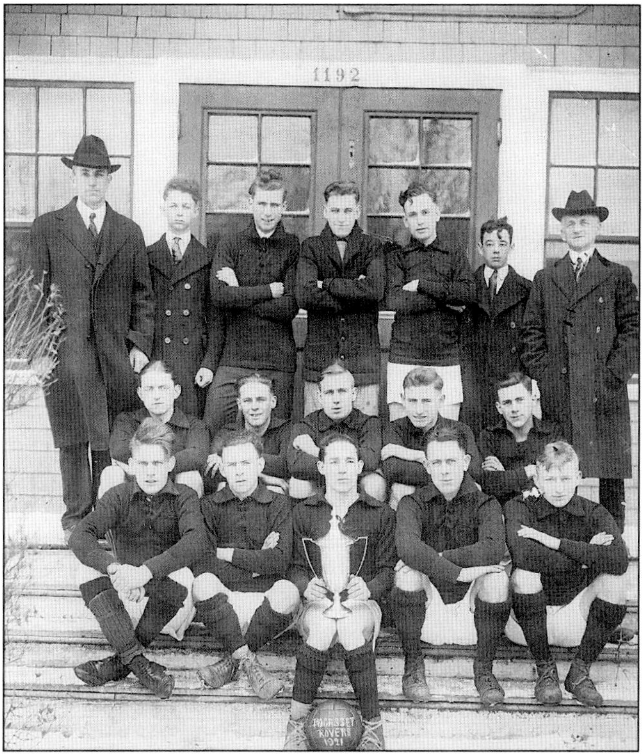

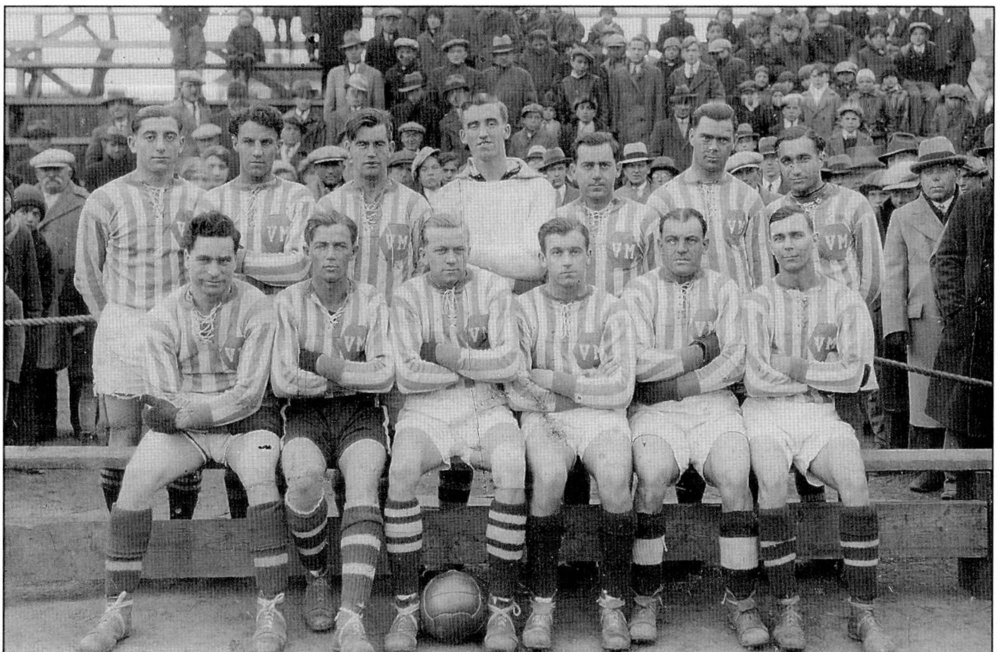

Victoria Mill sponsored this soccer team, one of many local teams at a time when soccer was king. The players are, from left to right, as follows: (front row) J. Ewart, J. McCrorie, C. Oborne, J. Smith, B. Barone, and T. Blackburn; (back row) J. Croce, A. Ferri, R. Caldwell, J. Johnston, A. Rainone, A. Tobin, and K. Croce. (Photograph courtesy of Carl Rainone.)

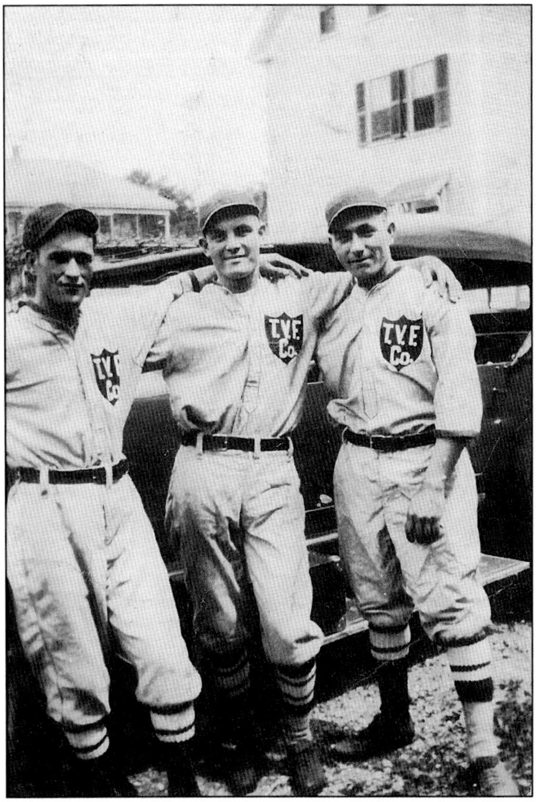

The Thornton Volunteer Fire Company sponsored a baseball team in the 1920s. This 1922 image shows, from left to right, Louie Ferrari, Bob Barone, and Carl "Nation" Simone. The latter two were also excellent soccer players. (Photograph courtesy of Carl Rainone.)

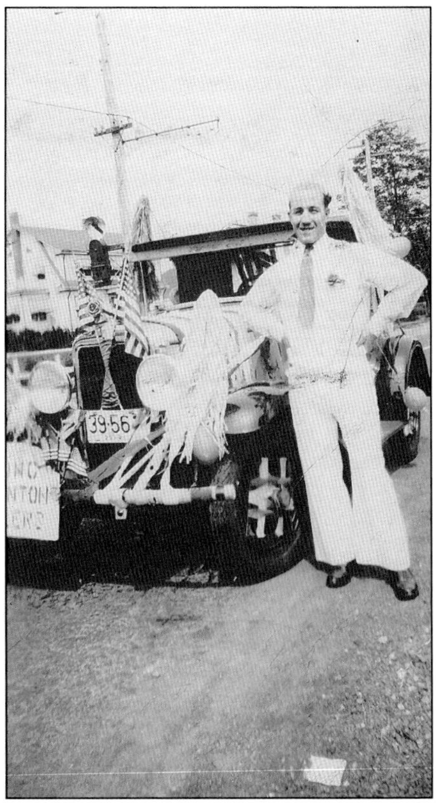

Anthony Ferri poses in front of a car decorated for the annual outing of the Thornton Bowlers in 1925. Bowling was very popular in the village, and their outing drew 100 men. The alleys were in the Ferri Block. (Photograph courtesy of Carl Rainone.)

Bonfires were an important part of celebrations in days gone by. As can be seen here, the participants were sometimes quite creative. This bonfire took place at Neutaconkanut Hill in the early 20th century. Well into the 1950s the local volunteer fire stations participated in building, burning, and watching over bonfires. (Photo courtesy of Harold & Judy Beaudoin.)

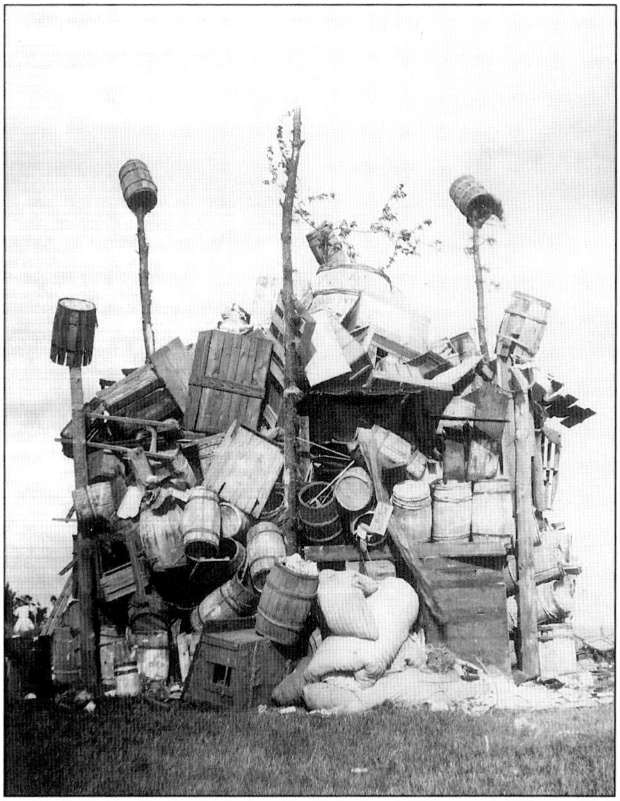

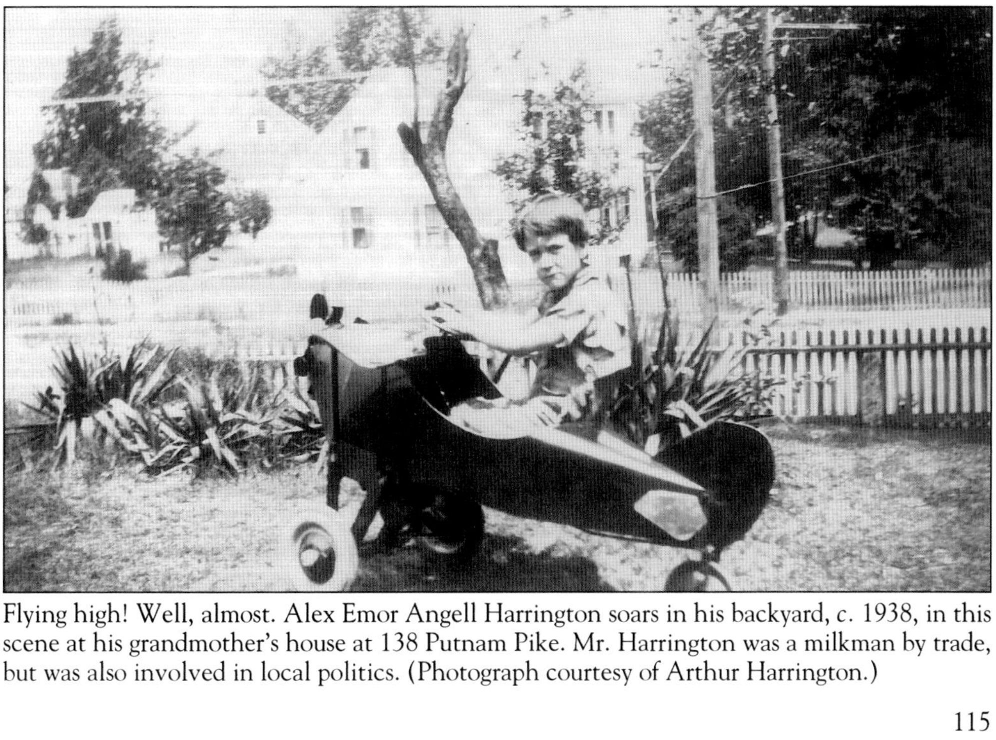

Flying high! Well, almost. Alex Emor Angell Harrington soars in his backyard, *c.* 1938, in this scene at his grandmother's house at 138 Putnam Pike. Mr. Harrington was a milkman by trade, but was also involved in local politics. (Photograph courtesy of Arthur Harrington.)

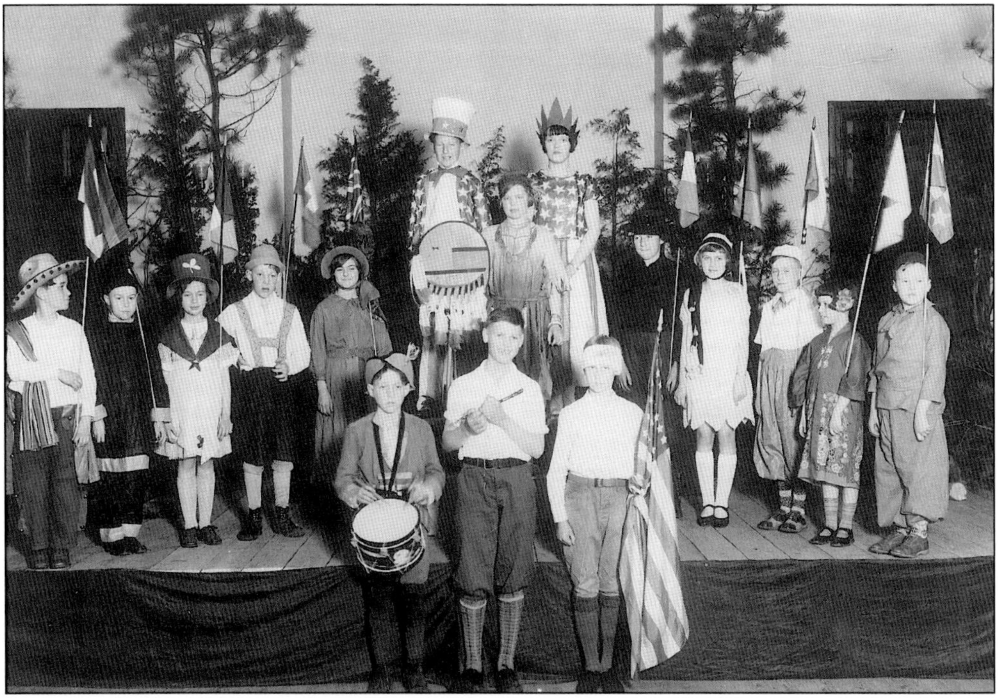

This interior view of the Hughesdale Congregational Church shows a children's cantata about 1929. It was a one-time event, held as a fund-raiser. The children are, from left to right, as follows: (in front of the stage) unknown, ? Kimball, and ? Kimball; (onstage) Wally Wilder, Louis Patton, unknown, ? Kimball, ? Waterman, Elena Patton, unknown, Dorothy Coffin, Charles Drew Jr., unknown, and Robert Drew. Uncle Sam is Harold Drew, and Luessa Wilder is Mrs. Uncle Sam. (Photograph courtesy of Mabel Sprague.)

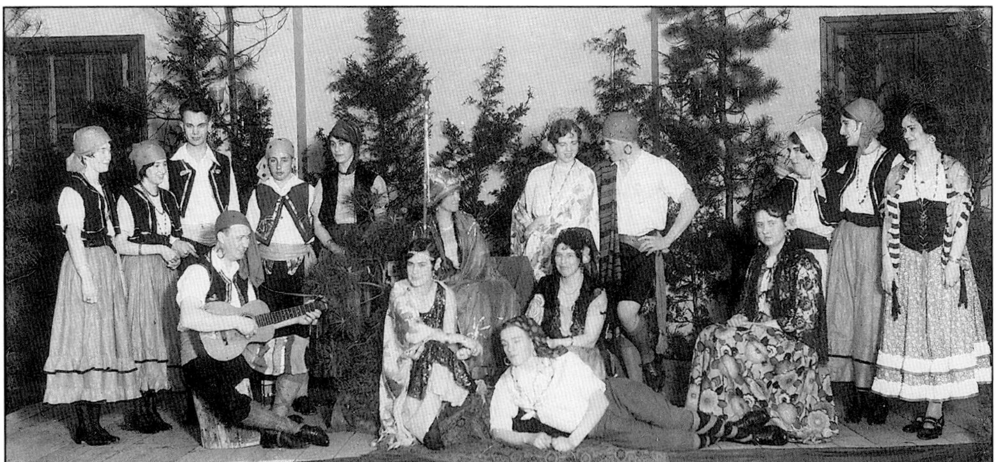

The adult's cantata was held at the same time and place as the children's cantata in the previous photograph. Shown here are, from left to right, as follows: (seated) Webb Wilder (on guitar), Eleanor Luther, unknown, Esther Patton, and Alice Atwood; (standing) Marian Luther, Wilma Waterman, Herbert Luther, ? Miller, Flora Luther, Gertrude Kimball, James Patton, Alice Brown?, Blanche Atwood, and Magel Wilder. The person lying on the stage is unknown. (Photograph courtesy of Mabel Sprague.)

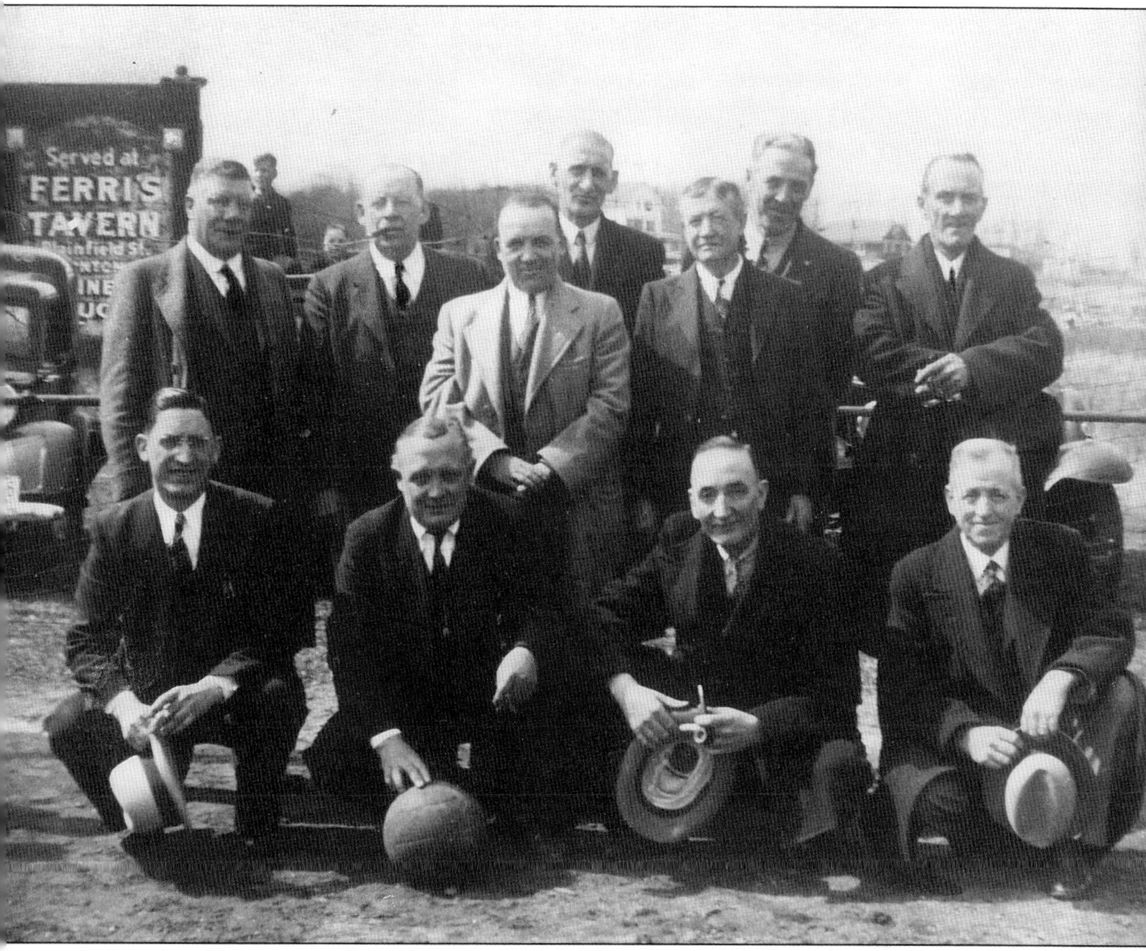

Gathered in Thornton in the 1930s are some of Johnston's movers and shakers, who combined to sponsor a local soccer team. To the far left in the first row is Pat Iafrate, a barber in Thornton. Two places to his left is Charlie Gaskin. Ferri's Tavern (left) was a popular eating, drinking, and dancing establishment in Thornton. (Photograph courtesy of Fred Iafrate.)

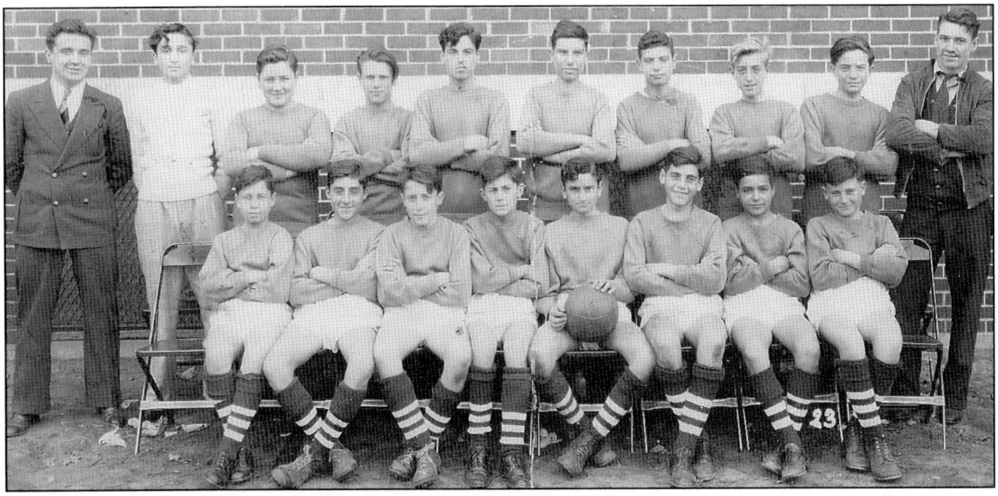

Thornton Junior High School's champion soccer team from 1937 poses outside the school. They played against other schools in the town. The players are, from left to right, as follows: (front row) James Iannuccilli, Mario "Cowboy" Ardente, unknown, unknown, John Macari, Al Salzillo, Freddie Ricci?, and George Ricci?; (back row) Ralph Mendozzi, Ray Pezzullo, Arthur Vacca, unknown, Ralph "Tattoo" Muscatelli, Angelo "Mo" Vitale, unknown, Anthony "Swede" Lanni, Al? Pitocco, and the team's coach. (Photograph courtesy of Dave Iannuccilli.)

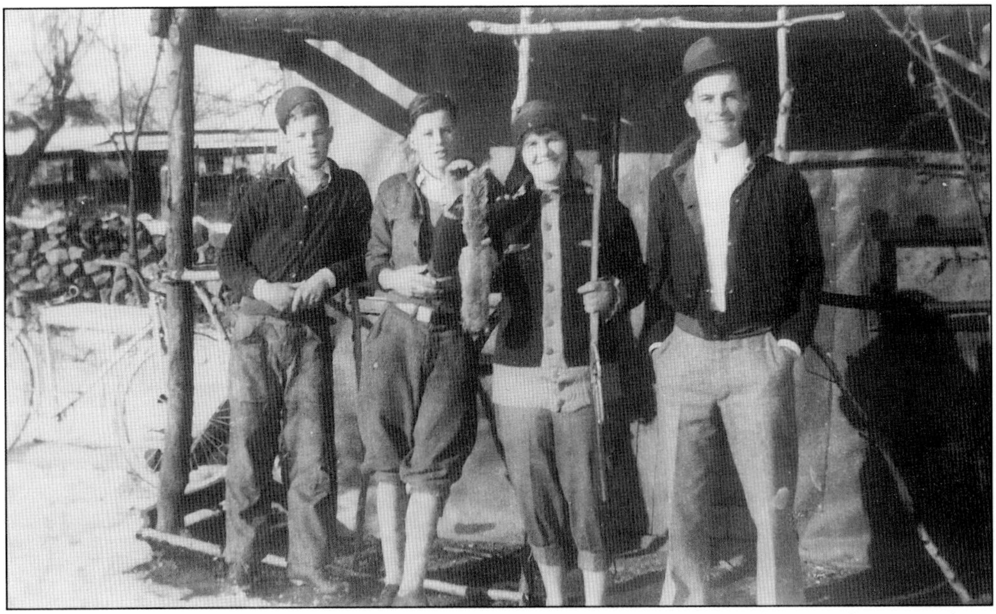

Four happy hunters show off their bounty—the three Morin boys and their mother pose for a photograph behind their house on Simmonsville Avenue after a hunting excursion. From left to right are Wilfred Morin, Irvin Morin, Sarah Morin, and Ernest Morin. (Photograph courtesy of Cecile Morin.)

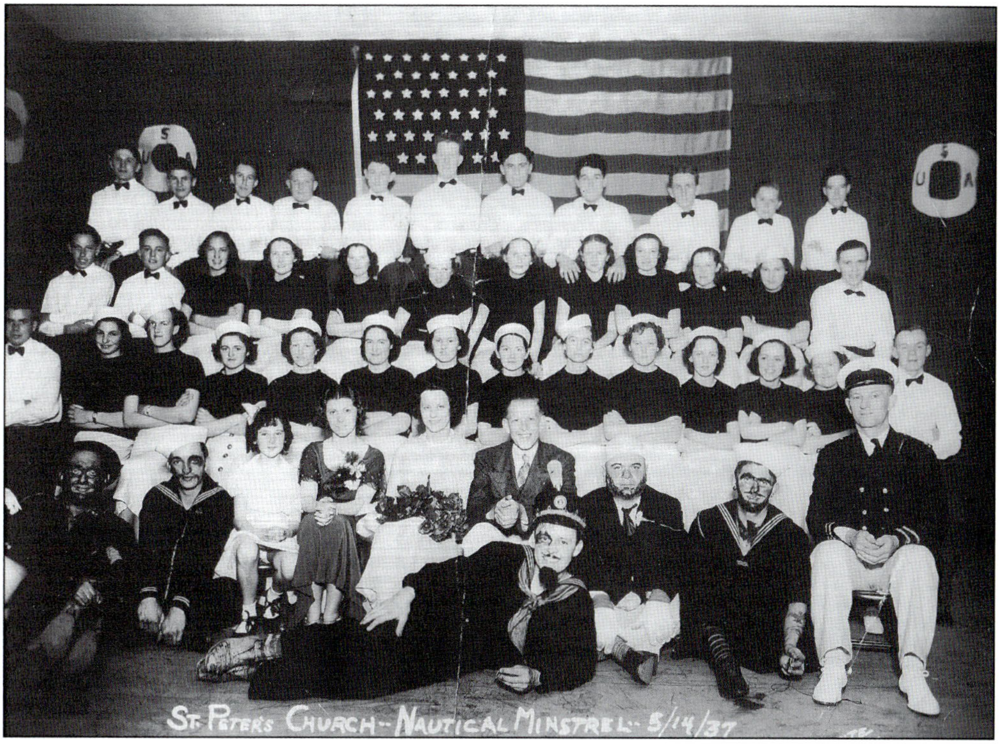

Minstrels were popular entertainment in the 1930s and '40s. This minstrel show took place at St. Peter's Church in 1937. The players are as follows: (front row) unknown, Tip McKay, ? Rushworth (tap dancer), three unknown, Rocco Scorpio, unknown, Paul Jache, and Gus Freiberger (in front); (middle row) Bill Robinson, ? Purnell, Gert (Newman) Rice, Ina Waterman, unknown, Dot Newman, Barbara Jache, Edith Hilton, Elizabeth Shippee, three unknown, Barbara (Rogers) Freiberger, and unknown; (back row) Hazel Jache (second from the left) and Helen Inman Forge (third from the left). (Photograph courtesy of Gert Newman Rice.)

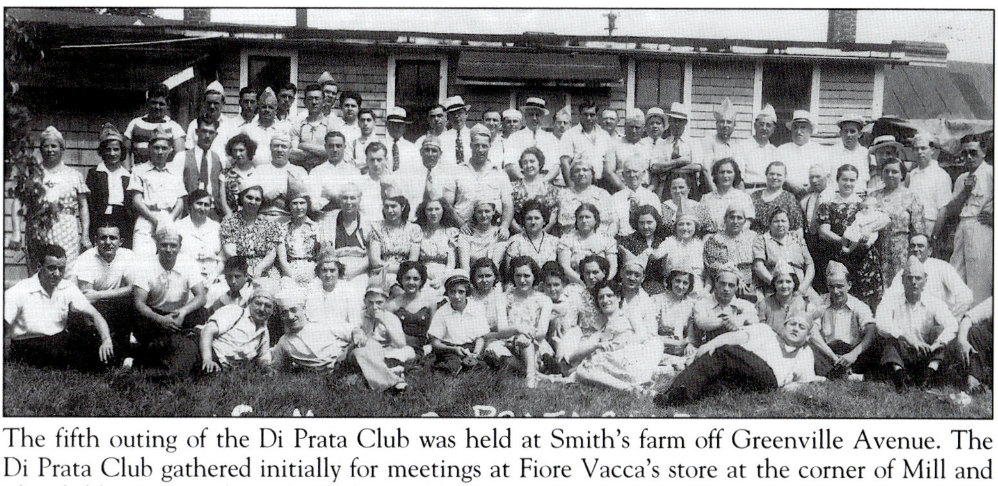

The fifth outing of the Di Prata Club was held at Smith's farm off Greenville Avenue. The Di Prata Club gathered initially for meetings at Fiore Vacca's store at the corner of Mill and Plainfield Streets. They played boccia, held dinners and outings, and marched in various parades. Many of the first members came from Prata Sanita in Italy. (Photograph courtesy of Carl Rainone.)

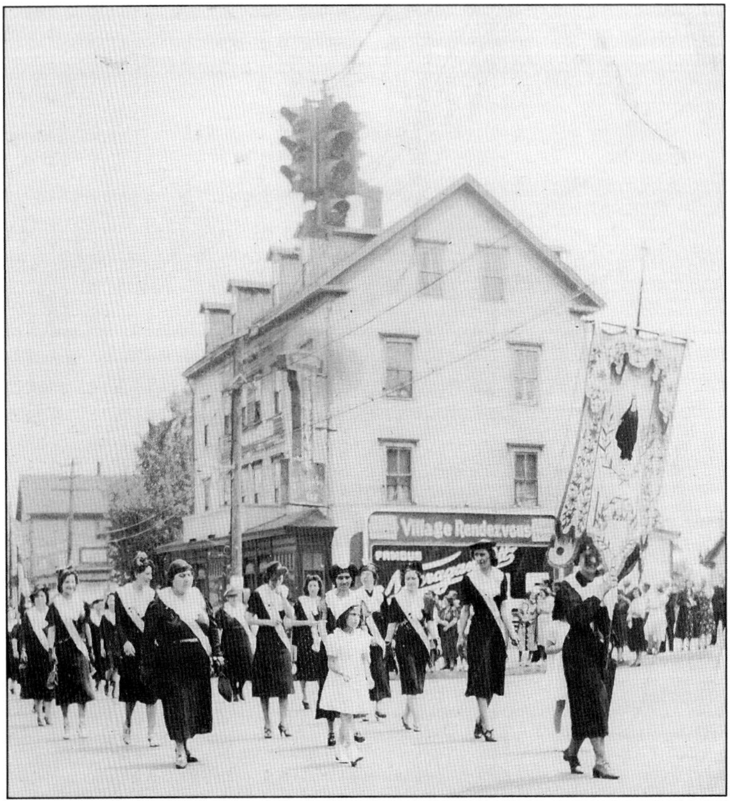

A woman's group takes part in one of the many parades held in Thornton during this century. In this parade from the 1930s, a marcher is carrying a flag honoring the Virgin Mary. Parades were held in honor of the various saints on their feast days. Groups from Thornton also marched in other towns, helping to strengthen the cultural bonds of the Italian-American community. (Photograph courtesy of Carl Rainone.)

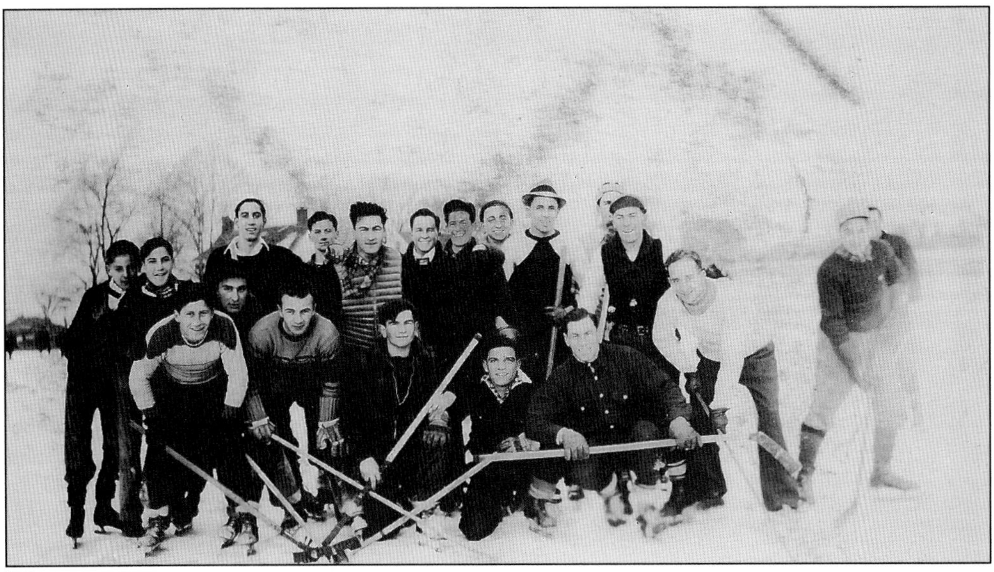

Local boys take a break from their hockey game in 1939 at Charlie Stone's Pond just off Plainfield Pike in Cranston. Youngsters from Thornton gathered here for many years to play the game. The Stones owned the property surrounding the pond, including the Major Thomas Fenner House, a 17th-century stone-ender. The farm sat across Plainfield Pike from Frog City. (Photograph courtesy of Carl Rainone.)

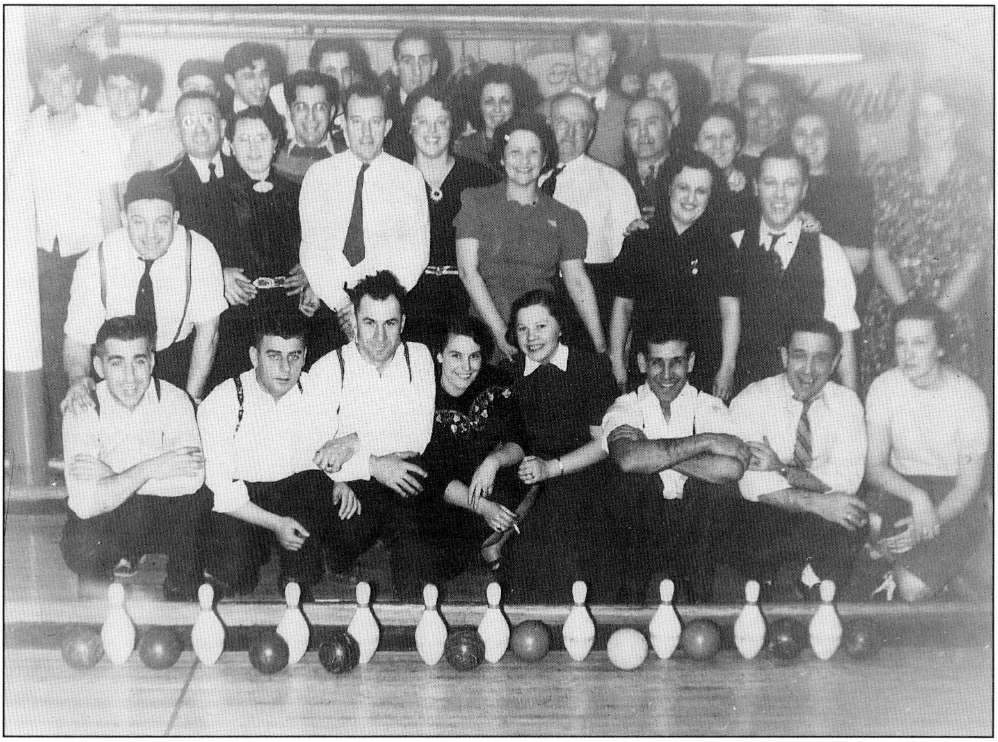

This happy group at the Thornton Bowling Alleys in the basement of the Ferri Block was captured on film in 1940. Rocco Barone and Henry D'Ambra built the lanes in the mid-1920s and hired Bob Barone to manage them. Bob (to the far left, second row) was president of the New England Duck Pin Bowling League and a professional soccer player. He ran the alleys through the war. Nick Ferri took over the alleys after Bob. (Photograph courtesy of Carl Rainone.)

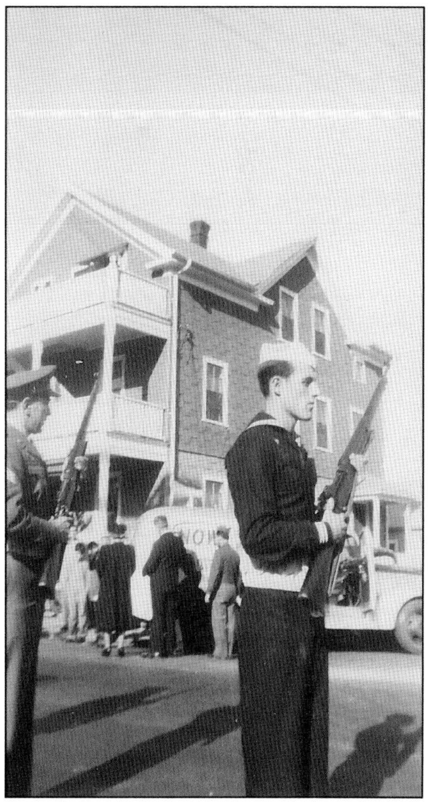

This Memorial Day scene from the 1940s was taken at the corner of Morgan and Atwood Avenues, where there is a memorial dedicated to Anthony Altieri, who was killed on Guam in 1944. The usual route of the parade started at Central Avenue and proceeded down Atwood Avenue into Thornton. At each memorial the honor guard fired a salute. It is also said that members of the band would stop at certain pubs along the way to quench their thirst. (Photograph courtesy of Rich LaFazia.)

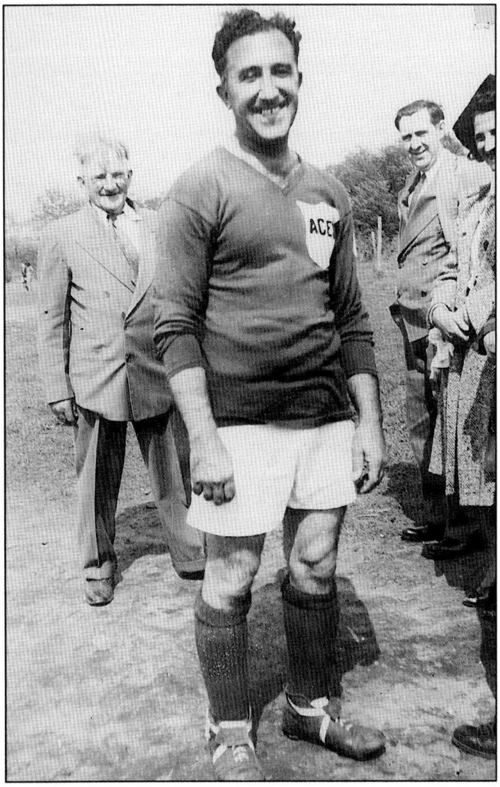

Tom Florie is seen during the latter stages of his soccer career. In his day he was one of America's best players. In the 1930 World Cup he scored a goal in the USA's victory over Belgium at Montevideo. In 1941, at the age of 43, he led the Pawtucket Rangers to a National Open championship. He lived most of his adult life in Hughesdale, where his wife, Marie, still resides. He died in 1966 at the age of 68. (Photograph courtesy of Carl Rainone.)

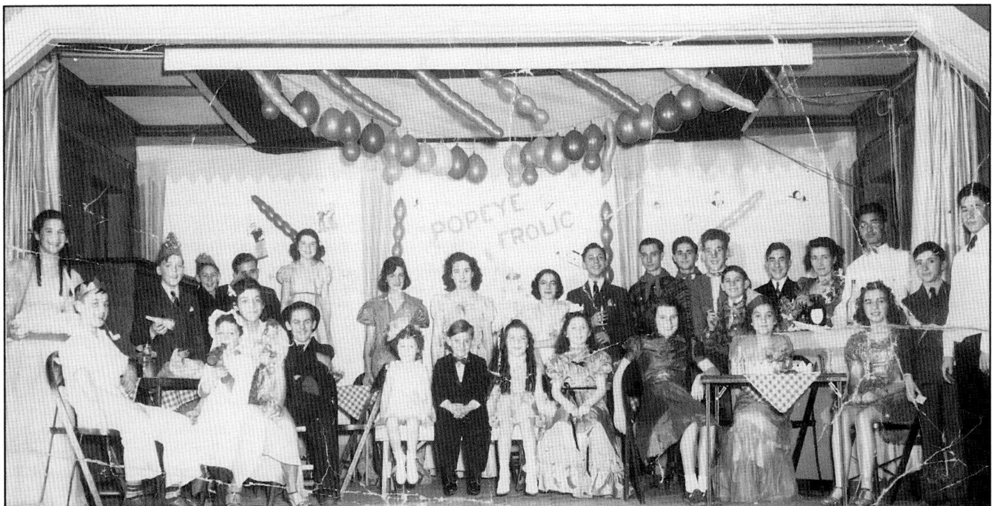

Created and run by Lillian Votolato, the Popeye Club met in Myrtle Hall. Once a year, the club would produce a performance, as in this Popeye Frolic from around 1940. Shown here are, from left to right, as follows: (front row) O. Cionci (the cigarette girl), G. Dalmazzi (Popeye), T. Cappelli (Sweet Pea), Anna Cappelli (Olive Oyl), J. Geary (Wimpy), E. Rossi, F. Tortolani, J. Caparrelli, unknown, D. Youde, F. Wells, unknown, A. Votolato, and A. Merolla; (back row) R. Tingle, M. Dalmazzi, A. Ferri, I. Imbeault, R. Pezza, Dot ?, M. Pezza, J. Cappelli, J. Fiontella, A. Carpentier, W. Tingle, J. Stabile, D. Merolla, L. Votolato, and P. Carpentier. (Photograph courtesy of Joan Caparrelli Ventetuolo.)

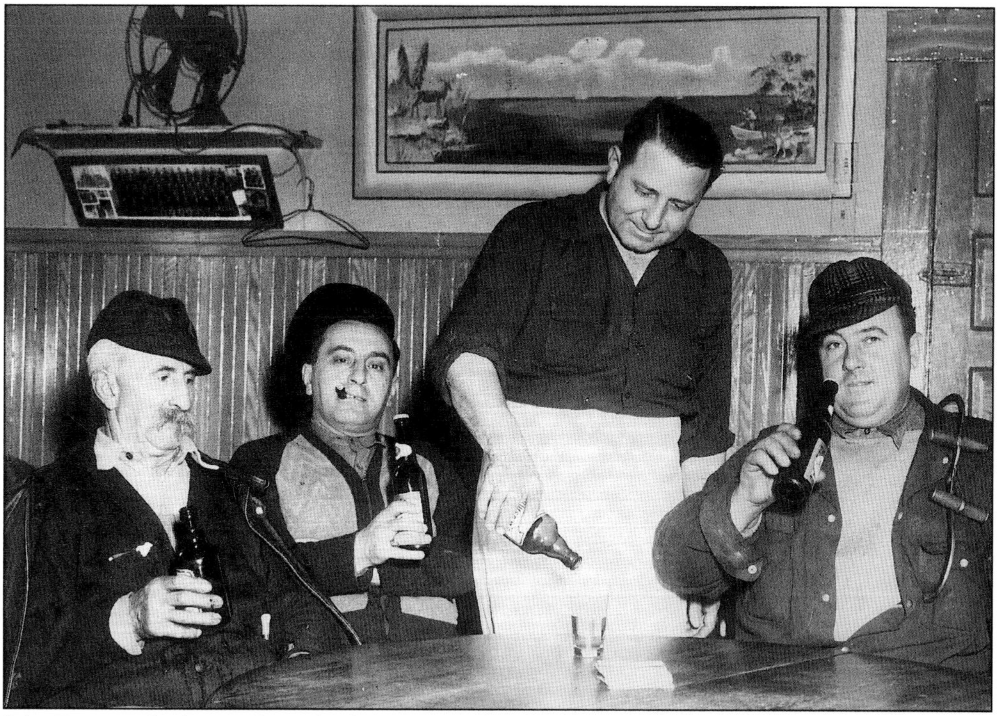

John Ricci is the bartender at his bar at 1 Zanfagna Street in Frog City. It was Ricci's Tap then, but now it is the Old Mill Tap. On the left is "Spaghetti," next to him is a LaFazia, and on the extreme right is Carl "Beattie" Cinami. (Photograph courtesy of Carl Rainone.)

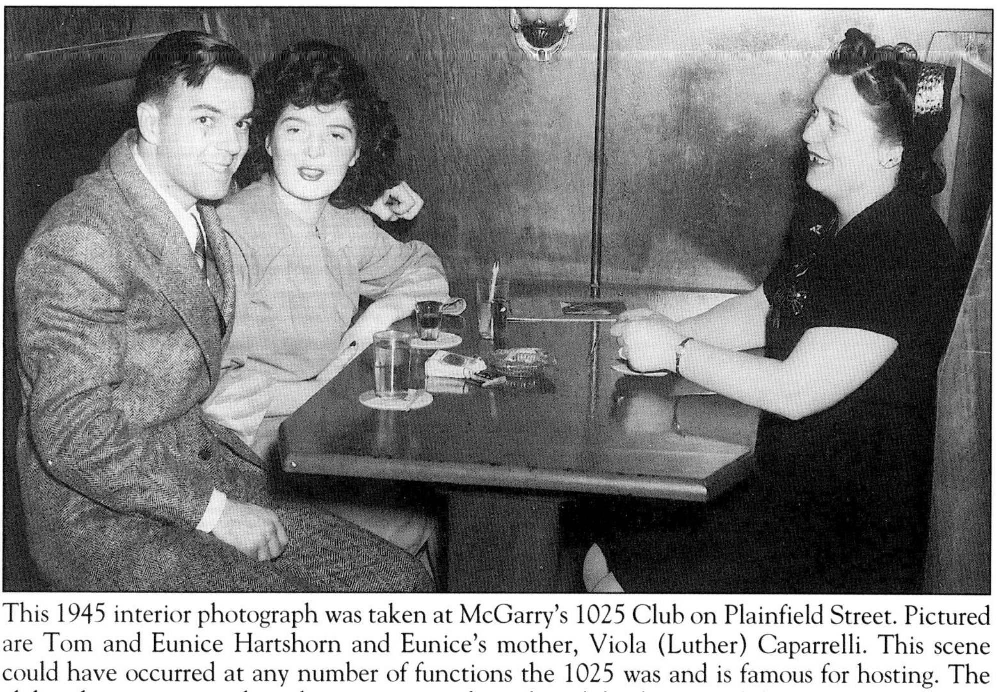

This 1945 interior photograph was taken at McGarry's 1025 Club on Plainfield Street. Pictured are Tom and Eunice Hartshorn and Eunice's mother, Viola (Luther) Caparrelli. This scene could have occurred at any number of functions the 1025 was and is famous for hosting. The club is known statewide as being a mecca for political fund-raisers. (Photograph courtesy of Tom and Eunice Hartshorn.)

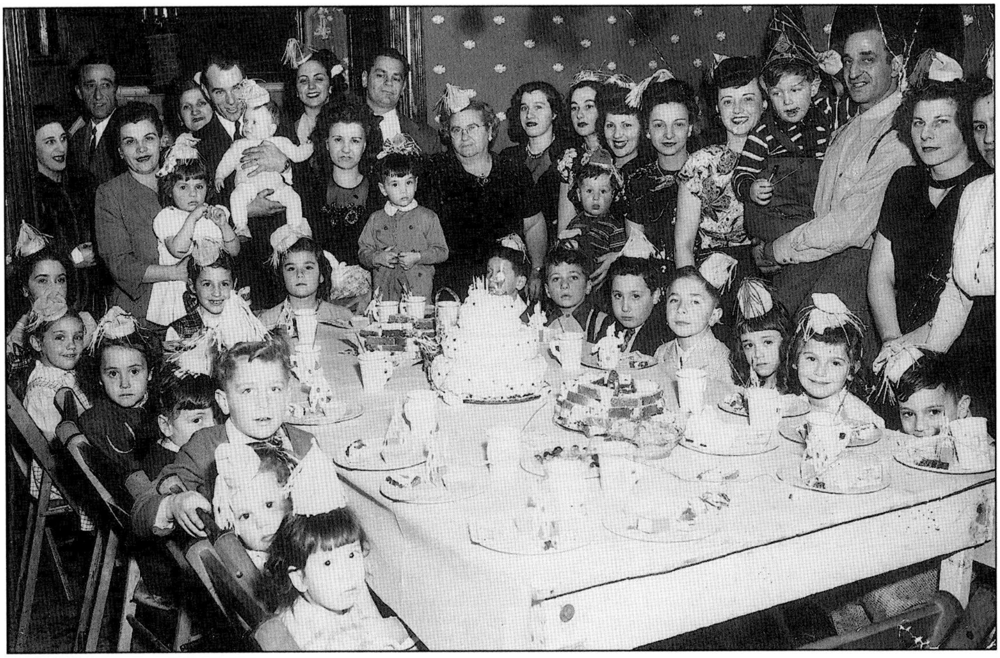

We have been told that this wonderful birthday scene was photographed about 50 years ago in Myrtle Hall on Plainfield Street. The only people identified are Beverly Votolato (second from the left, seated) and Barbra Votolato (at the far end of the table on the left, seated). (Photograph courtesy of Barbra Votolato McGuirl.)

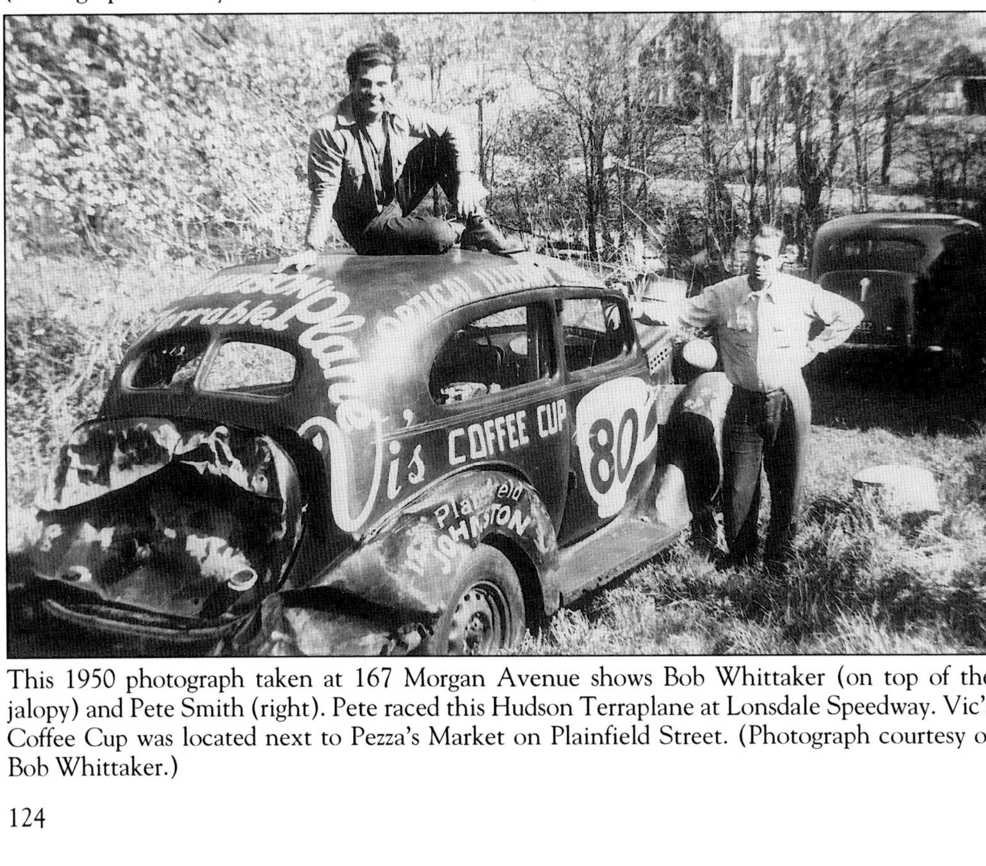

This 1950 photograph taken at 167 Morgan Avenue shows Bob Whittaker (on top of the jalopy) and Pete Smith (right). Pete raced this Hudson Terraplane at Lonsdale Speedway. Vic's Coffee Cup was located next to Pezza's Market on Plainfield Street. (Photograph courtesy of Bob Whittaker.)

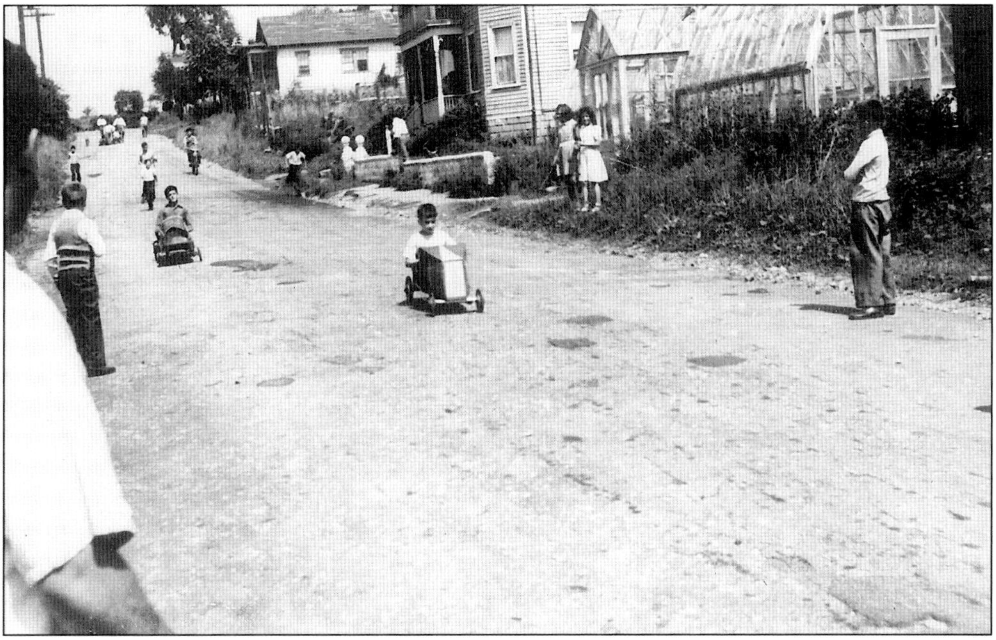

The soapbox derby was started by Leo Phillips in the late 1940s. It was said to be one of the first derbys in the state, and was run on Walnut Street and Maple Avenue on the north side of Plainfield Street. The soapboxes, or gigs, are seen here traveling down Maple Avenue. The greenhouses were owned by the Corbeil family. (Photograph courtesy of Lawrence Pezza.)

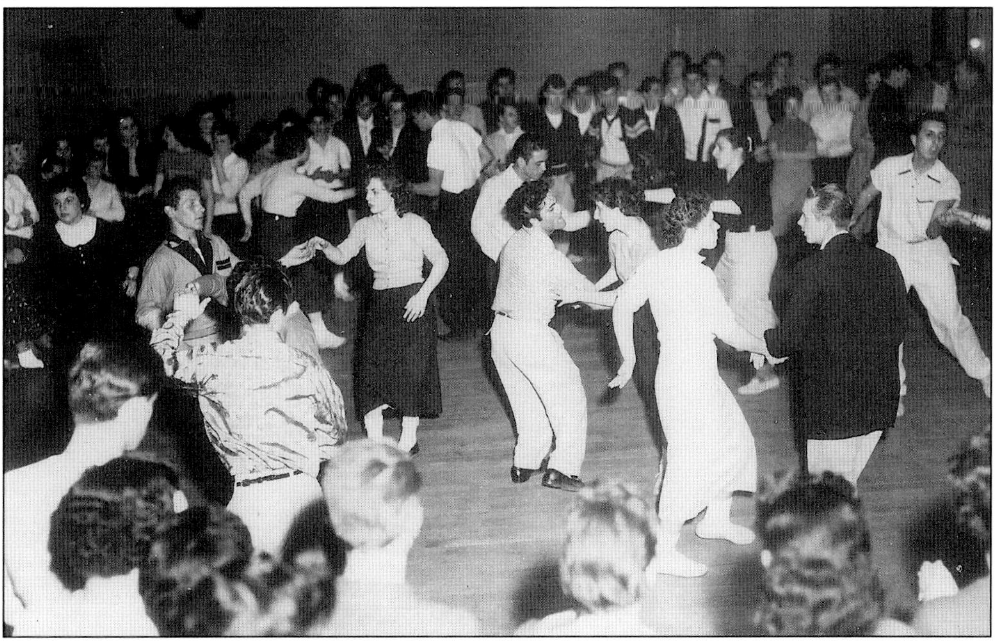

At Mario Votolato's Swinghaven Canteen in Myrtle Hall, the dancing was hot. In this late 1940s or early 1950s scene the kids are having a ball. Parents did not have to worry because Mario and his wife, Ann, ran a tight ship. The kids loved the dances, though, and the Votolatos ran them every Saturday from 1946 until 1964. (Photograph courtesy of Barbra Votolato McGuirl.)

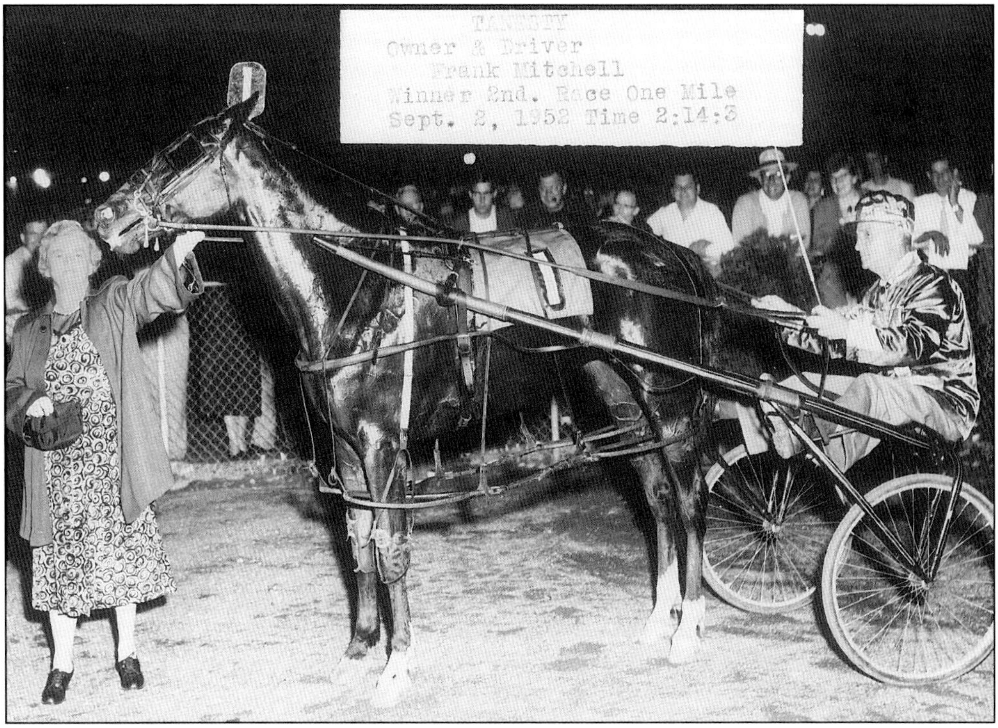

Frank Mitchell poses with his wife, Harriet, and his horse "Tanesty" after winning the second race at Foxboro on September 2, 1952. The horse was raised on the family farm behind Highland Cemetery off George Waterman Road. (Photograph courtesy of James E. Mitchell.)

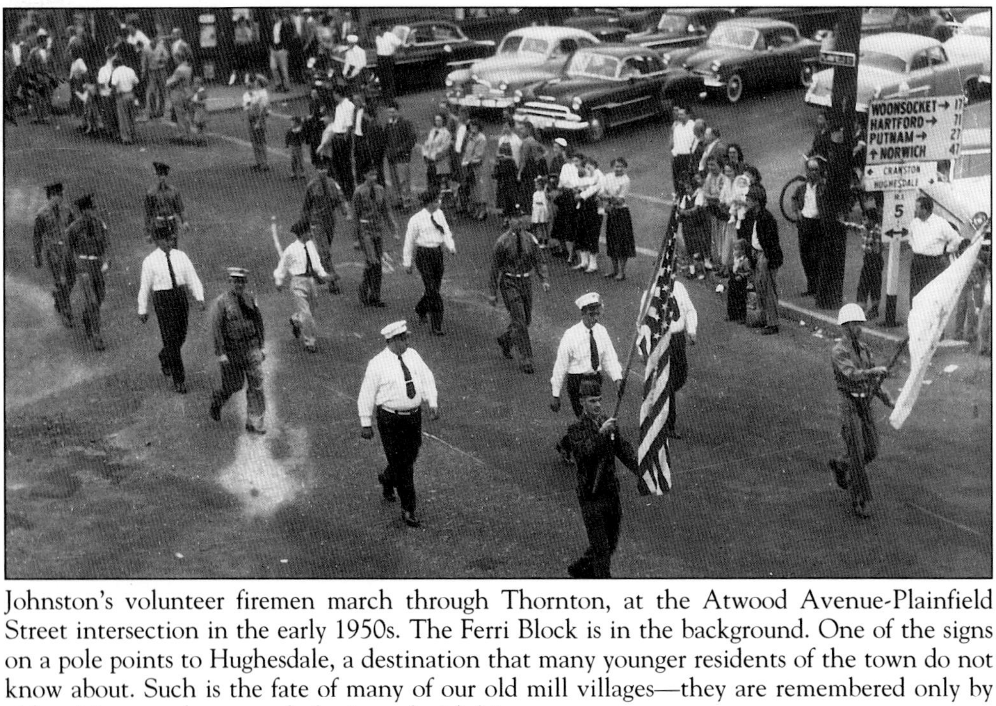

Johnston's volunteer firemen march through Thornton, at the Atwood Avenue-Plainfield Street intersection in the early 1950s. The Ferri Block is in the background. One of the signs on a pole points to Hughesdale, a destination that many younger residents of the town do not know about. Such is the fate of many of our old mill villages—they are remembered only by older citizens or those people fascinated with history.

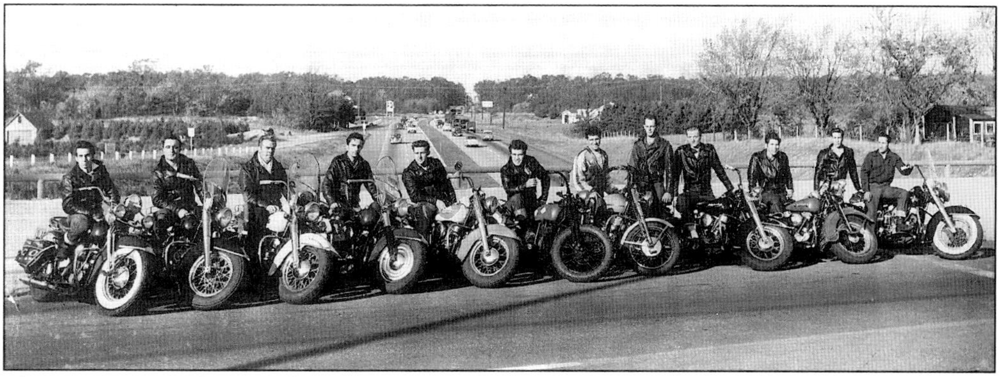

The Hurricane Riders are shown on the Route 117 bridge over Route 2 in Warwick. The club used to meet in a shack in back of the Cedar Grille on Hartford Avenue. One of the members, Vern Whittaker, died in a motorcycle accident in August of 1955, and the club broke up not long after.

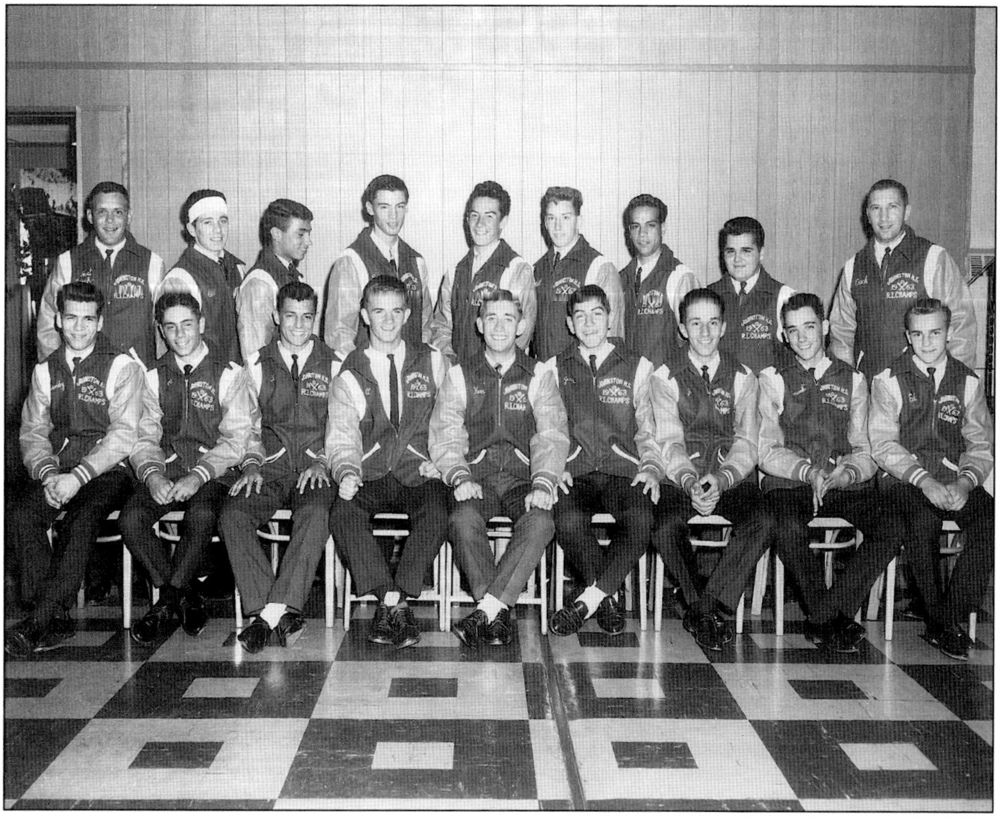

Johnston High School graduated its first class in 1963, and, in that year, its baseball team won the Rhode Island Interscholastic Championship, an amazing feat! The champs are, from left to right, as follows: (front row) L. Sanderson, D. Taraborelli, M. Steppo, S. Moore, K. Ainley, J. Petteruti, A. Giarusso, F. Jasparro, and E. Skovron; (back row) Assistant Coach R. Smith, T. Donnelly, D. Pisaturo, R. Ricci, R. Esposito, W. Geremia, M. Ursin, Equipment Manager C. Rego, and Coach E. DiSimone. (Photograph courtesy of Robert A. Smith.)

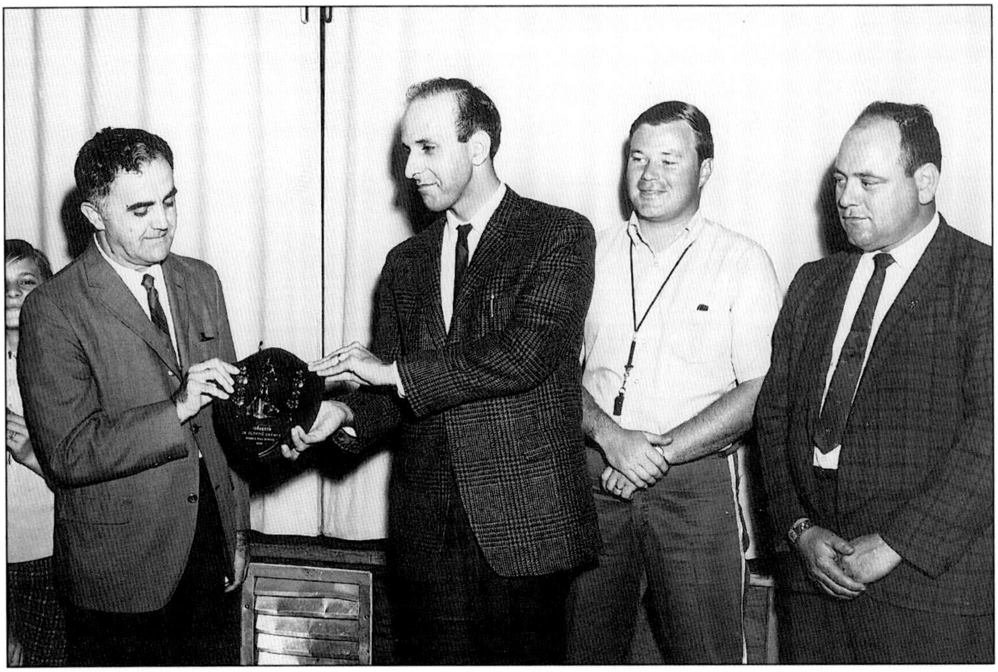

This 1968 photograph shows, from left to right, Winsor Hill School Principal Sandy LaFazia, Superintendent of Schools Dr. John DiSanto, Elementary School P.E. Supervisor Lee Swanson, and Recreation Department Director Dan Mazzulla. Swanson and Mazzulla supervised the sixth graders in town at an annual field day at Johnston Memorial Park. Ribbons were given to winning students, and a trophy was presented to the winning school. Boys and girls had their own events. Winsor Hill won the year this photograph was taken. (Photograph courtesy of Lee Swanson.)

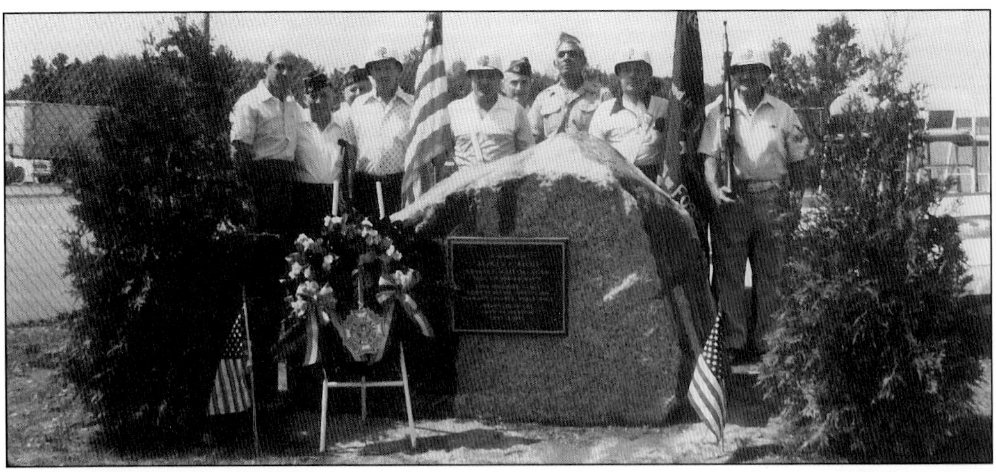

This monument on Mill Street was dedicated to Alfred A. Ricci, who was killed in 1944 off Normandy while on a PT boat. Mario "Cowboy" Ardente is in the center of the group. (Photograph courtesy of Mario Ardente.)